THIRD EDITION

The Heritage of Chinese Civilization

Albert M. Craig

Harvard University

Prentice Hall

Boston   Columbus   Indianapolis   New York   San Francisco   Upper Saddle River
Amsterdam   Cape Town   Dubai   London   Madrid   Milan   Munich   Paris   Montreal   Toronto
Delhi   Mexico City   São Paulo   Sydney   Hong Kong   Seoul   Singapore   Taipei   Tokyo

Executive Editor: Jeff Lasser
Editorial Project Manager: Rob DeGeorge
Editorial Assistant: Amanda Dykstra
Senior Marketing Manager: Maureen E. Prado Roberts
Marketing Assistant: Marissa O'Brien
Production Manager: Fran Russello
Manager, Visual Research: Beth Brenzel
Manager, Rights and Permissions: Zina Arabia
Image Permission Coordinator: Angelique Sharps
Manager, Cover Visual Research & Permissions: Karen Sanatar
Art Director: Jayne Conte
Cover Designer: Suzanne Behnke
Cover Image Credit: Freer Gallery of Art Smithsonian Institution
Full-Service Project Management: Joseph Barnabas Malcolm, PreMediaGlobal

Text Font: Caslon

Credits and acknowledgments borrowed from other sources and reproduced, with permission, in this
textbook appear on appropriate page within text.

Library of Congress Cataloging-in-Publication Data

Craig, Albert M.
  The heritage of Chinese civilization / Albert M. Craig. — 3rd ed.
    p. cm.
  Includes bibliographical references and index.
  ISBN-13: 978-0-205-79054-8
  ISBN-10: 0-205-79054-2
  1. China—History. I. Title.
  DS735.A2C73 2010
  951—dc22

                                            2010009898

Prentice Hall
is an imprint of

www.pearsonhighered.com

ISBN 10:   0-205-79054-2
ISBN 13: 978-0-205-79054-8

For Sarah Craig (1960–1992)

CONTENTS

CHAPTER **FIVE**

Modern China (1839–1949)   126

CHAPTER **SIX**

China, the Recent Decades   159

MAPS

DOCUMENTS

PREFACE

China was a birthplace of civilization. Of the original world civilizations, only China has continued down to the present. The civilizations of ancient Mesopotamia, Egypt, and India were all submerged or supplanted by subsequent waves of very different cultures. Chinese civilization, to be sure, was not static. It continued to evolve; but while absorbing outside influences, it was never wholly swamped by them. During the seventh and eighth centuries A.D., China's writing system, philosophy, and technology spread to Japan, Korea, and Vietnam, defining the area known today as East Asia. Its poetry, literature, and arts were no less influential. Today, China is a nuclear power with a fifth of the world's population. Its economy is growing apace. To understand today's world, one must understand China, and for that, we must understand its past.

This volume originally began as an expanded version of the China chapters of *The Heritage of World Civilizations*. In the second edition, the chapters were extensively revised, and the Romanization of Chinese names and terms was changed to *pinyin*. In this third edition, further changes and additions have been made in each chapter.

This work attempts to give a chronological framework and a short narrative of the sweep of Chinese history. It does not neglect the ruling dynasties, but it also treats social, economic, and cultural developments that cut across dynastic lines. For the instructor who wishes to approach Chinese history topically and assign monographs, documents, novels, and movies, the brevity of this text may prove an advantage.

Since brevity was a goal, the author asserts with seeming confidence many things that may be true only in the balance. Proper qualifications would take up many pages. The author has picked key historical variables for his reconstruction of the past. In doing so, he has inevitably left out other variables that are not without merit. Further readings from the works listed in the bibliographies at the end of each chapter may provide a counterpoint to the story told in the text.

Written history is an abstraction. In any society, change or stability is a consequence of the feelings and actions of hundreds of thousands or millions of people. Each person lives in a family, has social ties extending to the larger society, works for a living, and is protected and constrained by a structure of rule. The totality of such relationships shapes the course of a nation. The historian, at best, grasps bits and pieces of this past. In China, despite the fact that its written record in the premodern era surpassed that of any other nation, the vast majority of the people lived in obscurity and left no traces. Writing its history from surviving sources is like doing a jigsaw puzzle with most of the pieces missing.

It is always difficult to see the past in the terms in which it saw itself. Our contemporary assumptions intrude. Even studying the West—our own civilization—we catch only glimpses of what it meant to be, say, a merchant in medieval Hamburg.

How a Hangzhou merchant during the Southern Song dynasty saw family, society, and the universe is even more difficult to ascertain. But some inkling may be gleaned from original sources. To this end, poems, philosophy, essays, and scenes from novels are presented both in the narrative and in boxed quotations. The immediacy of these writings provides windows into the actual thought and feelings of the actors in China's history. They illuminate the history, and also remind us that Chinese living a thousand years ago had many of the same hopes, fears, joys, and sorrows that we have today. We recognize these shared feelings despite the powerful shaping of human experience by cultural modalities and social organization.

This volume contains many maps. Beijing in China's north is as different from Guangzhou in the near tropical southeast as Boston is from El Paso. Most place names that appear in the narrative may be found on chapter maps. The final section of each chapter attempts to place chapter materials in a larger historical or comparative perspective. Such comparisons advance our understanding but can only be taken so far.

A note on Chinese, which is not an easy language. Until twenty or so years ago, most Western scholarship on Chinese history used the Wade-Giles system to romanize Chinese names and terms. Today, most scholars and all newspapers use the *pinyin* system, which is the system used in China. I have used *pinyin* throughout. Thus, I write Mao Zedong, not Mao Tse-tung. On the whole, *pinyin* is not difficult for an English speaker. The "Way" in *pinyin* becomes "Dao," not "Tao," and that is what it sounds like in Chinese. But since the *pinyin* system was devised in the 1950s with Russian speakers in mind, several letters have values different from English. Their pronunciations should be kept in mind:

1. The old "hs" (as in Hsia dynasty) is now written "x" (so the dynastic name becomes Xia).

2. The old aspirated "ch'" (as in Ch'ing dynasty) is written "q" (so Qing dynasty).

3. The old "ts'" (as in Ts'ai Yuan-p'ei, a modern thinker) is now romanized as "c" (So Cai Yuanpei).

In China, as in Korea and Japan, the family name comes first. So the person in the previous example is Mr. Cai, not Mr. Yuanpei. Now and then, to bridge the transition to *pinyin* romanization, I put a more familiar name in parenthesis after the *pinyin*. For example: Jiang Jieshi (Chiang Kai-shek) or Guangzhou (Canton). Some book titles in the Suggested Readings use the old Wade-Giles system. For example, they use "Sung," rather than "Song" for the dynastic name. These can usually be understood by context.

In writing this book, I have drawn on many fine studies; my intellectual debts are legion and, as usual in a text, largely unacknowledged. But I would like to mention those persons to whom I owe a particular and personal debt: my first teachers in Chinese history—Benjamin Schwartz, Edwin Reischauer, Lien-sheng Yang, and

John Fairbank—and also the colleagues from whom I have learned so much over the years—Peter Bol, Paul Cohen, Nicola DiCosmo, Ronald Egan, Mark Elliott, Merle Goldman, William Kirby, Philip Kuhn, Dwight Perkins, Michael Puett, Ezra Vogel, and Robin Yates. And the following reviewers offered valuable suggestions: Henry Antkiewicz, East Tennessee State University; Yongtao Du, Washburn University; and Xiaorong Han, Butler University. I must also mention my wife, Teruko Craig, for her constant moral support and editorial advice. All errors are my own.

NEW TO THIS EDITION

In this edition, there are changes in every chapter:

- There is new coverage of early Buddhism
- New materials have been added on sea routes to China
- There is new coverage of the Ming and Manchu dynasties
- Coverage of contemporary China has been updated
- In Chapter 4, in response to suggestions from reviewers, the following changes were made:
  - The Ming and Qing dynasties are presented chronologically (in contrast with the thematic approach found in the second edition)
  - The Manchu elements in Qing rule are more clearly delineated
- Chapter 6 has been brought up to date and in some ways revamped.

It is not easy to keep up with the dynamism of contemporary China.

mysearchlab www.mysearchlab.com

Pearson's MySearchLab™ is the easiest way for students to start a research assignment or paper. Complete with extensive help on the research process and four databases of credible and reliable source material, MySearchLab™ helps students quickly and efficiently make the most of their research time.

ABOUT THE AUTHOR

Albert M. Craig is the Harvard-Yenching Research Professor of History Emeritus at Harvard University, where he has taught since 1959. A graduate of Northwestern University, he received his Ph.D. at Harvard University. He has studied at Strasbourg University and at Kyoto, Keio, and Tokyo universities in Japan. He is the author of *Choshu in the Meiji Restoration* (1961), *The Heritage of Japanese Civilization* (2011), and, with others, of *East Asia: Tradition and Transformation* (1989). He is the editor of *Japan, A Comparative View* (1973) and co-editor of *Personality in Japanese History* (1970). At present he is engaged in research on the thought of Fukuzawa Yukichi. For eleven years (1976–1987) he was the director of the Harvard-Yenching Institute. He has also been a visiting professor at Kyoto and Tokyo universities. He has received Guggenheim, Fulbright, and Japan Foundation Fellowships. In 1988 he was awarded the Order of the Rising Sun by the Japanese government.

CHAPTER ONE

Early China

Bronze vessel of the Shang dynasty.   The little elephant on top forms the handle of the lid. Wine was poured through the spout formed by the big elephant's trunk.
[Freer Gallery of Art, Smithsonian Institution, Washington, D.C.: Purchase, F1936.6]

CHAPTER OUTLINE

Origins: Old and New Stone Ages
Early Bronze Age: Shang
Later Bronze Age: Western Zhou
Iron Age: Eastern Zhou
Iron Age: Birth of Chinese Philosophy
Early Chinese Thought in Historical Perspective

ORIGINS: OLD AND NEW STONE AGES

Human life in China goes back several hundred thousand years to "Beijing (Peking) man" (*Homo erectus*), whose remains were first found on the North China plain but have since been found in other areas as well. Beijing man was about 5 feet tall and had a smaller cranial capacity than modern humans. Beijing man was similar to "Java man" and to varieties of *Homo erectus* found in Africa, the Middle East, and Europe. These early humans lived by hunting deer and other animals and by fishing and gathering. Men were slightly larger than women, and there was probably a division of labor by gender, with women doing the gathering. Nothing is known of their language capability, social relations, or beliefs, but we do know that they made chipped stone tools and cooked with fire. Bashed-in skulls suggest that they ate brains in some circumstances.

Large-brained modern human beings (*Homo sapiens*), who first evolved 100,000 years ago in Africa, entered China about 50,000 years ago, supplanting Beijing man. They used fire. They made tools with finer stone blades. The history of progress during the Old Stone Age is dimly perceived through successive layers of tools found in archaeological sites, and distinctive regional variations in the tools have been noted. They buried their dead. Population remained sparse, however, for humans were still subject to ecological constraints of the kind that today maintain a balance, for example, between deer and wolves in Alaska.

The New Stone Age or Neolithic in China dawned in the sixth millennium B.C. Of the thousands of Old Stone Age cultures in the world, only a few developed the combination of agriculture, pottery, domesticated animals, and better-polished stone tools that we characterize as the "New Stone Age." Better tools were useful both for hunting and for agriculture. Perhaps it was women, gathering while men hunted, who discovered how to plant and care for seeds and gave crops the constant attention they required from planting to harvest. New Stone Age people stored dry food in baskets and liquids in pottery jars. The greater production of food led to denser populations, and they built permanent settlements in clusters near their best fields. These changes transformed the prehistoric world as science is transforming our own.

Agriculture began in China between 5600 and 4000 B.C. in the basin of the southern bend of the Yellow River. This is the northernmost of East Asia's four great river systems (see Map 1–1). The others are the Yangzi River in central China, the West River in southern China, and the Red River in what is today northern Vietnam. All drain eastward into the Pacific Ocean. In recent millennia, the Yellow River has flowed through a deforested plain, cold in winter and subject to periodic droughts. But in the sixth millennium B.C., the area was warm and moist, with forested highlands in the west and swampy marshes to the east. The bamboo rat that today can be found only in semitropical Southeast Asia lived along the Yellow River.

Millet was the chief crop of China's agricultural revolution. Yam and taro may have been grown almost as early on China's southeastern coast, an extension of agriculture in Vietnam. Rice cultivation began in south China (and in what is today Vietnam and Thailand). Wheat, in time, entered China from the West.

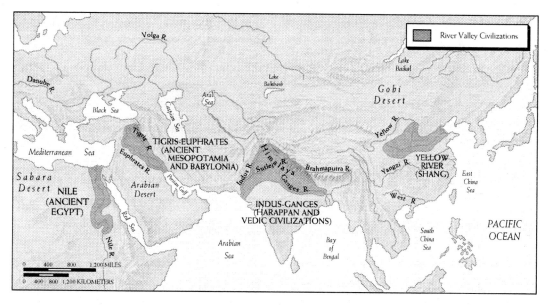

Map 1–1   The four great river valley civilizations to c. 1000 B.C.   By c. 2000 B.C., urban life was established along the Tigris and Euphrates rivers in Mesopotamia, the Nile River in Egypt, the Indus and Ganges rivers in India, and the Yellow River in China.

New Stone Age Chinese cleared land and burned its cover to plant millet, cabbage, and, later, rice and soybeans. When soil became exhausted, fields or whole villages were abandoned. Tools were of stone: axes, hoes, spades, and sickle-shaped knives. The early Chinese domesticated pigs, sheep, cattle, dogs, and chickens. Game was plentiful and hunting continued to be important to the village economy. In excavated garbage heaps of ancient villages are found the bones of deer, wild cattle, antelopes, rhinoceros, hares, and marmots. Grain was stored in pottery painted in bold, geometric designs of red and black. This pottery gave way to a harder, thin black pottery, made on a potter's wheel, which spread west along the Yellow River and south to the Yangzi. The tripodal shapes of Neolithic pots prefigure later Chinese bronzes.

Early cultivators wove fabrics of hemp and learned to produce silk from the cocoons of silkworms fed on mulberry leaves. They lived in wattle-and-daub pit-dwellings with wooden support posts and sunken, plastered floors. Their villages were located in isolated clearings along slopes of river valleys. Archaeological finds of weapons and remains of pounded earthen walls suggest tribal warfare between villages. Little is known about their religion, though some evidence suggests the worship of ancestral spirits. They practiced divination by applying heat to a hole drilled in the shoulder bone of an ox or the under-shell of a tortoise and then interpreting the resulting cracks in the bone. They buried their dead in cemeteries with jars of food. Tribal leaders wore rings and beads of jade.

EARLY BRONZE AGE: SHANG

The traditional history of China tells of three ancient dynasties:

2205–1766 B.C.	Xia
1766–1050 B.C.	Shang
1050–256 B.C.	Zhou

Until early in the twentieth century, modern historians thought the first two were legendary. Then, in the 1920s, archaeological excavations at "the wastes of Yin" near present-day Anyang uncovered the ruins of a walled city that had been a late Shang capital (see Map 1–2). Other Shang cities have been discovered

Map 1–2 Bronze Age China during the Shang dynasty, 1766–1050 B.C. Anyang was a late Shang dynasty capital. Xian and Luoyang were the capitals of the Western and the Eastern Zhou.

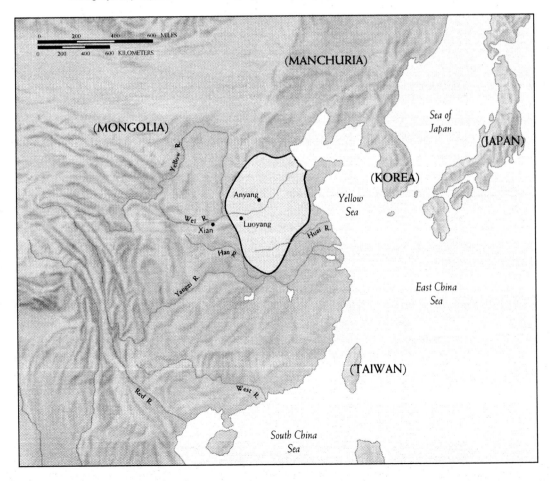

more recently. The ruins contained the archives of the department of divination of the Shang court, with thousands upon thousands of "oracle bones" incised with archaic Chinese writing. The names of kings on the bones fit almost perfectly those of the traditional historical record. The evidence that there actually was a Shang has led historians to suggest that the Xia may also have existed. Perhaps the Xia was a late Neolithic red-pottery kingdom or tribal confederation; some scholars tentatively identify a site just south of the Yellow River at Erlitou as the Xia capital. Did the Xia develop black pottery, bronze, and the earliest, still-missing stage of Chinese writing?

The characteristic political institution of Bronze Age China was the city-centered state. The largest was the Shang capital which frequently moved and lacked the monumental architecture of Egypt or Mesopotamia. The walled city contained public buildings, altars, and the residences of the aristocracy, and was surrounded by a sea of tribal villages. By late Shang times, several such cities were spotted across the North China plain. They were ruled by royal and noble clans. The Shang kings possessed political, economic, social, and religious authority. When they died, they were sometimes succeeded by younger brothers and sometimes by sons. The rulers of other city-states acknowledged their authority.

The military aristocracy went to war in chariots, supported by levies of foot soldiers. Their weapons were spears and powerful compound bows. Accounts tell of armies of 3,000 or 4,000 troops and of a battle involving 13,000. The Shang fought against barbarian tribes and, occasionally, against other city-states in rebellion against Shang rule. Captured prisoners were enslaved.

Three notable features of Shang civilization were writing, bronzes, and the appearance of social classes. Scribes at the Shang court may have kept records on strips of bamboo, but these have not survived. What survived are inscriptions on bronzes and the oracle bones. Some bones contain the question put to the oracle, the answer, and the outcome of the matter. Representative questions were: Which ancestor is causing the king's earache? If the king goes hunting at Qi, will there be a disaster? Will the king's child be a son? If the king sends his army to attack an enemy, will the deity help him? Was a sacrifice acceptable to ancestral deities?

What we know of Shang religion is based on the bones. The Shang Chinese believed in a supreme "Deity Above," who had authority over the human world. Also serving at the court of the Deity Above were lesser natural deities—the sun, moon, earth, rain, wind, and the six clouds. Even the Shang king sacrificed not to the Deity Above but to his own ancestors, who interceded with the Deity Above on his behalf. Kings, while alive at least, were not considered divine but were the high priests of the state.

In Shang times, as later, religion in China was often associated with cosmology. The Shang people observed the movements of the planets and stars and reported eclipses. Celestial happenings were seen as omens from the gods above. The chief cosmologists also recorded events at the court. The Shang calendar had a month of 30 days and a year

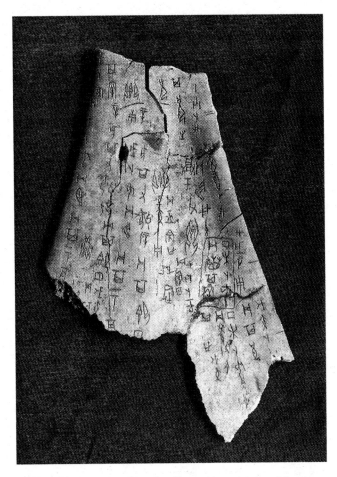

Inscribed oracle bone from the Shang dynasty city of Anyang
[From the Collection of the C. V. Starr East Asian Library, Columbia University]

of 360 days, and adjustments were made periodically by adding an extra month. The calendar was used by the king to tell his people when to sow and when to reap.

Bronze appeared in China about 2000 B.C., 1,000 years later than in Mesopotamia and 500 years later than in India. Its origins are debated. Archaeological sites stretching from the Fertile Crescent in the Middle East across central Asia suggest that bronze made its way east over the course of the third millennium B.C. But the Shang may have developed bronze technology independently: Shang methods of casting were more advanced than those of Mesopotamia, and the designs on Shang bronzes emerge directly from the preceding black-pottery culture. Bronze was used for weapons, armor, and chariot fittings, and for a variety of ceremonial vessels of amazing fineness and beauty.

CHINESE WRITING

The Chinese system of writing dates back at least to the Shang dynasty (1766–1050 B.C.) when animal bones and tortoise shells (the so-called oracle bones) were incised for the purpose of divination. About half of the 3,000 characters used in Shang times have been deciphered. They evolved over the centuries into the 50,000 characters found in the largest dictionaries today. But even now only about 3,000 or 4,000 are in common use. A scholar may know twice that number.

Characters developed from little pictures. Note the progressive stylization. By 200 B.C., the writing had become standardized and close to the modern form of the printed character.

	Shang (1400 B.C.)	Zhou (600 B.C.)	Seal Script (200 B.C.)	Modern
Sun	日	日	日	日
Moon	月	月	月	月
Tree	木	木	米	木
Bird	鳥	鳥	鳥	鳥
Mouth	口	口	口	口
Horse	馬	馬	馬	馬

Other characters combined two pictures to express an idea. The following examples use modern characters:

Sun	日	+ moon	月	= bright	明	
Mouth	口	+ bird	鳥	= to chirp	鳴	
Woman	女	+ child	子	= good	好	
Tree	木	+ sun	日	= east	東	

It was a matter of convention that the sun behind a tree meant the rising sun in the east and not the setting sun in the west.

Characters were formed several other ways. In one, a sound element was combined with a meaning element. Chinese has many homophones, or words with the same sound. The character 台, for example, is read *tai* and means "elevation" or "to raise up." But in spoken Chinese, there are other words with the same sound that mean "moss," "trample," a "nag," and "idle." Thus

Tai	台	+ grass	艹	= moss	苔	
Tai	台	+ foot	足	= trample	跆	
Tai	台	+ horse	馬	= a nag	駘	
Tai	台	+ heart	心	= idle	怠	

In each case, the sound comes from the 台, and the meaning from the second element. Note that the 台 may be at the bottom, the top, or the right. This positioning, too, is a matter of convention.

Table by author; calligraphy by Teruko Craig.

LANGUAGES OF EAST ASIA

The two main language families in present-day East Asia are the Sinitic and Ural-Altaic. They are as different from each other as they are from European tongues. The Sinitic languages are Chinese in all of its varieties, Tibetan, and Burmese. Vietnamese and Thai may be Sinitic or, though heavily influenced by Chinese, may originally be from another language family. Within Chinese are several mutually unintelligible dialects. Standard Chinese, based on the Beijing dialect, is further from Cantonese (the language spoken in Guangzhou; formerly, Canton) than Spanish is from French. Ural-Altaic languages are spoken to the east, north, and west of China. They include Japanese, Korean, Manchurian, Mongolian, the Turkic languages, and, in Europe, distantly, Finnish and Hungarian.

Among the Shang, as in other early river valley civilizations, the increasing control of nature through agriculture and metallurgy was accompanied by the emergence of a highly stratified society in which the many were compelled to serve the few. A monopoly of bronze weapons enabled aristocrats to exploit other groups. A hierarchy of class defined life in the Chinese city-state. The king and the officials of his court lived within the walled city. Their houses were spacious, built above the ground, that rested with roofs supported by rows of wooden pillars that rested on foundation stones. Their lifestyle was, for ancient times, opulent: They wore fine clothes, feasted at banquets, and drank wine from bronze vessels. In contrast, a far larger population of agricultural workers lived outside the city in cramped pit-dwellings. Their lives were meager and hard; archaeological excavations of their underground hovels have uncovered only earthenware pots.

Nowhere was the gulf between the royal lineage and the baseborn more apparent than in the Shang institution of human sacrifice. One Shang tomb 39 feet long, 26 feet wide, and 26 feet deep contained the decapitated bodies of humans, horses, and dogs, as well as ornaments of bone, stone, and jade. When a king died, hundreds of slaves or prisoners of war, together with some who had served the king during his lifetime, might be buried with him. Sacrifices were also made when a palace or an altar was built.

HUMAN SACRIFICE IN EARLY CHINA

By the seventh century B.C., human sacrifice had become less frequent, but it still happened. This poem was composed when Duke Mu of the state of Qin died in 631. The poem suggests that despite religious belief and the honor accorded the victims, they may not have gone gladly to the grave. Note the identification of Heaven with "that blue one," the sky.

Today it is believed honorable to die in war for one's nation. How is that different from dying to serve one's lord in the afterlife?

"Kio" sings the oriole
As it lights on the thorn-bush.
Who went with Duke Mu to the grave?
Yen-hsi of the clan Tzu-chu.
Now this Yen-hsi
Was the pick of all our men;
But as he drew near the tomb-hole

His limbs shook with dread.
That blue one, Heaven,
Takes all our good men.
Could we but ransom him
There are a hundred would give their lives.

"Kio" sings the oriole
As it lights on the mulberry-tree.
Who went with Duke Mu to the grave?
Chung-hang of the clan Tzu-chu.
Now this Chung-hang
Was the sturdiest of all our men;
But as he drew near the tomb-hole
His limbs shook with dread.
That blue one, Heaven,
Takes all our good men.
Could we but ransom him
There are a hundred would give their lives.

From *The Book of Songs*, trans. by Arthur Waley (New York: Grove Press, 1960), p. 311.

LATER BRONZE AGE: WESTERN ZHOU

The Zhou people, during the centuries of Shang rule, lived to the west in the valley of the Wei River, a tributary of the Yellow River, and near the present-day city of Xian. Culturally closer to the Neolithic black-pottery culture, they were less civilized and more warlike than the Shang. References to the Zhou in the Shang oracle bones indicate that the Shang had relations with them—sometimes friendly, sometimes hostile. According to the traditional historical record, the last Shang kings were weak, cruel, and tyrannical. By 1050 B.C., the Shang had been debilitated by campaigns against nomads in the north and rebellious tribes in the east. Taking advantage of this opportunity, the Zhou made alliances with disaffected city-states and swept in, conquering the Shang.

In most respects, the Zhou continued the Shang pattern of life and rule. The agrarian-based city-centered state continued to be the basic unit of society; it is estimated that there were about two hundred of them in the eighth century B.C. The Zhou social hierarchy was not unlike that of the Shang, with kings and lords at the top, officials and warriors below them, and peasants and slaves at the bottom. Slaves served primarily as domestic servants. Being backward themselves, the Zhou assimilated Shang culture, extending without interruption the development of Chinese ideographic writing. The Zhou also maintained the practice of casting bronze ceremonial vessels, though their vessels lacked the fineness that set the Shang above the rest of the Bronze Age world.

Early China	
4000 B.C.	Neolithic agricultural villages
1766 B.C.	Bronze Age city-states, aristocratic charioteers, pictographic writing
771 B.C.	Iron Age territorial states
500–300 B.C.	Age of philosophers
221 B.C.	Qin unifies China

The Zhou kept their capital in the west but set up a secondary capital at Luoyang, along the southern bend of the Yellow River (see Map 1–2). They appointed their kinsmen or other aristocratic allies to rule in other city-states. The Chinese term (*fengjian*) used to characterize this system of decentralized aristocratic rule is sometime translated as "feudal." This is not inappropriate since such appointments were largely in the gift of the Zhou king, and military support, as needed, was expected in return. Later Chinese historians would contrast the decentralized Zhou system with the highly centralized "bureaucratic" (*junxian*) system of the dynasties that followed.

Blood or lineage ties were essential to the Zhou pattern of rule. The Zhou king was the head of the senior branch of the family, and he performed the sacrifices to the

Deity Above for the entire family. The rankings of the lords of other princely states, which, for want of better terms, are usually translated into the titles of English feudal nobility—duke, marquis, earl, viscount, and baron—reflected their degree of closeness to the senior line of Zhou kings.

One difference between the Shang and the Zhou was in the nature of the political legitimacy each claimed. The Shang kings, descended from shamanistic (priestly) rulers, had a built-in religious authority and needed no theory to justify their rule. But the Zhou, having conquered the Shang, needed a rationale for why they, and not the Shang, were now the rightful rulers. Their argument was that Heaven (the word for the supreme being that gradually replaced "Deity Above" during the early Zhou), appalled by the wickedness of the last Shang king, had withdrawn its mandate to rule from the Shang, awarding it instead to the Zhou. This concept of the Mandate of Heaven was subsequently invoked by every dynasty in China down to the twentieth century. The ideograph for Heaven is related to that for man, and the concept originally had human, or anthropomorphic, overtones. In the later Zhou, however, although it continued to have a moral will, Heaven became less anthropomorphic and more of an abstract metaphysical force.

IRON AGE: EASTERN ZHOU

In 771 B.C., the Wei valley capital of the Western Zhou was overrun by barbarians. The explanation of the event in Chinese tradition calls to mind the story of "the boy who cried wolf." To please his favorite concubine, the infatuated Western Zhou king repeatedly lit bonfires signaling a barbarian attack. His concubine would clap her hands in delight at the sight of the army assembled in martial splendor. But the army tired of the charade, and when invaders actually came, the king's beacons were ignored. The king was killed and the Zhou capital sacked. The heir to the throne, with some members of the court, escaped to the secondary capital at Luoyang, 200 miles to the east and just south of the bend in the Yellow River, beginning the Eastern Zhou period.

The first phase of the Eastern Zhou is sometimes called the Spring and Autumn period after the classic history by that name, and lasted until 481 B.C. After their flight to Luoyang, the Zhou kings were never able to reestablish their old authority. By the early seventh century B.C., Luoyang's political power was nominal, although it remained a center of culture and ritual observances. Kinship and religious ties to the Zhou house had worn thin, and it no longer had the military strength to reimpose its rule. During the seventh and sixth centuries B.C., the political configuration in China was an equilibrium of many little principalities on the north-central plain surrounded by larger, wholly autonomous territorial states along the borders of the plain (see Map 1–3). The larger states consolidated the areas within their borders, absorbed tribal peoples, and expanded, conquering states on their periphery.

To defend themselves against the more aggressive territorial states, and in the absence of effective Zhou authority, smaller states entered into defensive alliances.

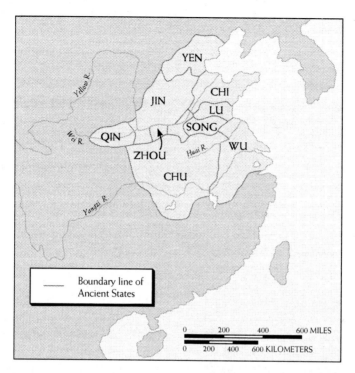

Map 1–3   Early Iron Age territorial states in China during the sixth century B.C.   After the fall of the Western Zhou in China in 771 B.C., large territorial states formed and became increasingly independent of the later Zhou kings.

The earliest alliance, in 681 B.C., was directed against the half-barbarian state of Chu, which straddled the Yangzi in the south. Princes and lords of smaller states elected as their hegemon (or military overlord) the lord of a northern territorial state and pledged him their support. At the formal ceremony that established the alliance, a bull was sacrificed. The hegemon and other lords smeared its blood on their mouths and before the gods swore oaths to uphold the alliance. That the oaths were not always upheld can be surmised from the Chinese expression "to break an oath while the blood is still wet on one's lips." During the next two centuries, alliances shifted and hegemons changed. At best, alliances only slowed down the pace of military aggrandizement.

The second phase of the Eastern Zhou is known as the Warring States period after a chronicle of the same name treating the years from 401 B.C. to 256 B.C. By the fifth century B.C., all defensive alliances had collapsed. Strong states swallowed their weaker neighbors. The border states grew in size and power. Interstate stability disappeared. By the fourth century B.C., only eight or nine great territorial states remained as contenders. The only question was which one would defeat the others and go on to unify China.

Three basic changes in Chinese society contributed to the rise of large territorial states. One was the expansion of population and agricultural lands. The walled cities of the Shang and Western Zhou had been like oases in the wilds, bounded by plains, marshes, and forests. Game was plentiful, and hunting, along with the pasturage of sheep and cattle, supplemented agriculture. But in the Eastern Zhou, as population grew, wilds began to disappear, the economy became almost entirely agricultural, and hunting became an aristocratic pastime. Friction arose over boundaries as states began to abut. These changes accelerated in the late sixth century B.C. after the start of the Iron Age. Iron tools cleared new lands and plowed deeper, raising yields and increasing agricultural surpluses. Irrigation and drainage canals became important for the first time. Serfs gave way to independent farmers, who bought and sold land. By the third century B.C., China had about twenty million people, making it the most populous country in the world, a distinction it has never lost.

The second development was the rise of commerce, which further disrupted the formerly stable agricultural economy. Roads built for war were used by merchants. Goods were transported by horses, oxcarts, riverboats, and the camel, which entered China in the third century B.C. The products of one region were traded for those of another. Copper coins joined bolts of silk and precious metals as the media of exchange. Rich merchants rivaled in lifestyle the landowning lower nobility. New outer walls were added to cities to provide for expanded merchant quarters. Bronze bells and mirrors, clay figurines, lacquer boxes, and musical instruments found in late Zhou tombs give ample evidence that the material and artistic culture of China leaped ahead during this period, despite endemic wars.

The third change that benefited larger states was a new kind of army. Cavalry armed with crossbows replaced the war chariots of the old aristocracy that had been practical only on level terrain. Most fighting was done by conscript foot soldiers. The upstart armies of the territorial states numbered in the hundreds of thousands. Against these, little states were helpless. The old nobility gave way to professional commanders. The old aristocratic etiquette, which affected behavior even in battle, gave way to military tactics that were bloody and ruthless. Prisoners were often massacred.

Change also affected government. Lords of the new territorial states began to style themselves as kings, taking the title that only Zhou royalty had enjoyed previously. At some courts, the hereditary nobility began to decline, supplanted by ministers appointed for their knowledge of statecraft. To survive, new states had to transform their agricultural and commercial wealth into military strength. To collect taxes, conscript soldiers, and administer the affairs of state required records and literate officials. Academies were established to fill the need. Beneath the ministers, a literate bureaucracy developed. Its members were referred to as *shi*, a term that had once meant "warrior" but gradually came to mean "scholar-bureaucrat." The *shi* were of mixed social origins, including petty nobility, literate members of the old warrior class, landlords, merchants, and rising commoners. From this class came the philosophers who created the "one hundred schools" and transformed the culture of China.

IRON AGE: BIRTH OF CHINESE PHILOSOPHY

Shang bronzes are breathtakingly beautiful, but they also have an archaic strangeness. Like Mayan stone sculpture, they are products of a culture so far removed from our own as to be almost incomprehensible. By contrast, the humanism of the Confucian writings and poetry of the Eastern Zhou (771–256 B.C.) speaks to us directly. However much the philosophies of these centuries grew out of the earlier matrix of archaic culture, they mark a break with it and the beginning of what we think of today as the Chinese tradition.

The philosophical revolution of Iron Age China, we note, had parallels in other parts of the globe. In South Asia, there rose Hinduism and Buddhism. In the eastern Mediterranean, there appeared Greek philosophy and the monotheistic Judaism from which would later develop the world religions of Christianity and Islam. The simultaneity of their appearance was striking. Confucius, Laozi, the Hebrew prophets, Buddha, and Socrates, if not exact contemporaries, were born within a few hundred years of each other in the first millennium B.C. The founders of these great philosophies and religions based their teachings on intensely personal experiences that cannot be analyzed in historical terms. Yet we can examine their historical contexts and note certain similarities.

1. All of the philosophical and religious revolutions occurred in or near one of the original river valley civilizations: the Yellow River, the Nile, the Tigris–Euphrates, and along the Indus and Ganges. These areas contained the most advanced cultures of the ancient world. They had sophisticated agriculture, cities with many literate inhabitants, and specialized trades and professions. In short, they had the material preconditions for breakthroughs in religion and thought.

2. Each revolution was born of a crisis in the ancient world. The appearance of iron meant better tools and weapons and, by extension, greater riches and more powerful armies. Old societies began to change and then to disintegrate. Old aristocratic and priestly codes of behavior broke down, producing a demand for more universalized rules of behavior, that is to say, for ethics. The very relation of humans to nature and to the universe seemed to be changing. These conditions led to new visions of social and political order. The similarity between the Chinese sage-king, the Jewish Messiah, and Plato's philosopher-king is more than accidental. Each, responding to a crisis in the ancient world, would restore order in a troubled society by reconnecting ethics to history.

3. What distinguished the visions embodied in the new religions and philosophies was their universalism. Each held that its doctrines were true for all people and times. Because of this, Buddhism, Christianity, and Islam became missionary religions, and Greek and Chinese philosophies could spread far beyond their countries of origin. Confucianism eventually spread to Vietnam, Korea, and Japan—countries with customs quite different from those of China. It could provide a basis for social ethics and law in those countries because its moral teachings transcended particular Chinese institutions.

4. The number of philosophical and religious revolutions can almost be counted on the fingers of one hand. The reason is not that human creativity dried up after 300 B.C. but that subsequent breakthroughs and advances tended to occur within the original traditions, which, absorbing new energies, continued to evolve. This is demonstrated in China by developments within Confucianism during the Han (206 B.C.–220 A.D.) and Song (960–1279 A.D.) dynasties. Once a cultural pattern was set, it usually endured. Each major culture was resistant to others and rarely displaced. In China, the greatest challenge to Confucianism was Buddhism, which won a permanent position in the culture. But Confucianism kept or regained its primacy.

Most of the one hundred schools of the Zhou—if, in fact, there were that many—are unknown today. Many writings disappeared in the book burning of the Qin dynasty (256–221 B.C.). But even apart from the three major schools of Confucianism, Daoism, and Legalism, enough have survived to convey a sense of the range and vitality of Zhou thought:

Rhetoricians. This school taught the arts of persuasion to be used in diplomatic negotiations. Its principal work instructed the rulers of territorial states by using historical anecdote. A practical work, it was popular for its humor and lively style.

Logicians. This school taught logic and relativity. For example, one proposition was: "The south has no limit and has a limit." Another was: "A white horse is not a horse." That is to say, the concept of *horse* is not the same as the concept of *white horse.*

Strategists. *The Art of War* by Sunzi became the classic of military science in China and is studied today by guerrillas and in military academies around the world. It praises the general who wins victories without battles and also talks of supplies, spies, propaganda, and organizing states for war.

Cosmologists. This school described the functions of the cosmos in terms of *yin* and *yang*, the complementary negative and positive forces of nature, and in terms of the five elements (metal, wood, earth, fire, and water). Its ideas were later absorbed by other schools.

Mohists. Mozi (470–391 B.C.) was an early critic of Confucius. His goals were peace, wealth, and the increase of population. He taught an ethic of universal love—to overcome a selfish human nature. He preached discipline and austerity and was critical of whatever lacked utility, including music, other arts, elaborate funerals, wasteful rites, and, above all, war. To achieve his goals, Mozi argued for a strong state: Subjects must obey their rulers, who, in turn, must obey Heaven. Heaven will punish evil and reward good. To promote peace, Mozi organized his followers into military units to aid states that were attacked.

Thinkers of Zhou China	
551–479 B.C.	Confucius
Fourth century B.C.	Laozi (Daoism)
370–290 B.C.	Mencius (Confucian)
300–237 B.C.	Xunxi (Confucian)
? –233 B.C.	Han Feizi (Legalist)

Confucianism

Confucius was born in 551 B.C. in a minor state in what is today Shandong Province in north China. He probably belonged to the lower nobility or the knightly class, because he received an education in writing, music, and rituals. His father died when Confucius was young, so he may have known privation. He made his living by teaching. He traveled with his disciples from state to state, seeking a ruler who would put

Confucius, depicted wearing the robes of a scholar of a later age.
[Photo Credit: INTERFOTO/Personalities/Alamy]

his ideas into practice. Although he may once have held a minor position, his ideas were rejected as impractical. He died in 479 B.C., honored as a teacher and scholar but having failed to find a ruler to advise. The name *Confucius* is the Latinized form of Kong Fuzi, or Master Kong, as he is known in China.

We know of Confucius only through *The Analects*, his sayings collected by his disciples, or perhaps by their disciples. They are mostly in the form of "The Master said," followed by his words. The picture that emerges is of a man of moderation, propriety, optimism, good sense, and wisdom. In an age of cruelty and superstition, he was humane, rational, and upright, demanding much of others and more of himself. Asked about death, he replied, "You do not understand even life. How can you understand death?"[1] Asked about how to serve the spirits and the gods, in which he did not disbelieve, he answered, "You are not able even to serve man. How can you serve the spirits?"

CONFUCIUS DEFINES THE GENTLEMAN

For over two thousand years in China, the cultural ideal was the gentleman, who combined knowledge of the ancient sages with an inner morality and outer propriety.

How does the injunction "to repay an injury with straightness" compare to the Christian injunction to turn the other cheek? Which do you think is more appropriate?

The Master said, "I never enlighten anyone who has not been driven to distraction by trying to understand a difficulty or who has not got into a frenzy trying to put his ideas into words."

"When I have pointed out one corner of a square to anyone and he does not come back with the other three, I will not point it out to him a second time."

The Master said, "Yu, shall I tell you what it is to know. To say you know when you know, and to say you do not when you do not, that is knowledge."

The Master said, "Is it not a pleasure, having learned something, to try it out at due intervals? Is it not a joy to have friends come from afar? Is it

not gentlemanly not to take offence when others fail to appreciate your abilities?"

Someone said, "Repay an injury with a good turn. What do you think of this saying?" The Master said, "What, then, do you repay a good turn with? You repay an injury with straightness, but you repay a good turn with a good turn."

Lin Fang asked about the basis of the rites. The Master said, "A noble question indeed! With the rites, it is better to err on the side of frugality than on the side of extravagance; in mourning, it is better to err on the side of grief than on the side of formality."

The Master said, "The gentleman agrees with others without being an echo. The small man echoes without being in agreement."

The Master said, "The gentleman is at ease without being arrogant; the small man is arrogant without being at ease."

The Master said, "There is no point in seeking the views of a gentleman who, though he sets his heart on the Way, is ashamed of poor food and poor clothes."

Confucius, *The Analects*, trans. by D. C. Lau (New York: Penguin Classics, 1979), © D. C. Lau, 1979.

---

[1]This quotation and all quotations from Confucius in this passage are from Confucius, *The Analects*, trans. by D. C. Lau (Penguin Books, 1979).

Confucius described himself as a transmitter and a conservator of tradition, not an innovator. He idealized the early Shang and Zhou kings as paragons of virtue and particularly saw early Zhou society as a golden age. He sought the secrets of this golden age in its writings. Some of these writings, along with later texts, became the Confucian classics, which through most of subsequent Chinese history, had an authority not unlike that of Scripture in the West. Five of the thirteen classics were the following:

1. *The Book of Changes.* (also known as the *Classic of Divination*). A handbook for diviners, it was later seen as containing metaphysical truths about the universe.

2. *The Book of History.* Documents and speeches from the early Zhou, some authentic. Chinese tradition holds that it was edited by Confucius. It was interpreted as the record of sage-kings.

3. *The Book of Poetry.* Some three hundred poems from the early Zhou. Representing a sophisticated literary tradition, they include love songs as well as poems of friendship, ritual, and politics. Many were given political and moral interpretations in later times.

4. *The Book of Rites.* Rituals and rules of etiquette. Rites were important to Confucians, both as a support for proper behavior and because they were seen as corresponding to forces within nature.

5. *The Spring and Autumn Annals.* A brief record of the major occurrences from 722 B.C. to 481 B.C. in the state where Confucius was born. In the Chinese tradition, this book was edited by Confucius and reflects his moral judgments on historical figures of that era.

Basing his teachings on these writings, Confucius proposed to end the turmoil of his own age by returning to the good old ways of the early Zhou. When asked about government, he said, "Let the ruler be a ruler, the subject a subject, the father a father, the son a son." (The five Confucian relationships were ruler–subject, father–son, husband–wife, older brother–younger brother, and friend–friend.) If everyone fulfilled the duties of his or her status, then harmony would prevail. Confucius understood the fundamental truth that the well-being of a society depends on the morality of its members. His vision was of an unbroken social harmony extending from the individual family member to the monarch.

But a return to the early Zhou was impossible. China was undergoing a dynamic transition from hundreds of small city-states to a few large territorial states. Specialized classes were emerging. Old rituals no longer worked. It was thus not enough to stress basic human relationships. The genius of Confucius was to transform the old aristocratic code into a new ethic that any educated Chinese could practice. His reinterpretation of the early Zhou tradition can be seen in the concept of the *junzi*. This term literally meant "the son of the ruler" (or the aristocrat). Confucius redefined it to mean a person of noble behavior with the inner virtues of humanity, integrity, righteousness, altruism, and loyalty, and an outward demeanor and propriety to match.

This redefinition was not unlike the change in the meaning of *gentleman* in England from "one who is gentle-born" to "one who is gentle-behaved." But whereas *gentleman* remained a fairly superficial category in the West, in China, *junzi* went deeper. Confucius saw ethics as grounded in nature. The true *junzi* was in touch with his own basic nature, which, in turn, was a part of the cosmic order. Confucius expressed this saying: "Heaven is the author of the virtue that is in me." Confucius's description of his own passage through life goes far beyond the question of good manners: "At fifteen I set my heart on learning; at thirty I took my stand; at forty I came to be free from doubts; at fifty I understood the Decree of Heaven; at sixty my ear was attuned; at seventy I followed my heart's desire without overstepping the line."

Confucius often contrasted the gentleman with the small or common person. The gentleman, educated in the classics and cultivating the Way (dao), understands moral action. The common people, in contrast, "can be made to follow the path but not to understand it." Good government for Confucius depended on the appointment to office of good men, who would serve as examples for the multitude: "Just desire the good yourself and the common people will be good. The virtue of the gentleman is like wind; the virtue of the small man is like grass. Let the wind blow over the grass and it is sure to bend." Beyond the gentleman was the sage-king, who possessed an almost mystical virtue and power. For Confucius, the early Zhou kings were clearly sages. But Confucius wrote, "I have no hopes of meeting a sage. I would be content if I met someone who is a gentleman."

Confucius's preoccupation with the gentleman also explains his rejection by twentieth century Chinese intellectuals and revolutionaries. The dictum that a gentleman does not seek profit or engage in physical labor clashes with modern needs and ideas of equality. Confucius's view of women was equally regressive: They were difficult to get along with and were enemies of virtue. In the *Analects*, a collection of the sayings of Confucius that was almost like a play with an all male cast, he lamented, "I suppose I should give up hope. I have yet to meet the man who is as fond of virtue as he is of beauty in women."[2]

Confucianism was not adopted as the official philosophy of China until the second century B.C., during the Han dynasty. But two other important Confucian philosophers had appeared in the meantime. Mencius (370–290 B.C.) represents an idealistic extension of Confucius's thought. His interpretation was accepted during most of subsequent history. He is famous for his argument that humans tend toward the good just as water runs downward. The role of education, therefore, is to uncover

[2]*Analects*, 1979.

and cultivate that innate goodness. Moreover, just as humans tend toward the good, so does Heaven possess a moral will. The will of Heaven is that a government should see to the education and well-being of its people. The rebellion of people against a government is the primary evidence that Heaven has withdrawn its mandate. At times in Chinese history, only lip service was paid to a concern for the people. In fact, rebellions occurred more often against weak governments than against harsh ones. But the idea that government ought to care for the people became a permanent part of the Confucian tradition.

The other influential Confucian philosopher was Xunzi (300–237 B.C.), who represents a tough-minded extension of Confucius's thought. Xunzi felt Heaven was amoral, indifferent to whether China was ruled by a tyrant or by a sage. He believed that human nature was bad or, at least, that desires and emotions, if unchecked and unrefined, led to social conflict. So he emphasized etiquette and education as restraints on an unruly human nature, and good institutions, including punishments and rewards, as a means for shaping behavior. His ideas exerted a powerful influence on thinkers of the Legalist school.

Daoism

It is often said that the Chinese were Confucian while in office and Daoist in their private lives. Daoism offered a refuge from the burden of social responsibilities. The classics of the school are the *Laozi*, dating from the fourth century B.C., and the *Zhuangzi*, dating in part from the same century and in part from a century or two later.

The central concept is the *Dao*, or Way. It is mysterious, ineffable, and cannot be named. It is the creator of the universe, the sustainer of the universe, and the process or flux of the universe. The *Dao* functions on a cosmic, not a human, scale. As the *Laozi* put it, "Heaven and Earth are ruthless, and treat the myriad creatures as straw dogs; the sage (in accord with the *Dao*) is ruthless, and treats the people as straw dogs."[3]

What does it mean to be a sage? How does a human join the rhythms of nature? The answer given by the *Laozi* is by regaining or returning to an original simplicity. Various similes describe this state: "to return to the infinite," "to return to being a babe," or "to return to being the uncarved block." To attain this state, one must "learn to be without learning." Knowledge is bad because it creates distinctions, because it leads to the succession of ideas and images that interfere with participation in the *Dao*. One must also learn to be without desires beyond the immediate and simple needs of nature: "The nameless uncarved block is but freedom from desire."

---

[3]All quotations from the *Laozi* are from *Lao-Tzu: Tao Te Ching*, trans. by D. C. Lau (Penguin Books, 1963).

DAOISM

Can inner, transformative, religious experience take people beyond everyday worldly concerns and imbue them with moral charisma or moral authority? What other religions might call "supernatural," Daoism sees as truly natural.

How does the "Way" in Daoism compare with Confucius's use of the same term?

Laozi Tells of the Way of the Sage

The way that can be spoken of
Is not the constant way;
The name that can be named
Is not the constant name.
The nameless was the beginning of heaven and earth;
The named was the mother of the myriad creatures.
The spirit of the valley never dies
This is called the mysterious female.
The gateway of the mysterious female
Is called the root of heaven and earth.
Dimly visible, it seems as if it were there,
Yet use will never drain it.
There is a thing confusedly formed,
Born before heaven and earth.
Silent and void
It stands alone and does not change,
Goes round and does not weary.
It is capable of being the mother of the world.
I know not its name
So I style it "the way."
When the way prevails in the empire, fleet footed horses are relegated to ploughing the fields; when the way does not prevail

in the empire, war-horses breed on the border.
One who knows does not speak; one who speaks does not know.
Therefore the sage puts his person last and it comes first,
Treats it as extraneous to himself and it is preserved.
Is it not because he is without thought of self that he is able to accomplish his private ends?

Zhuangzi Compares Governmental Office to a Dead Rat

When Hui Tzu was prime minister of Liang, Chuang Tzu (Zhuangzi) set off to visit him. Someone said to Hui Tzu, "Chuang Tzu is coming because he wants to replace you as prime minister!" With this Hui Tzu was filled with alarm and searched all over the state for three days and three nights trying to find Chuang Tzu. Chuang Tzu then came to see him and said, "In the south there is a bird called the Yuan-ch'u—I wonder if you've ever heard of it? The Yuan-ch'u rises up from the South Sea and flies to the North Sea, and it will rest on nothing but the Wu-t'ung tree, eat nothing but the fruit of the Lien, and drink only from springs of sweet water. Once there was an owl who had gotten hold of a half-rotten old rat, and as the Yuan-ch'u passed by, it raised its head, looked up at the Yuan-ch'u, and said, 'Shoo!' Now that you have this Liang state of yours, are you trying to shoo me?"

Laozi selection from *Lao-Tzu: Tao Te Ching*, trans. by D. C. Lau (New York: Penguin Classics, 1963). © D. C. Lau. Zhuangzi selection from *The Complete Works of Chuang-Tzu*, trans. by B. Watson. © 1968 by Columbia University Press. Reprinted by permission of the publisher.

If the sage treats the people as straw dogs, it would appear that he is beyond good and evil. But elsewhere in the *Laozi*, the sage is described as one who "excels in saving people." If not a contradiction, this is at least a paradox. The resolution is that the sage is clearly beyond morality but is not immoral or even amoral. Quite to the contrary, by being in harmony with the *Dao*, the sage is impeccably moral—as one who clings to the forms of morality or makes morality a goal could never be. So in the *Laozi* it is written, "Exterminate benevolence, discard rectitude, and the people will again be filial; exterminate ingenuity, discard profit, and there will be no more thieves and bandits."

In these words, we also see the basis for the political philosophy of Daoism, which is summed up by the expression "not doing" (*wu wei*). What this means is something between "doing nothing" and "being, but not acting." This concept has some overlap with Confucianism. The Confucian sage-king, we recall, exerts a moral force by dint of his internal accord with nature. A perfect Confucian sage could rule without doing. Confucius said, "If there was a ruler who achieved order without taking any action, it was, perhaps, Shun [an early Zhou sage emperor]. There was nothing for him to do but to hold himself in a respectful posture and to face due south." In Daoism, all true sages had this Shun-like power to rule without action: "The way never acts yet nothing is left undone. Should lords and princes be able to hold fast to it, the myriad creatures will be transformed of their own accord." Or, says the *Laozi*, "I am free from desire and the people of themselves become simple like the uncarved block." The sage acts without acting, and "when his task is accomplished and his work is done, the people will say, 'It happened to us naturally.'"

Along with the basic Daoist prescription of becoming one with the *Dao* are two other assumptions or principles. One is that any action pushed to an extreme will initiate a countervailing reaction in the direction of the opposite extreme. The other is that too much government, even good government, can become oppressive by its very weight. As the *Laozi* put it, "The people are hungry; it is because those in authority eat up too much in taxes that the people are hungry. The people are difficult to govern; it is because those in authority are too fond of action that the people are difficult to govern." Elsewhere, the same idea was expressed in even homelier terms: "Govern a large state as you would cook small fish," that is, without too much stirring.

Legalism

The third great current in classical Chinese thought, and by far the most influential in its own age, was Legalism. Like the philosophers of other schools, the Legalists were concerned to end the wars that plagued China. True peace, they felt, required a united country and thus a strong state. They favored conscription and considered war a means of extending state power.

The Legalists did not seek a model in the distant past. In ancient times, said one, there were fewer people and more food, so it was easier to rule; the different conditions of the present day require new principles of government. Nor did the Legalists model their state on a heavenly order of values. Human nature is selfish, argued both of the leading Legalists, Han Feizi (d. 233 B.C.) and Li Si (d. 208 B.C.). It is human to like rewards or pleasure and to dislike punishments or pain. If laws are severe and

LEGALISM

According to Legalism, the state can only regulate behavior, it cannot affect the inner dimensions of human life. Rewards and punishments, furthermore, are far more efficient in controlling behavior than moral appeals.

Do the tenets of Legalism have any modern parallels? What do you think of Legalism as a philosophy of government? As an approach to the problem of crime? How does Legalism compare with other approaches to law, leadership, and government?

Han Feizi Argues for the Efficacy of Punishments

Now take a young fellow who is a bad character. His parents may get angry at him, but he never makes any change. The villagers may reprove him, but he is not moved. His teachers and elders may admonish him, but he never reforms. The love of his parents, the efforts of the villagers, and the wisdom of his teachers and elders—all the three excellent disciplines are applied to him, and yet not even a hair on his shins is altered. It is only after the district magistrate sends out his soldiers and in the name of the law searches for wicked individuals that the young man becomes afraid and changes his ways and alters his deeds. So while the love of parents is not sufficient to discipline the children, the severe penalties of the district magistrate are. This is because men became naturally spoiled by love, but are submissive to authority. . . .

That being so, rewards should be rich and certain so that the people will be attracted by them; punishments should be severe and definite so that the people will fear them; and laws should be uniform and steadfast so that the people will be familiar with them. Consequently, the sovereign should show no wavering in bestowing rewards and grant no pardon in administering punishments, and he should add honor to rewards and disgrace to punishments—when this is done, then both the worthy and the unworthy will want to exert themselves. . . .

Han Feizi Attacks Confucianism

There was once a man of Sung who tilled his field. In the midst of his field stood the stump of a tree, and one day a hare, running at full speed, bumped into the stump, broke its neck, and died. Thereupon the man left his plow and kept watch at the stump, hoping that he would get another hare. But he never caught another hare, and was only ridiculed by the people of Sung. Now those who try to rule the people of the present age with the conduct of government of the early kings are all doing exactly the same thing as that fellow who kept watch by the stump. . . .

Those who are ignorant about government insistently say: "Win the hearts of the people." If order could be procured by winning the hearts of the people, then even the wise ministers Yi Yin and Kuan Chung would be of no use. For all that the ruler would need to do would be just to listen to the people. Actually, the intelligence of the people is not to be relied upon any more than the mind of a baby. If the baby does not have his head shaved, his sores will recur; if he does not have his boil cut open, his illness will go from bad to worse. However, in order to shave his head or open the boil someone has to hold the baby while the affectionate mother is performing the work, and yet he keeps crying and yelling incessantly. The baby does not understand that suffering a small pain is the way to obtain a great benefit.

Now, the sovereign urges the tillage of land and the cultivation of pastures for the purpose of increasing production for the people, but they think the sovereign is cruel. The sovereign regulates penalties and increases punishments for the purpose of repressing the wicked, but the people think the sovereign is severe. Again he levies taxes in cash and in grain to fill up the granaries and treasuries in order to relieve famine and provide for the army, but they think the sovereign is greedy. Finally, he insists upon universal military training without personal favoritism, and urges his forces to fight hard in order to take the enemy captive, but the people think the sovereign is violent. These four measures are methods for attaining order and maintaining peace, but the people are too ignorant to appreciate them.

impartial, if what strengthens the state is rewarded and what weakens the state is punished, then a strong state and a good society will ensue.

Laws, therefore, should contain incentives for loyalty and bravery in battle, and for obedience, diligence, and frugality in everyday life. The Legalists despised merchants as parasites and approved of productive farmers. They particularly despised purveyors of doctrines different from their own and criticized rulers who honored philosophers while ignoring their philosophies.

Legalism was the philosophy of the state of Qin, which destroyed the Zhou in 256 B.C. and unified China in 221 B.C. Because Qin laws were cruel and severe and because Legalism put human laws above an ethic modeled on Heaven, later generations of Chinese have execrated its doctrines. They saw it, not without justification, as a philosophy that consumed its founders: Han Feizi became an official of the Qin state but was eventually poisoned in a prison cell by Li Si, who was jealous of his growing influence. Although Li Si became prime minister of Qin, he was killed in 208 B.C. in a political struggle with a court eunuch. Yet, for all of the abuse heaped on Legalist doctrines, their legacy of administrative and criminal laws became a vital part of subsequent dynastic China. Even Confucian statesmen could not do without them.

EARLY CHINESE THOUGHT IN HISTORICAL PERSPECTIVE

The era of religious and philosophical revolutions in the ancient world is sometimes called the "axial age." Subsequent developments, this term suggests, revolved about the axes of these doctrines. If the philosophical revolution of the Zhou is compared with others, it is unlike Judaic monotheism or its second-stage offshoots, Christianity and Islam, unlike Hinduism or Buddhism, and most like the development in ancient Greece with its contending schools of philosophy. When Mao Zedong in 1956 said, "Let the one hundred flowers bloom"—encouraging a momentary easing of intellectual oppression— he was referring back to the creative era of the Zhou when many philosophies abounded.

Of the two, Greek thinkers were more speculative, more concerned with numbers and the world of nature. Chinese thinkers were usually more practical, more strongly oriented toward the social and political. Even the Daoist sages, who were intrinsically apolitical, found it necessary to offer a political philosophy.

Chinese philosophy also had far greater staying power than the Greek. Only a few centuries after the glory of Athens, Greek philosophy was submerged by Christianity.

It became the handmaiden of theology and did not reemerge as an independent force until the Renaissance. In contrast, Chinese philosophy, though challenged for centuries by Buddhism, reasserted itself and kept its dominance down to the early twentieth century. How were these early Chinese philosophies, especially the Confucian, able to maintain such a grip on China when the cultures of every other part of the world fell under the sway of religions?

Part of the answer is that Confucianism, which in later dynasties usually had state support, was always counterbalanced by a plethora of popular religions with gods and demons, heavens and hells. Most Chinese participated in such religions. Their temples became established in every village and town throughout China. Only among the literati of later dynasties, who studied in the rarified atmosphere of Confucian academies, was a "pure" philosophical Confucianism to be found.

Another part is that Confucianism had a religious dimension, but one with assumptions very different from religions with Judaic roots. In the Christian or Islamic worldview, there is a God, who, however concerned with humankind, is not of this world. This conception leads to dualism, the distinction between an other world, which is supernatural, and this world, which is natural. In the Chinese worldview, the two spheres are not so separate: The cosmos is single, continuous, and nondualistic. It includes Heaven, earth, and man. Heaven is above. Earth is below. Man stands in between, ideally governed by a wise ruler who regulates or harmonizes the cosmological forces of Heaven and earth by the power of his virtue and by performing the sacrifices.

The form that this cosmology took under the last Manchu dynasty can be seen today in the city of Beijing. The Temple of Heaven is in the south; the Temple of Earth is in the northeast; and the Imperial Palace is, symbolically at least, in between. To say that the emperor's sacrifices at the Temple of Heaven were secular (and, therefore, not religious) or religious (and not secular) misses the point. It projects our own dualistic assumptions onto China. Similarly, when we speak of the Daoist sage becoming one with nature, it is not the nature of a present-day natural scientist; rather, it is a nature that contains metaphysical and cosmological forces of a kind that our worldview might label as religious.

REVIEW QUESTIONS

1. "The 'New Stone Age' is a shorthand designation for many complex changes in China's society and economy." How did these give rise to civilization?

2. What are the distinguishing characteristics of the Shang, Eastern Zhou, and Western Zhou eras?

3. What conditions gave rise to the one hundred schools of philosophy?

4. What was China's predicament in the fourth century B.C., and what solutions were offered by Confucianism, by Daoism, and by Legalism?

SUGGESTED READINGS

CHANG, K. C. *The Archaeology of Ancient China*, 4th ed. (1986). The standard work on the subject.

CHANG, K. C. *Art, Myth, and Ritual: The Path to Political Authority in Ancient China* (1983). A study of the relation between shamans, gods, agricultural production, and political authority during the Shang and Zhou dynasties.

CHANG, K. C. *Shang Civilization* (1980).

CREEL, H. G. *The Origins of Statecraft in China* (1970). On the political structure of the Western Zhou kingdom.

CREEL, H. G. *What Is Taoism? And Other Studies in Chinese Cultural History* (1970).

DE BARY, W. T., and BLOOM, I. (compilers). *Sources of the Chinese Tradition*, 2nd ed. (1999). A selection of basic sources for all of Chinese history. Invaluable.

DI COSMO, N. *Ancient China and Its Enemies: The Rise of Nomadic Power in East Asia* (2002). Excellent study of an important dimension of Chinese history.

FINGARETTE, H. *Confucius: The Secular as Sacred* (1998). An insightful study of Confucius.

GRAHAM, A. C. *Disputers of the Tao* (1989). On early Zhou intellectual history.

HAWKES, D. *Ch'u Tz'u: The Songs of the South* (1985). Zhou poems from the southern state of Chu, superbly translated.

HSU, C. Y. *Ancient China in Transition: An Analysis of Social Mobility 722–222 B.C.* (1965). A study of the Eastern Zhou dynasty.

HSU, C. Y. *Western Chou Civilization* (1988).

KEIGHTLEY, D. N., ED. *The Origins of Chinese Civilization* (1983).

LAU, D. C., TRANS. *Confucius: The Analects* (1979).

LAU, D. C., TRANS. *Lao-Tzu: Tao Te Ching* (1963).

LEWIS, M. E. *Sanctioned Violence in Early China* (1990).

LI, C., ED. *The Sage and Second Sex: Confucianism, Ethics, and Gender* (2000). Gender in Confucian thought.

LI, X. Q. *Eastern Zhou and Qin Civilizations* (1986). This work includes interpretations based on archaeological finds.

LOEWE, M., and Shaughnessy, E. L. Ed. *The Cambridge History of Ancient China: From the Origins of Civilization to 221 B.C.* (1999).

MITE, F. W. *Intellectual Foundations of China* (1971).

PUETT, M. *To Become a God: Sacrifice and Self-Divinization in Early China* (2002).

PUETT, M. *The Ambivalence of Creation: Debates Concerning Innovation and Artifice in Early China* (2001).

SCHWARTZ, B. I. *The World of Thought in Ancient China* (1985).

WALEY, A., TRANS. *The Book of Songs* (1960).

WALEY, A. *Three Ways of Thought in Ancient China* (1956). A readable but sound introduction to Confucianism, Daoism, and Legalism.

WATSON, B., TRANS. *Han Feizi: Basic Writings* (2003).

WATSON, B., TRANS. *Xunzi: Basic Writings* (2003).

WATSON, B., TRANS. *Zhuangzi: Basic Writings* (2003).

WELCH, H. *Taoism, the Parting of the Way* (1967). A most readable and insightful account.

CHAPTER TWO

China's First Empire (221 B.C.–220 A.D.) and Its Aftermath (220–589 A.D.)

Court figures painted on ceramic tiles in a Han dynasty tomb.

[Denman Waldo Ross Collection and gift of C. T. Loo. Photograph © 2007 Courtesy Museum of Fine Arts, Boston]

CHAPTER OUTLINE

Qin Unification of China

Former Han Dynasty (206 B.C.–8 A.D.)

Later Han Dynasty (25–220 A.D.) and Its Aftermath (220–589 A.D.)

Han Thought and Religion

China's First Empire in Historical Perspective

One hallmark of Chinese history is its striking continuity of culture, language, and geography. The Shang and Zhou dynasties were centered in north China along the Yellow River or its tributary, the Wei River. The capitals of China's first empire were in exactly the same areas, and north China would remain China's political center down through history to the present. If Western civilization had experienced similar continuity, it would have progressed from Thebes in the valley of the Nile to Athens on the Nile, Rome on the Nile, and then, in time, to Paris, London, and Berlin on the Nile, and each of these centers of civilization would have spoken Egyptian and written in Egyptian hieroglyphics.

The many continuities in its history did not mean, however, that China was unchanging. One key turning point came in the third century B.C. when the old, quasi-feudal, multistate Zhou system gave way to a centralized bureaucratic government. The new centralized state built an empire stretching from the steppe in the north to Vietnam in the south.

The history of the first empire is composed of three segments: The Qin (pronounced chin) dynasty, the Former Han dynasty, and the Later Han dynasty. The English word *China* is derived from the name of the first dynasty. The Qin overthrew the previous Zhou dynasty in 256 B.C., and went on to unify China in 221 B.C. In reshaping China, the Qin developed such momentum that it became overextended and collapsed a single generation after the unification. The succeeding Han dynasties each lasted about two hundred years, the Former Han from 206 B.C. to 8 A.D., the Later Han (founded by a descendant of the Former Han rulers), from A.D. 25 to A.D. 220. Historians usually treat each of the Han dynasties as a separate period of rule, although they were almost back to back and shared many institutions and cultural traits. So deep was the impression left by these two dynasties on the Chinese that even today they call themselves—in contrast to Mongols, Manchus, Tibetans, and other minorities—the "Han people," and their ideographs, "Han writing."

QIN UNIFICATION OF CHINA

Among the territorial states of the late Zhou era, the Qin had advantages. It was strategically located on the Wei River in northwest China—the same region from which the Zhou had launched their expansion a millennium earlier. Behind the mountain passes that led out onto the Yellow River plain, it was easy to defend and a secure base from which to launch attacks on other states. Its agricultural economy was prosperous. The Qin built canals to irrigate 200 square miles of the Chengdu plain, which supported its population of about 5 million. Then, in the late fourth century B.C., it conquered a part of Sichuan, another of the most fertile regions of ancient China. A visitor from another state described the Qin population as "simple and unsophisticated" and obedient to officials. The Qin welcomed Legalist administrators, who developed innovative policies to enrich the country and strengthen its military. Despite harsh laws, farmers moved to Qin from other regions of China, attracted by the order and stability of its society. Qin armies had been forged by centuries of warfare against the nomadic raiders, whose lands half encircled the Qin. To counter these raiders, its armies adopted nomadic skills, developing cavalry in the fourth century B.C. Other states regarded the Qin as culturally crude, but recognized the formidable strength of its tough and ruthless military.

In 246 B.C., the man who would unify China succeeded to the Qin throne at age thirteen. Historical sources give conflicting accounts of his character: On the one hand, he was vigorous, intelligent, and decisive; on the other, secretive, superstitious, and cruel in the fashion of his age. On one occasion, he expressed to his entourage his displeasure on viewing the many carriages of his minister Li Si. This was reported to Li Si, who reduced the number accordingly. "The emperor, realizing that he had an informer, became angry. When nobody would admit guilt, he had all those who had been with him at the time arrested and executed."[1]

He is famous as a Legalist autocrat; but he was also appreciated by his ministers, whose advice he usually followed. In 232 B.C., at the age of twenty-seven, he began the campaigns that destroyed the six remaining territorial states. On completing his conquests in 221 B.C., to raise himself above the kings of the former territorial states, he adopted the glorious title we translate as "emperor"—a combination of ideographs hitherto used only for gods or mythic heroes. Then, aided by officials of great talent, the First Emperor set about applying to all of China the reforms that had been tried and found effective in his own realm. During the eleven years before his death in 210 B.C., his accomplishments were stupendous.

Having conquered the civilized world of north China and the Yangzi River basin, the First Emperor sent armies to conquer new lands. His armies marched south to the northern edge of the Red River basin in what is now Vietnam, and also occupied China's southeastern coast in the area of the present-day city of Guangzhou (or Canton) (see Map 2–1). In the north and the northwest, they fought against the Xiongnu, Altaic-speaking Hunnish nomads organized in a tribal confederation. During the previous age, northern border states had built long walls to protect settled lands from incursions by such horse-riding raiders. The Qin emperor had these joined into a single Great Wall that extended 1,400 miles from the Pacific Ocean into Central Asia. (By way of comparison, Hadrian's Wall in England, built by the Romans for a similar purpose, was 73 miles long.) Construction of the Great Wall cost the lives of vast numbers of conscripted laborers—by some accounts, 100,000; by others, as many as

[1]Derk Bodde, "The State and Empire of Ch'in" in *Cambridge History of China*, Volume 1 (1986), p. 71.

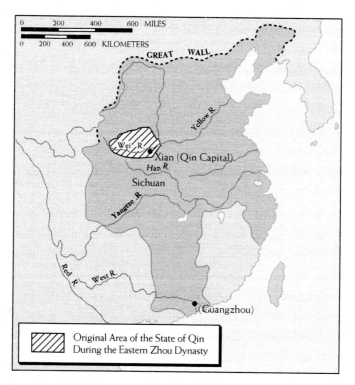

Map 2–1   The unification of China by the Qin state.   Between 232 B.C. and 221 B.C., the Qin state expanded and unified China.

one million. Among those deported to work on the Great Wall were "officials who had not been upright in handling court cases."

The most significant Qin reform was the establishment of a central government over all of China. Li Si, Legalist minister and confidant of the First Emperor, extended the Qin system of bureaucratic government to the territories of all the newly conquered states. He divided China into forty prefectures, which were further subdivided into counties. The county heads were responsible to prefects, who, in turn, were responsible to the central government. Officials were chosen by ability. Bureaucratic administration was impersonal, based on laws to which all, peasants and aristocrats alike, were subject. No one, for example, escaped Qin taxation. This kind of bureaucratic centralism broke sharply with the old Zhou pattern in which members of the ruler's family held quasi-feudal principalities. Furthermore, to ensure the smooth functioning of local offices, aristocrats of the conquered states were removed from their lands and resettled in the capital, near present-day Xian. They were housed in mansions on one side of the river, from which they could gaze across at the enormous main palace of the First Emperor.

Other reforms further unified the First Emperor's vast domain. Roads were built radiating out from the capital city. The emperor decreed a system of uniform weights and measures. He unified the Chinese writing system, establishing standard ideographs to replace the great variety that had hitherto prevailed. He established uniform axle lengths for carts. Even ideas did not escape the drive toward uniformity. Following the precepts of Legalism, the emperor and his advisers launched a campaign for which they subsequently have been execrated throughout Chinese history. They collected and burned the books of Confucianism and other schools, and executed (or, by one interpretation, buried alive) several hundred scholars opposed to the Legalist philosophy. Only useful books on history, agriculture, forestry, divination, and medicine were spared. Li Si argued that "those who use the past to criticize the present" should be put to death. He singled out the Confucian *Book of Songs* and *Book of Documents* as particularly seditious; possession of these works was made a crime.

Modern historians question the traditional negative judgment of the Qin made by Confucian historians. They point out that the First Emperor upheld morality, including the Confucian values of humanity, righteousness, and filial piety. They note that while Qin laws were strict, their application was usually tailored to fit the circumstances. They also stress the emperor's contribution to the unity of China.

When the First Emperor died in 210 B.C., intrigues broke out at the court. A jealous eunuch advisor persuaded the inept Second Emperor to execute Li Si. (Li suffered the "five mutilations" and then was cut in two at the waist in a public square.) No one of equal wisdom replaced him. Rebellions arose. The Qin, it became clear, had changed too much too quickly. To pay for the roads, canals, and the Great Wall, burdensome taxes had been levied on the people. Commoners hated conscription and labor service, and nobles resented their loss of status. Merchants were despised and exploited; scholars, except for Legalists, were oppressed. A Chinese historian wrote afterward: "The condemned were an innumerable multitude; those who had been tortured and mutilated formed a long procession on the roads. From princes and ministers down to the humblest people everyone was terrified and in fear of their lives."[2] At the end, the Qin was destroyed by the domino effect of its own legal codes. When the generals sent to quell a rebellion were defeated, they joined the rebellion rather than return to the capital and incur the severe punishment decreed for failure. The Qin collapsed in 206 B.C.

In 1974, a farmer digging a well near Xian discovered the army of 8,000 life-sized terra-cotta horses and soldiers that guarded the tomb of the First Emperor.

---

[2]C. P. Fitzgerald, *China, a Short Cultural History* (New York, Praeger, 1935), p. 147.

The historical record of the tomb itself—as yet unexcavated—tells of a ceiling depicting the constellations of Heaven, walls of bronze, a floor with a replica of the Qin empire with rivers of quicksilver. The tomb also contained traps with armed crossbows to discourage break-ins. Surrounding the tomb are the remains of horses, noblemen, and criminals sacrificed to accompany in death the emperor whose dynasty was to have lasted for 10,000 generations.

The Dynastic History of China's First Empire	
256–206 B.C.	Qin dynasty
206 B.C.–8 A.D.	Former Han dynasty
25–220 A.D.	Later Han dynasty

Life-size fully armed terra-cotta warriors stand in rows in deep trenches around the tomb of the First Emperor, Qin Shihuangdi, in central China.

[O. Louis Mazzatenta/National Geographic Image Collection]

FORMER HAN DYNASTY (206 B.C.–8 A.D.)

The Dynastic Cycle

Confucian historians of China have seen a pattern in every dynasty of long duration. They call it the *dynastic cycle*. The stages of the cycle are interpreted in terms of the "Mandate of Heaven." The cycle begins with internal wars that eventually lead to the military unification of China. Unification is proof that Heaven has given the unifier the mandate to rule. Strong and vigorous, the first ruler, in the process of consolidating his political power, restores peace and order to China. His rule is harmonious. Economic growth follows, almost automatically. The peak of the cycle is marked by public works, further energetic reforms, and aggressive military expansion. During this phase, China appears invincible. But then the cycle curves downward. The costs of expansion, coupled with an increasing opulence at the court, leads to a drain on tax revenues just as they are beginning to decline. The vigor of monarchs wanes. Intrigues develop at the court. The central controls loosen, and provincial governors and military commanders gain autonomy. Finally, canals and other public works fall into disrepair, floods and pestilence occur, rebellions break out, and the dynasty collapses. In the view of Confucian historians, the last emperors in a cycle are not only politically weak but morally culpable.

Early Years of the Former Han Dynasty

The first sixty years of the Han were the early phase of its dynastic cycle. After the collapse of the Qin, one rebel general gained control of the Wei River basin and went on to unify China. He became the first emperor of the Han dynasty and is known by his posthumous title of Gaozu. He rose from plebeian origins to become emperor, which would happen only once again in Chinese history. Gaozu built his capital at Chang'an, not far from the capitals of the previous dynasties. It took Gaozu and his immediate successors many years to consolidate their power because they consciously avoided actions that would remind the populace of the hated Qin despotism. They made punishments less severe and reduced taxes. Good government prevailed, the economy rebounded, granaries were filled, and vast cash reserves accumulated. Later historians often singled out the early Han rulers as model sage emperors.

Han Wudi

The second phase of the dynastic cycle began with the rule of Wudi (the "martial emperor"), who came to the throne in 141 B.C. at the age of sixteen and ruled for fifty-four years. Wudi was daring, vigorous, and intelligent but also superstitious, suspicious, and vengeful. He wielded tremendous personal authority.

Building on the prosperity achieved by his predecessors, Wudi initiated new economic policies. He had a canal built from the Yellow River to the capital in northwest China, linking the two major economic regions of north China. He established "ever-level granaries" throughout the country so that the surplus from bumper crops could be bought up and then resold at a time of scarcity. To increase revenues, he levied taxes on merchants, debased the currency, and sold some offices. Wudi also moved against merchants who had built fortunes in untaxed commodities by reestablishing government monopolies—a practice of the Qin—on copper coins, salt, iron, and liquor. For fear of Wudi, no one spoke out against the monopolies, but a few years after his death, a famous debate was held at the court.

Known after the title of the chronicle as the "Salt and Iron Debate," it was frequently cited thereafter in China, and in Japan and Korea as well. On one side, quasi-Legalist officials argued that the state should enjoy the profits from the sale of salt and iron. On the other side, Confucians argued that these resources should be left in private hands, for the moral purity of officials would be sullied by dealings with merchants. The Confucian scholars who compiled the chronicle made themselves the winner in the debate; but state monopolies became a regular part of Chinese government finance.

Wudi also aggressively expanded Chinese borders—a policy that would characterize every strong dynasty. His armies swept south into what is today northern Vietnam, where Chinese rule lasted for over 1,000 years, and northeast across Manchuria to establish a military outpost in northern Korea that would last until A.D. 313

Xiongnu

The principal threat to the Han was from the Xiongnu (pronounced Shiung-nu), a nomadic, pastoral people, who had formed a tribal confederation or empire to the north. Their mounted archers could raid China and flee before an army could be sent against them. To combat them, Wudi employed the entire repertoire of policies that would become standard thereafter. When possible he "used the barbarian to control the barbarian," making allies of border nomads against more distant tribes. Allies were permitted to trade with Chinese merchants; they were awarded titles and honors; and their kings were sent Chinese princesses as brides. Poems capture the pathos of these women exiled to grassy steppes far from China. When trade and titles did not work, he used military might. Between 129 B.C. and 119 B.C., Wudi sent several armies of over 100,000 troops into the steppe, destroying Xiongnu power south of the Gobi Desert in southern Mongolia. To establish a strategic line of defense aimed at the heart of the Xiongnu empire further to the west, he then sent 700,000 Chinese colonists to the arid Gansu panhandle (roughly, from Lanzhou to Yumen) and extended the Great Wall to the Yumen (Jade Gate) outpost at the eastern end of the Tarim Basin. From this outpost, Chinese influence was extended over the rim oases of Central Asia, opening the Silk Road that linked Chang'an to points further west (see Map 2–2).

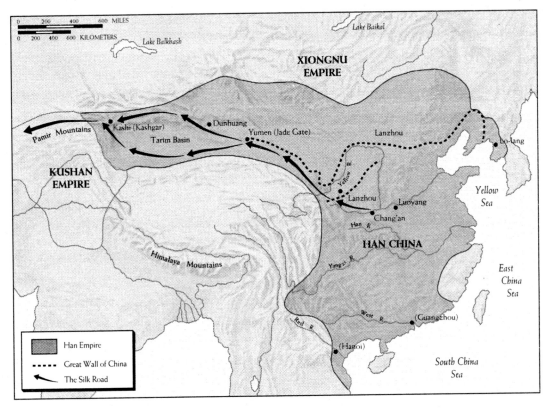

Map 2–2 The Han Empire 206 B.C.–220 A.D. At the peak of the Han expansion, Han armies advanced far out into the steppe north of the Great Wall and west into Central Asia. The Silk Road to Rome passed through the Tarim Basin to the Kushan empire, and on to western Asia and the Middle East.

Government During the Former Han

At the founding of the Han, only the western half of the empire, divided into commanderies, was under direct court rule. The eastern half was broken up into ten semi-autonomous states, ruled by kings who had been allies of Gaozi, the first emperor, during his rise to power. The Han recognition of these Zhou-like "feudal" states was a necessity and also a token of how different Han rule was from the centralized bureaucracy of the hated Qin. But as the Han court consolidated its power, it replaced the kings with the sons or brothers of emperors. Next, these kingdoms were divided into smaller units and brought under stronger imperial control. By the end of the first century of Han rule, only a few small kingdoms remained. Basically, despite its surface repudiation of the Qin and all its works, the Han had reinstituted the Qin form of centralized bureaucratic administration.

CHINESE WOMEN AMONG THE NOMADS

The first of these selections is the lament of Xijun, a Chinese lady sent by Wudi in about 105 B.C. to be the wife of a nomad king of the Wusun people of Central Asia. When she arrived, she found her husband to be old and decrepit. He saw her only once or twice a year, when they drank a cup of wine together. They could not converse, as they had no language in common. The second selection, written centuries later, is by the Tang poet Du Fu, who visited the village of another woman sent to be the wife of a nomad king.

What does the fate of the women in these poems suggest about the foreign policy of the rulers of ancient China?

1

My people have married me
In a far corner of Earth;
Sent me away to a strange land,
To the king of the Wu-sun.
A tent is my house,
Of felt are my walls;
Raw flesh my food
With mare's milk to drink.

Always thinking of my own country,
My heart sad within.
Would I were a yellow stork
And could fly to my old home!

2

Ten thousand ranges and valleys approach the
*   Ching Gate*
And the village in which the Lady of Light was
*   born and bred.*
She went out from the purple palace into the
*   desert-land;*
She has now become a green grave in the yel-
*   low dusk.*
Her face!—Can you picture a wind of the
*   spring?*
Her spirit by moonlight returns with a tinkling
Telling her eternal sorrow.

1. From *Chinese Poems* by Arthur Waley. Copyright © 1946 by George Allen and Unwin Ltd., London, p. 43. Reprinted by permission of the Arthur Waley Estate.

2. From *The Jade Mountain: A Chinese Anthology* by Witter Bynner, trans. Copyright © 1929 and renewed 1956 by Alfred A. Knopf, Inc. Reprinted by permission of Alfred A. Knopf, a division of Random House, Inc.

Officials were organized by grades and were paid salaries in grain, plus cash or silk. They were recruited by sponsorship or recommendation: It was the duty of provincial officials to recommend promising candidates. A school established at Chang'an was said to have had 30,000 students by the Later Han. The bureaucracy grew until, by the first century B.C., there were more than 130,000 officials—perhaps not too many for a population that, by that time, had reached sixty million.

During the Han dynasty, this Legalist structure of government became partially Confucianized. It did not happen overnight. The first Han emperor, Gaozu, despised Confucians as bookish pedants—he once urinated in the hat of a scholar. But Confucian ideas proved useful. The Mandate of Heaven provided a moral basis for dynastic rule. A respect for old records and the written word fit in well with the vast bookkeeping the empire entailed. Gradually, the Confucian classics were accepted as the standard for education. By 135 B.C., virtually all officials had been trained in its doctrines.

BAN ZHAO'S ADMONITIONS FOR WOMEN

Ban Zhao (45–116 A.D.) was the sister of the famous historian Ban Gu. Her guide to morality, *Admonitions for Women,* was widely used during the Han dynasty. Humility is one of the seven womanly virtues about which she wrote; the others are resignation, subservience, self-abasement, obedience, cleanliness, and industry.

Given the range of female personalities in Chinese society, what are some of the likely responses to this sort of moral education? Are the virtues listed by Ban Zhao more likely to be associated with weakness or with strength of character?

Humility

In ancient times, on the third day after a girl was born, people placed her at the base of the bed, gave her a pot shard to play with, and made a sacrifice to announce her birth. She was put below the bed to show that she was lowly and weak and should concentrate on humbling herself before others. Playing with a shard showed that she should get accustomed to hard work and concentrate on being diligent. Announcing her birth to the ancestors showed that she should

focus on continuing the sacrifices. These three customs convey the unchanging path for women and the ritual traditions.

Humility means yielding and acting respectful, putting others first and oneself last, never mentioning one's own good deeds or denying one's own faults, enduring insults and bearing with mistreatment, all with due trepidation. Industriousness means going to bed late, getting up early, never shirking work morning or night, never refusing to take on domestic work, and completing everything that needs to be done neatly and carefully. Continuing the sacrifices means serving one's husband-master with appropriate demeanor, keeping oneself clean and pure, never joking or laughing, and preparing pure wine and food to offer to the ancestors.

There has never been a woman who had these three traits and yet ruined her reputation or fell into disgrace. If a woman loses these three traits, she will have no name to preserve and will not be able to avoid shame.

Reprinted with the permission of The Free Press, a division of Simon & Schuster, Inc. From *Chinese Civilizations: A Sourcebook* by Patricia Buckley Ebrey. © 1993 by Patricia Buckley Ebrey.

Confucianism was seen as shaping moral men who would be upright officials, even in the absence of external constraints, for Confucius had taught the transformation of self by ethical cultivation and had presented a vision of benevolent government by men who were virtuous as well as talented. To be sure, no one attempted to replace laws with a code of etiquette, but increasingly, laws were interpreted and applied by men with a Confucian education.

The court during the Han dynasty exhibited features that would appear in later dynasties as well. All authority centered on the emperor, who was the all-powerful "son of Heaven." The will of a strong adult emperor was paramount. When the emperor was weak, however, or ascended to the throne when still a child, others competed to rule in his name. Four contenders for this surrogate role appeared and reappeared through Chinese history: court officials, the empress dowager, court eunuchs, and military commanders.

THE POSITION OF WOMEN

In the teachings of Confucius, a woman first obeyed her parents, then her husband, and finally her son—as the new family head. Descent was traced through the male line. A woman left her family and her ancestors at marriage to join those of her husband. A millennium before footbinding began in China, Fu Xuan (217–278 A.D.), a male poet, wrote this lament.

"Leaves her home" means to marry. How does the imagery in this verse differ from Western poems that you know?

Woman

How sad it is to be a woman!
Nothing on earth is held so cheap.
Boys stand leaning at the door
Like Gods fallen out of Heaven.
Their hearts brave the Four Oceans,
The wind and dust of a thousand miles.
No one is glad when a girl is born:
By her the family sets no store.
When she grows up, she hides in her room

Afraid to look a man in the face.
No one cries when she leaves her home—
Sudden as clouds when the rain stops.
She bows her head and composes her face,
Her teeth are pressed on her red lips:
She bows and kneels countless times.
She must humble herself even to the servants.
His love is distant as the stars in Heaven,
Yet the sunflower bends towards the sun.
Their hearts more sundered than water and
* fire—*
A hundred evils are heaped upon her.
Her face will follow the year's changes:
Her lord will find new pleasures.
They that were once like substance and
* shadow*
Are now as far as Hu from Ch'in [two distant
* places]*
Yet Hu and Ch'in shall sooner meet
Than they whose parting is like Ts'an and
* Ch'en [two stars].*

A. Waley, *Translations from the Chinese* (1919, renewed 1947), pp. 84–85.

Court officials were selected for their ability to govern. They staffed the apparatus of government and advised the emperor directly. Apart from the emperor himself, they were usually the most powerful men in China, yet their position was often precarious. Few officials escaped being removed from office or banished once or twice during their careers, and of the seven prime ministers who served Wudi, five were executed by his order.

Of the emperor's many wives, the empress dowager was the one whose child had been named as the heir to the throne. Her influence sometimes continued even after her child became an adult emperor. But she was most powerful as a regent for a child emperor. On Gaozu's death in 195 B.C., for example, Empress Lu became the regent for her child, the new emperor. Aided by her relatives, she seized control of the court and murdered a rival, and when her son was about to come of age, she had him killed and a younger son made the heir in order to continue her rule as regent. When she died in 180 B.C., loyal adherents of the imperial family who had opposed her rule massacred her relatives.

Court eunuchs came mostly from families of low social status. They were brought to the court as boys, castrated, and assigned to work as servants in the emperor's harem. They were thus in contact with the future emperor from the day he was born, became his childhood confidants, and often continued to advise him after he had gained the throne. Emperors found eunuchs useful as counterweights to officials. But to the scholars who wrote China's history, the eunuchs were greedy half men, given to evil intrigues.

Military leaders, whether generals or rebels, were the usual founders of dynasties. In the later phase of dynasties, regional military commanders often became semi-independent rulers. A few even usurped the throne. Yet they were less powerful at the Chinese court than they were, for example, in imperial Rome, partly because the military constituted a separate social stratum, lower in prestige than the better educated civil officials. It was also partly because the court took great pains to prevent its generals from establishing a base of personal power. An appointment to command a Han army was given only for a specific campaign, and commanders were appointed in pairs so that each would check the other.

Tomb figure of standing attendant from the Former Han dynasty, second century B.C.
[The Asia Society, New York: Mr. and Mrs. John D. Rockefeller 3rd Collection. 1979.110. Photograph by Lynton Gardiner]

Another characteristic of government during the Han and subsequent dynasties was that its functions were limited. It collected taxes, maintained military forces, administered laws, supported the imperial household, and carried out public works that were beyond the powers of local jurisdictions. But government in a district that remained orderly and paid its taxes was left largely in the hands of local notables and large landowners. This pattern was not, to be sure, unique to China. Most premodern governments, even those that were bureaucratic, floated on top of local society and only occasionally reached down and interfered in the everyday lives of their subjects.

The Silk Road

Roman ladies loved, and Roman moralists inveighed against, diaphanous gowns of Chinese silk. Wealthy Chinese coveted Roman glass and gold. Yet no camel train traveled from Chang'an all the way to Rome. Precious cargoes, moving more easily than persons, were passed across empires, like batons in relay races, from one network of merchants to another.

The route, during the Han and later dynasties, began with a network of Chinese or Central Asian traders, which stretched from the Chinese capital to Lanzhou in northeastern China, through the Gansu corridor to Dunhuang. It then crossed the inhospitable Tarim Basin, intermittently under Chinese military control, from oasis to oasis, to Kashi (Kashgar). From Kashi, the route continued in a northerly sweep to Tashkent, Samarkand, and Bukhara or in a southerly sweep to Teheran, Baghdad, and Damascus, and finally on to the Mediterranean ports of Tyre, Antioch, and Constantinople—which traded with Rome. Of goods departing Chang'an, only a minute portion reached Rome—which was not a destination as much as the center of the westernmost trade net. Of goods consigned to Roman commerce, only the thinnest trickle reached China.

The Silk Road, and the alternate, more distant, and equally perilous oceanic route, points up China's isolation from other high centers of civilization. The "journey" took more than half a year; the distance was measured in thousands of miles; camel caravans at times traveled as little as 15miles a day. The route was hazardous, the climate extreme. Crossing deserts and mountain passes, travelers experienced cold, hunger, sandstorms, and bandits.

Most Chinese foreign trade was limited to their immediate steppe neighbors. Chinese exported silk, lacquer, metalwork, and later jewels, musk and rhubarb (as a digestive for nomadic stomachs). They imported horses for their army, cattle, sheep, donkeys, jade (from Khotan), woolens, medicines, indigo, and the occasional exotic animal. Only the most precious goods made their way to distant empires. Silk—valuable, light, and compact—was ideal. Romans and Chinese had only the vaguest idea of where the other was located, and knew nothing of the other's civilization. Romans thought silk came from a plant.

Exotic goods hawked in distant bazaars lend an aura of romance to the Silk Road, but its true significance was as a transmission belt. In an early age, China may have borrowed the chariot, compound bow, wheat, domesticated horses, and the stirrup from western Asia. Even the idea of mold-casting bronze may have come from beyond China's frontiers. Chinese technologies of papermaking, iron-casting, water-powered mills, and shoulder collars for draft animals, and then the compass and gunpowder, spread slowly to the West, sometimes over centuries. Seeds of trees and plants went in both directions, as did germs. During the late Han (the second century A.D.), the Roman empire lost a quarter of its population to an epidemic that, some say, appeared in China forty years later with equally dire results. During the fourteenth century A.D., bubonic plague may have spread through the Mongol empire from southwestern China to Central Asia to the Middle East, and then on to Europe as the Black Death. Missionary religions traveled the Silk Road east: Buddhism from the end of the Han dynasty and Islam centuries later.

Decline and Usurpation

During the last decade of Wudi's rule in the early first century B.C., military expenses ran ahead of revenues. His successor cut back on military costs, eased economic controls, and reduced taxes. But over the next several generations, large landowners began to use their growing influence in provincial politics to avoid paying taxes. State revenues declined. The tax burden on smaller landowners and free peasants grew heavier. In 22 B.C., rebellions broke out in several parts of the empire. At the court, too, a decline set in. There was a succession of weak emperors. Intrigues, nepotism, and factional struggles grew apace. Even officials began to sense that the dynasty no longer had Heaven's approval. The dynastic cycle approached its end.

Many at the court urged Wang Mang, the regent for the infant emperor and a nephew of an empress, to take the throne and begin a new dynasty. Wang Mang refused several times—to demonstrate a commendable lack of eagerness—and then accepted in A.D. 8. He drew up a program of sweeping reforms based on ancient texts. He was Confucian, yet relied on new institutional arrangements, rather than moral reform, to improve society. He revived ancient titles, expanded state monopolies, abolished private slavery (about 1 percent of the population), made loans to poor peasants, and then moved to confiscate large private estates.

These reforms alienated many. Merchants disliked the monopolies. Large landowners resisted the expropriation of their lands. Nature also conspired to bring down Wang Mang: The Yellow River overflowed its banks and changed its course, destroying the northern Chinese irrigation system. Several years of poor harvests produced famines. The Xiongnu overran China's northern borders. In A.D. 18, the Red Eyebrows, a peasant secret society, rose in rebellion. In A.D. 23, rebels attacked Chang'an, and Wang Mang was killed and eaten by rebel troops. Wang Mang had tried to found a new dynasty from within a decrepit court without an independent military base. The attempt was futile. Internal wars continued in China for two more years until a large landowner, who had become the leader of a rebel army, emerged triumphant in A.D. 25. Because he was from a branch line of the imperial family, his new dynasty was viewed as a restoration of the Han.

LATER HAN DYNASTY (25–220 A.D.) AND ITS AFTERMATH (220–589 A.D.)

First Century

The founder of the Later Han moved his capital east to Luoyang. Under the first emperor and his two successors, there was a return to strong central government and a laissez-faire economy. Agriculture and population recovered from the devastation of war. By the end of the first century A.D., China was as prosperous as it had been during the good years of the Former Han. The shift from pacification and recuperation to military expansion came earlier than in the previous dynasty. Even during the reign of the first emperor, south China and Vietnam were retaken. Dissension among the Xiongnu enabled the Chinese to secure an alliance with southern tribes in A.D. 50, and in A.D. 89, Chinese armies crossed the Gobi Desert and defeated the northern Xiongnu. This defeat sparked the migrations, some historians say, that brought the Xiongnu to the southern Russian steppes and then, in the fifth century A.D., to Europe, where they were known as the Huns of Attila. In A.D. 97, a Chinese general led an army as far west as the shores of the Caspian Sea. The Chinese expansion in inner Asia, coupled with more lenient government policies toward merchants, facilitated the camel caravans that carried Chinese silk across the Tarim Basin to Iran, Palestine, and Rome.

Decline During the Second Century

Until A.D. 88, Later Han emperors were vigorous; afterward, they were ineffective and short-lived. Empresses plotted to advance the fortunes of their families. Emperors turned for help to palace eunuchs, whose power at times surpassed that of officials. In A.D. 159, a conspiracy of eunuchs in the service of an emperor slaughtered the family of a scheming empress dowager and ruled at the court. When officials and students protested against the eunuch dictatorship, over 100 were killed and over 1,000 were tortured or imprisoned. A reaction occurred in 189–190 A.D., when a general deposed one emperor, installed another, killed the empress dowager, and massacred more than 2,000 eunuchs at the court. The destruction of eunuch power upset the previous balance, giving ambitious generals, already active in regional politics, a larger role at the court.

In the countryside, large landowners who had been powerful from the start of the dynasty grew more so. They harbored private armies. Farmers on the estates of the mighty were reduced to serfs. The landowners used their influence to avoid taxes. Great numbers of free farmers fled south for the same purpose. The remaining freeholders paid ever heavier taxes and labor services. Many peasants turned to neo-Daoist religious movements—the Yellow Turbans in the east and the Five Pecks of Rice Band in Sichuan—that provided the ideology and organization to channel their discontent into action. In A.D. 184, rebellions organized by members of the religious movements broke out against the government. Han generals suppressed the rebellions but stayed on to rule in the provinces they had pacified. In A.D. 220, they deposed the last Han emperor.

Aftermath of Empire

For more than three-and-a-half centuries after the fall of the Han, China was disunited. For several generations, it was divided into three kingdoms, whose heroic warriors and scheming statesmen were made famous by wandering storytellers. These figures later peopled the *Romance of the Three Kingdoms*, a great romantic epic of Chinese literature.

Chinese history during the post-Han centuries had two characteristics. The first was that great aristocratic landowning families played the dominant role. With vast estates, huge numbers of serfs, fortified manor houses, and private armies, they were beyond the control of most governments. Because they took over many of the functions of local government, some historians describe post-Han China as having reverted to the quasi-feudalism of the Zhou. The second characteristic of these centuries was that northern and southern China developed in quite different ways.

In the south, there followed a succession of ever weaker dynasties with capitals at Nanjing. Although these six southern states were called dynasties—and the entire period of Chinese history from A.D. 220 to A.D. 589 is called the Six Dynasties era after them—they were in fact short-lived kingdoms, plagued by intrigues, usurpations, and *coups d'état*. They frequently warred with northern states and were in constant fear of their own generals. The main developments in the south were (1) continuing economic growth and the emergence of Nanjing as a thriving center of commerce; (2) the ongoing absorption of tribal peoples into Chinese society and culture; (3) large-scale immigrations of Chinese fleeing the north; and (4) the spread of Buddhism and its penetration to the heart of Chinese culture.

In the north, state formation depended on the interaction of nomads and Chinese. During the Han dynasty, Chinese invasions of the steppe had led to the incorporation of semi-Sinicized Xiongnu as the northernmost tier of the Chinese defense system—just as Germanic tribes had acted as the teeth and claws of the late Roman empire. But as the Chinese state weakened, the highly mobile nomads broke loose, joined with other tribes, and began to invade China. The short-lived states that they formed are usually referred to as the "Sixteen Kingdoms." One kingdom was founded by invaders of Tibetan stock. Most spoke Altaic languages: the Xianbi (proto-Mongols), the Tuoba (proto-Turks), and the Ruan Ruan (who would later appear in eastern Europe as the Avars). But differences of language and stock were less important than these tribes' similarities:

1. All began as steppe nomads with a way of life different from that of agricultural China.

THE PEACH BLOSSOM SPRING

The poet Tao Qian wrote in A.D. 380 of a lost village without taxes and untouched by the barbarian invasions and wars of the post-Han era. The simplicity and naturalness of his utopian vision were in accord, perhaps, with certain strains of Neo-Daoist thought. It struck a chord in the hearts of Chinese, and then Koreans and Japanese, inspiring a spate of paintings, poetry, and essays.

Utopias are often based on religion, but this one is not. What does this suggest regarding the Chinese view of human nature?

During the T'ai-yuan period of the Ch'in [Qin] dynasty a fisherman of Wuling once rowed upstream, unmindful of the distance he had gone, when he suddenly came to a grove of peach trees in bloom. For several hundred paces on both banks of the stream there was no other kind of tree. The wild flowers growing under them were fresh and lovely, and fallen petals covered the ground—it made a great impression on the fisherman. He went on for a way with the idea of finding out how far the grove extended. It came to an end at the foot of a mountain whence issued the spring that supplied the stream. There was a small opening in the mountain and it seemed as though light was coming through it. The fisherman left his boat and entered the cave, which at first was extremely narrow, barely admitting his body; after a few dozen steps it suddenly opened out onto a broad and level plain where well-built houses were surrounded by rich fields and pretty ponds. Mulberry, bamboo and other trees and plants grew there, and crisscross paths skirted the fields. The sounds of cocks crowing and dogs barking could be heard from one courtyard to the next. Men and women were coming and going about their work in the fields. The clothes they wore were like those of ordinary people. Old men and boys were carefree and happy.

When they caught sight of the fisherman, they asked in surprise how he had got there. The fisherman told the whole story, and was invited to go to their house, where he was served wine while they killed a chicken for a feast. When the other villagers heard about the fisherman's arrival they all came to pay him a visit. They told him that their ancestors had fled the disorders of Ch'in times and, having taken refuge here with wives and children and neighbors, had never ventured out again; consequently they had lost all contact with the outside world. They asked what the present ruling dynasty was, for they had never heard of the Han, let alone the Wei and the Chin. They sighed unhappily as the fisherman enumerated the dynasties one by one and recounted the vicissitudes of each. The visitors all asked him to come to their houses in turn, and at every house he had wine and food. He stayed several days. As he was about to go away, the people said, "There's no need to mention our existence to outsiders."

After the fisherman had gone out and recovered his boat, he carefully marked the route. On reaching the city, he reported what he had found to the magistrate, who at once sent a man to follow him back to the place. They proceeded according to the marks he had made, but went astray and were unable to find the cave again.

From *The Poetry of Ta'o Ch'ien* by J. R. Hightower. Copyright © 1970 Clarendon Press, pp. 254–255. Reprinted by permission of Oxford University Press.

---

2. After forming states, all became at least partially Sinicized. Chinese from great families, which had preserved Han traditions, served as their tutors and administrators.

3. All were involved in wars—among themselves, against southern dynasties, or against conservative steppe tribes that resisted Sinicization.

4. Buddhism was powerful in the north as in the south. As a universal religion, it acted as a bridge between "barbarians" and Chinese—just as Christianity was a unifying force in post-Roman Europe. The barbarian rulers of the north were especially attracted to its magical side. Usually Buddhism was made the state religion. Of the northern states, the most durable was the Northern Wei (386–534 A.D.), famed for its Buddhist sculpture.

HAN THOUGHT AND RELIGION

Poems describe the splendor of Chang'an and Luoyang: broad boulevards, tiled gateways, open courtyards, watchtowers, and imposing walls. Most splendid of all were the palaces of the emperors, with their audience halls, vast chambers, harem quarters, and parks containing artificial lakes and rare animals and birds. But today, little remains of the grandeur of the Han. Whereas Roman ruins abound in Italy and circle the Mediterranean, in China, nothing remains above ground. Only from the pottery, bronzes, musical instruments, gold and silver jewelry, lacquerware, and clay figurines that were buried in tombs do we gain an inkling of the rich material culture of the Han period. And only from paintings on the walls of tombs do we know of its art. But a wealth of written records convey the sophistication and depth of Han culture. Perhaps the two most important areas were philosophy and history.

Han Confucianism

A major accomplishment of the early Han was the recovery of texts that had been lost during the Qin persecution of scholars. Some were retrieved from the walls of houses where they had been hidden; scholars reproduced others from memory. Debate arose regarding the relative authenticity of the old and new texts—a controversy that has continued until modern times. In 51 B.C. and again in A.D. 79, councils were held to determine the true meaning of the Confucian classics. In A.D. 175, an approved, official version of the texts was inscribed on stone tablets.

In about A.D. 100, the first Chinese dictionary was compiled. Containing about 9,000 characters, it helped promote a uniform system of writing. In Han times, as today, Chinese from the north could not converse with Chinese from the southeastern coast. But a common written language bridged differences of pronunciation, contributing to Chinese unity.

It was also in Han times that scholars began writing commentaries on the classics, a major activity for scholars throughout Chinese history. Scholars learned the classics by heart and used classical allusions in their writing.

Han philosophers extended Zhou Confucianism by adding to it the teachings of cosmological naturalism. Zhou Confucianists had assumed that the moral force of a virtuous emperor would not only order society but also harmonize nature. Han Confucianists explained why. Dong Zhongshu (c. 179–104 B.C.), for example, held that all nature was a single, interrelated system. Just as summer always followed spring, so did one color, one virtue, one planet, one element, one number, and one officer of the court always take precedence over another. All reflected the systematic workings of *yin* and *yang* and the five elements. And just as one dresses appropriately to the season, so was it important for the emperor to choose policies appropriate to the sequences inherent in nature. If he was moral, if he acted in accord with Heaven's natural system, then all would go well. But if he acted inappropriately, then Heaven would send a portent as a warning—a blue dog, a rat holding its tail in its mouth, an eclipse, or a comet. If the portent went unheeded, wonders and then misfortunes would follow. It was the Confucian scholars, of course, who claimed to understand nature's messages and advised the emperor.

It is easy to criticize Han philosophy as a pseudoscientific and mechanistic view of nature. But it represented a new effort by the Chinese to encompass and comprehend the interrelationships of the natural world. This effort led to inventions like the seismograph and to advances in astronomy, music, and medicine. It was also during the Han that the Chinese invented paper, the wheelbarrow, the sternpost rudder, and the compass (known as the "south-pointing chariot").

History

The Chinese were the greatest historians of the premodern world. They wrote more history than anyone else, and what they wrote was usually more accurate. Apart from the *Spring and Autumn Annals* and the scholarship of Confucius himself, history writing in China began during the Han dynasty. Why the Chinese were so history-minded has been variously explained: because the Chinese tradition is this-worldly; because Confucians were scholarly and their veneration for the classics carried over to the written word; and because history was seen as a lesson book (the Chinese called it a mirror) for statesmen, and thus a necessity for the literate men who operated the centralized Chinese state.

The practice of using actual documents and firsthand accounts of events began with Sima Qian (d. 85 B.C.), who set out to write a history of the known world from the most ancient times down to the age of the Emperor Wudi. His *Historical Records* consisted of 130 substantial chapters (with a total of over 700,000 characters) divided into "Basic Annals"; "Chronological Tables"; "Treatises" on rites, music, astronomy, the calendar, and so on; "Hereditary Houses"; and 70 chapters of "Biographies," including descriptions of foreign peoples. A second great work, *The Book of the Han*, was written by Ban Gu (d. A.D. 92). It applied the analytical schema of Sima Qian to a single dynasty, the Former Han, and established the pattern by which each dynasty wrote the history of its predecessor.

A second century Chinese seismograph. When an earthquake occurs, a weight suspended in the vase swings in the direction of the quake. This moves a lever, dropping a ball from the dragon head on that side of the vase into the mouth of a waiting frog.
[Michael Holford/Michael Holford Photographs]

Neo-Daoism

As the Han dynasty waned, the effort to realize the Confucian ethic in the sociopolitical order became increasingly difficult. Some scholars abandoned Confucianism altogether in favor of new doctrines and new social organizations.

Daoist millenarian sects, which had little relation to earlier philosophical Daoism, appeared. Their leaders were educated men, who created a liturgy and a hierarchical church. They venerated Laozi as a god who had given men the text of the Laozi as a revelation. They also studied other Daoist texts as guides for a troubled age. One such sect in eastern China was known as the "Yellow Turbans." The yellow headgear of its adherents represented earth, which would triumph over fire, the guiding element of the Later Han dynasty. Peasant armies of the sect rebelled in A.D. 184; their goal was to establish a "Great Peace," but the sect was suppressed soon afterwards. Another sect in western China (eastern Sichuan) was known as the "Way of the Celestial Masters" or the "Five Pecks of Rice Band." That much rice, a tithe of sorts, was contributed by each member. This sect, too, had a church organization, was theocratic and messianic, and emphasized loyalty, filial piety, and the cure of diseases by religious practice. During the Tang dynasty, these sects and their scriptures and hierarchical clergy were recognized by the state.

Another long-standing concern of Chinese thinkers, which gained a new force in this era, was the quest for immortality. Some sought it in dietary restrictions and yoga-like meditation, some in sexual abstinence or orgies. Others, seeking elixirs to prolong life, dabbled in alchemy, and although no magical elixir was ever found, the schools of alchemy to which the search gave rise are credited with the discovery of medicines, dyes, glazes, and gunpowder. Still another intellectual movement was "Mysterious (or Dark) Learning." Its members were concerned with the proper response to circumstances. They admired Laozi and Zhuangzi but held Confucius in even greater esteem. They stressed the teachings in the *Analects* and criticized the Han emphasis on the five classics.

The most charming thinkers of this era were the practitioners of "pure conversation." Withdrawing from Wei dynasty court society, they saw the natural as the pleasurable, engaged in witty repartee, discussed poetry and philosophy, played the lute, and drank wine. Famous among them were the Seven Sages of the Bamboo Grove. One sage was always accompanied by a servant carrying a jug of wine and a spade—the first one for his enjoyment and the other to dig his grave should he die. Another wore no clothes at home. When criticized, he replied that the cosmos was his home, and his house his clothes. "Why are you in my pants?" he asked a discomfited visitor. Still another took a boat to visit a friend on a snowy night, but on arriving at his friend's door, turned around and went home. When pressed for an explanation, he said that it had been his pleasure to go, and that when the impulse died, it was his pleasure to return. These anecdotes reveal a scorn for convention coupled with an admiration for inner spontaneity, however eccentric.

The lines of demarcation between these several movements were not always clear. Some adherents of Mysterious Learning praised the Seven Sages, but others criticized them as frivolous. Neo-Daoists and scholars of Mysterious Learning might emphasize some of the same texts but interpret them differently. Also, apart from the movements described earlier, other folk religions abounded. They contained an amalgam of beliefs, practices, and superstitions. They had priests, shamans, seers, and sorceresses, and pantheons of gods and immortals. We know of them principally through the harsh criticisms written by scholars. Such popular cults have continued down to modern times, though with many Buddhist accretions. They are sometimes called "Daoist" but this use of the name is almost meaningless.

SIMA QIAN ON THE WEALTHY

More than half of the chapters in Sima Qian's *Historical Records* (early first century B.C.) were biographies of extraordinary men and women. He wrote of scholars, wandering knights, diviners, harsh officials and reasonable officials, wits and humorists, doctors, and moneymakers. The following is his description of the vibrant economic life of Han cities and his judgments regarding the wealthy.

What economic "principles" can you derive from this passage? Can you detect an echo of Sima Qian's claims in current debates on economic policy?

Anyone who in the market towns or great cities manages in the course of a year to sell the following items: a thousand brewings of liquor; a thousand jars of pickles and sauces; a thousand jars of sirups; a thousand slaughtered cattle, sheep, and swine; a thousand chung of grain; a thousand cartloads or a thousand boat-lengths of firewood and stubble for fuel; a thousand logs of timber; ten thousand bamboo poles; a hundred horse carriages; a thousand two-wheeled ox carts; a thousand lacquered wooden vessels; brass utensils weighing thirty thousand catties; a thousand piculs of plain wooden vessels, iron vessels, or gardenia and madder dyes; two hundred horses; five hundred cattle; two thousand sheep or swine; a hundred male or female slaves; a thousand catties of tendons, horns, or cinnabar; thirty thousand catties of silken fabric, raw silk, or other fine fabrics; a thousand rolls of embroidered or patterned silk; a thousand piculs of fabrics made of vegetable fiber or raw or tanned hides; a thousand pecks of lacquer; a thousand jars of leaven or salted bean relish; a thousand catties of globefish or mullet; a thousand piculs of dried fish; thirty thousand catties of salted fish; three thousand piculs of jujubes or chestnuts; a thousand skins of fox or sable; a thousand piculs of lamb or sheep skins; a thousand felt mats; or a thousand chung

of fruits or vegetables—such a man may live as well as the master of an estate of a thousand chariots. The same applies for anyone who has a thousand strings of cash [i.e., a million in cash] to lend out on interest. Such loans are made through a moneylender, but a greedy merchant who is too anxious for a quick return will only manage to revolve his working capital three times while a less avaricious merchant has revolved his five times. These are the principal ways of making money. There are various other occupations which bring in less than twenty percent profit, but they are not what I would call sources of wealth.

Thrift and hard work are without doubt the proper way to gain a livelihood. And yet it will be found that rich men have invariably employed some unusual scheme or method to get to the top. Plowing the fields is a rather crude way to make a living, and yet Qin Yang did so well at it that he became the richest man in his province. Robbing graves is a criminal offense, but T'ien Shu got his start by doing it. Gambling is a wicked pastime, but Huan Fa used it to acquire a fortune. Most fine young men would despise the thought of traveling around peddling goods, yet Yung Lo-ch'eng got rich that way. Many people would consider trading in fats a disgraceful line of business, but Yung Po made a thousand catties of gold at it. Vending sirups is a petty occupation, but the Chang family acquired ten million cash that way. It takes little skill to sharpen knives, but because the Chih family didn't mind doing it, they could eat the best of everything. Dealing in dried sheep stomachs seems like an insignificant enough trade, but thanks to it the Cho family went around with a mounted retinue. The calling of a horse doctor is a rather ignominious profession, but it enabled Chang Li to own a house so large that he had to strike a bell to summon the servants. All of these men got where they did because of their devotion and singleness of purpose.

From this we may see that there is no fixed road to wealth, and money has no permanent master. It finds its way to the man of ability like the spokes of a wheel converging upon the hub, and from the hands of the worthless it falls like shattered tiles. A family with a thousand catties of gold may stand side by side with the lord of a city; the man with a hundred million cash may enjoy the pleasures of a king. Rich men such as these deserve to be called the "untitled nobility," do they not?

From *Records of the Grand Historian of China*, trans. by Burton Watson. Copyright © 1961 by Columbia University Press. Reprinted by permission of the publisher.

THE CASTRATION OF SIMA QIAN

Why did the historian Sima Qian permit himself to be castrated? When he incurred the wrath of the Emperor Wudi for defending a general defeated by the Xiongnu and was condemned to suffer this shame in 98 B.C., why did he not choose an honorable suicide? Read his explanation.

A man has only one death. That death may be as weighty as Mount T'ai, or it may be as light as a goose feather. It all depends upon the way he uses it. It is the nature of every man to love life and hate death, to think of his relatives and look after his wife and children. Only when a man is moved by higher principles is this not so. Then there are things which he must do. The brave man does not always die for honor, while even the coward may fulfill his duty. Each takes a different way to exert himself. Though I might be weak and cowardly and seek shamefully to prolong my life, yet I know full well the difference between what ought to be followed and what rejected. How could I bring myself to sink into the shame of ropes and bonds? If even the lowest slave and scullery maid can bear to commit suicide, why should not one like myself be able to do what has to be done? But the reason I have not refused to bear these ills and have continued to live, dwelling among this filth, is that I grieve that I have things in my heart that I have not been able to express fully, and I am shamed to think that after I am gone my writings will not be known to posterity.

I too have ventured not to be modest but have entrusted myself to my useless writings. I have gathered up and brought together the old traditions of the world which were scattered and lost. I have examined the deeds and events of the past and investigated the principles behind their success and failure, their rise and decay, in one hundred and thirty chapters. I wished to examine into all that concerns heaven and man, to penetrate the changes of the past and present, completing all as the work of one family. But before I had finished my rough manuscript, I met with this calamity. It is because I regretted that it had not been completed that I submitted to the extreme penalty without rancor. When I have truly completed this work, I shall deposit it in some safe place. If it may be handed down to men who will appreciate it and penetrate to the villages and great cities, then though I should suffer a thousand mutilations, what regret would I have?

W. T. de Bary, W. T. Chan, and B. Watson, eds., *Sources of Chinese Tradition* (New York: Columbia University Press, 1960), pp. 272–273.

Buddhism

Central Asian missionaries, following trade routes east, brought Buddhism to China in the first century A.D. It was at first viewed as a new Daoist sect—not surprising since early translators used Daoist terms to render Buddhist concepts. *Nirvana*, for example, was translated as "not doing" (*wu-wei*). In the second century A.D., confusion about the two religions led to the very Chinese view that Laozi had gone to India, where the Buddha had become his disciple, and that Buddhism was the Indian form of Daoism.

Then, as the Han sociopolitical order collapsed in the third century A.D., Buddhism spread rapidly. We are reminded of the spread of Christianity at the end of the Roman empire. Although an alien religion in China, Buddhism had advantages over Daoism:

1. It was a doctrine of personal salvation, offering several routes to that goal.

2. It contained high standards of personal ethics.

3. It had systematic philosophies, and during its early centuries in China, it continued to receive inspiration from India.

4. It drew on the Indian tradition of meditative practices and psychologies, which were the most sophisticated in the world.

By the fifth century A.D., Buddhism had spread over all of China (see Map 2–3). Occasionally it was persecuted by Daoist emperors—in the north between A.D. 446

Map 2–3 The spread of Buddhism and Chinese states in A.D. 500. Buddhism originated in a Himalayan state in northwest India. It spread in one wave south in India and on to Southeast Asia as far as Java. It also spread into northwest India, Afghanistan, Central Asia, and then to China, Korea, and Japan.

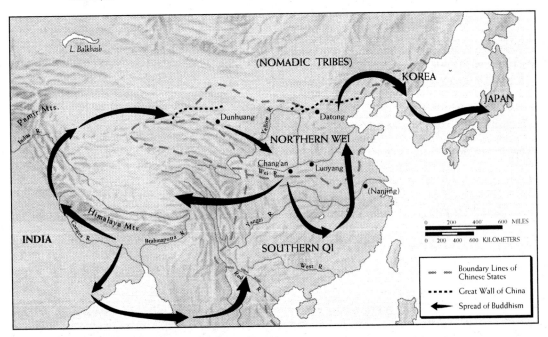

and A.D. 452 and again between A.D. 574 and A.D. 578. But most courts supported Buddhism. The "Bodhisattva Emperor" Wu of the southern Liang dynasty three times gave himself to a monastery and had to be ransomed back by his disgusted courtiers. Temples and monasteries abounded in both the north and the south. There were communities of nuns as well as of monks. Chinese artists produced Buddhist painting and sculpture of surpassing beauty, and thousands of monk-scholars labored to translate sutras and philosophical treatises. Chinese monks went on pilgrimages to India. The record left by Fa Xian, who traveled to India overland and back by sea between A.D. 399 and A.D. 413, became a prime source of Indian history. The Tang monk Xuanzang went to India from A.D. 629 until A.D. 645. Several centuries later, his pilgrimage was novelized as *Journey to the West* (later dubbed *Monkey* by Arthur Waley in his abridged English translation). The novel joins faith, magic, and adventure.

A comparison of Indian and Chinese Buddhism highlights some distinctive features of its spread. Buddhism in India had begun as a reform movement. Forget speculative philosophies and elaborate metaphysics, taught the Buddha, and concentrate on simple truths: Life is suffering, the cause of suffering is desire, death does not stop the endless cycle of birth and rebirth; only the attainment of *nirvana* releases one from the "wheel of *karma*." Thus, in this most otherworldly of the world's religions, all of the cosmic drama of salvation was compressed into the single figure of the Buddha meditating under the Bodhi tree. Over the centuries, however, Indian Buddhism developed contending philosophies and conflicting sects and, having become virtually indistinguishable from Hinduism, was reabsorbed after A.D. 1000.

In China, there were a number of sects with different doctrinal positions, but the Chinese genius was syncretic. It took in the sutras and meditative practices of early Buddhism. It took in the Mahayana philosophies that depicted a succession of Buddhas, cosmic and historical, past and future, all embodying a single ultimate reality. It also took in the sutras and practices of Buddhist devotional sects. Finally, in the Tiantai sect, the Chinese joined together these various elements as different levels of a single truth. Thus the monastic routine of a Tiantai monk would include reading sutras, sitting in meditation, and also practicing devotional exercises.

Socially, too, Buddhism adapted to China. Ancestor worship demanded heirs to perform the sacrifices. Without progeny, ancestors might become "hungry ghosts." Hence, the first son would be expected to marry and have children, whereas the second son, if he were so inclined, might become a monk. The practice also arose of holding Buddhist masses for dead ancestors. Still another difference between China and India was the more extensive regulation of Buddhism by the state in China. Just as Buddhism was not to threaten the integrity of the family, so Buddhism was not to reduce the taxes paid on land. As a result, limits were placed on the number of monasteries, nunneries, and monastic lands, and the requirement was made that the state must give its permission before men or women abandoned the world to enter a religious establishment. The regulations, to be sure, were not always enforced.

CHINA'S FIRST EMPIRE IN HISTORICAL PERSPECTIVE

Were there world-historical forces that produced at roughly the same time great empires in China, India, and the Mediterranean? Certainly these empires had similar features. All three arose after revolutions in thought. The Han built on Zhou thought (it would be hard to imagine the Han bureaucratic state without Legalism and Confucianism), just as Rome used Greek thought and the Mauryan empire used Buddhist thought. In each case, the conception of universal political authority that sustained the empire derived from earlier philosophies. All three were Iron Age empires, joining their respective technologies with new organizational techniques to create superb military forces.

The differences between the empires are also instructive. Contrast China and Rome. In China, the pervasive culture—the only higher culture in the area—was Chinese even before the first empire arose. This culture had been slowly spreading for centuries and in places outran the polity. Even the culture of the Chu peoples south of the Yangzi, while viewed as "semibarbarian" by northern Chinese, was only a variation of the common culture. Thus cultural unity paved the way for political unity. In contrast, the polyglot empire of Rome encompassed quite different peoples, including older civilizations. The genius of Rome, in fact, was to fashion a government and a set of laws that could contain its cultural diversity.

Geographically, Rome had an easier time of it, for the Mediterranean offered direct access to most parts of the empire and was a thoroughfare for commerce. China, in contrast, was largely landlocked. It was composed of several regional economies, each of which, located in a segment of a river basin separated from others by natural barriers, looked inward. It was the genius of Chinese administration to overcome physical and spatial barriers and integrate the country politically.

The second difference was that government in Han China was more orderly, more complex, and more competent than that of Rome. For example, civil officials controlled the Chinese military almost until the end, whereas in later Roman times, emperor after emperor was set on the throne by the army or the Praetorian Guard. The Roman empire was not a Chinese-type, single-family dynasty.

The third difference was in the military dynamics of the two empires. Roman power was built over centuries. Its history is the story of one state growing in power by increments, imposing its will on others, and little by little piecing together an empire. Not until the early centuries A.D. was the whole empire in place. China, in contrast, remained a multistate system right up to 232 B.C. and then, in a sudden surge, was unified by one state in the space of eleven years. The greater dynamism of China can be explained, perhaps, by the military challenge it faced along its northern border: an immense Hunnish nomadic empire, far more united than the tribes that threatened Rome. Because the threat was more serious than that posed to Rome by any European barbarian enemy, the Chinese response was correspondingly massive.

REVIEW QUESTIONS

1. How did Legalism help the Qin to unify China? What other factors played a part? What were the main features of Qin administration? Why did the Qin collapse?

2. What is the "dynastic cycle"? In what sense is it a Confucian moral rationalization? Was a cycle of administrative and military decline especially true of Chinese government, or can we see the same pattern elsewhere?

3. Who were the players who sought power at the court? Did the means they used reflect differences in their positions?

4. Did Buddhism "triumph" in China in the same sense in which Christianity triumphed in the Roman world? Compare China to the Roman empire. What problems did both face and how did they try to resolve them?

SUGGESTED READINGS

BODDE, D. *China's First Unifier* (1938). A Study of the Qin unification of China, as seen through the life of the Legalist philosopher and statesman Li Si.

CH'U, T. T. *Han Social Structure* (1972).

CH'U, T. T. *Law and Society in Traditional China* (1961). Treats the sweep of Chinese history from 202 B.C. to A.D. 1911.

COTTERELL, A. *The First Emperor of China* (1981).

COULBORN, R. *Feudalism in History* (1965). One chapter interestingly compares the quasi-feudalism of the Zhou with that of the dynasties that followed the Han.

DIEN, A. *State and Society in Early Medieval China* (1991). The centuries after the fall of the Han dynasty.

FAIRBANK, J. K., REISCHAUER, E. O., AND CRAIG, A. M. *East Asia: Tradition and Transformation* (1989). A fairly detailed, pioneering single-volume history covering China, Japan, and other countries in East Asia from antiquity to modern times.

FAIRBANK, J. K. AND TWITCHETT D. (eds.), *Cambridge History of China* (1978–1998). A multivolume work, each volume by multiple authors, representing the state of scholarship at the time each volume appeared. Volume 1 (published in 1986) treats the Qin and Han empires, 221 B.C.–220 A.D.

GERNET, J. *A History of Chinese Civilization* (1982). An early survey of Chinese history.

GRAF, D.A. AND HIGHAM, R. *A Military History of China* (2002).

HSU, C. Y. *Han Agriculture* (1980). A study of the Han agrarian economy.

HSU, C. Y. *Ancient China in Transition* (1965). On social mobility during the Eastern Zhou era.

LEVI, J. *The Chinese Emperor* (1987). A novel about the first Qin emperor based on scholarly sources.

LOEWE, M. *Everyday Life in Early Imperial China* (1968). A social history of the Han dynasty.

NEEDHAM, J. *The Shorter Science and Civilization in China* (1978). An abridgement of the multivolume work on the same subject with the same title—minus *Shorter*—by the same author.

ROBINET, I. *Taoism: Growth of a Religion* (1987). A survey of Daoist religion.

SULLIVAN, M. *The Arts of China* (1967). An excellent survey history of Chinese art.

WANG, Z. S. *Han Civilization* (1982).

WATSON, B. *The Columbia Book of Chinese Poetry* (1986).

WATSON, B. *Records of the Grand Historian of China*, Vols. 1 and 2 (1961). Selections from the *Shiji* by Sima Qian.

WATSON, B. *Ssu-ma Ch'ien, Grand Historian of China* (1958). A study of Sima Qian, China's premier historian.

WOOD, F. *The Silk Road: Two Thousand Years in the Heart of Asia* (2003). A lively narrative illustrated with photos and paintings.

WRIGHT, A. *Buddhism in Chinese History* (1959).

YU, Y. S. *Trade and Expansion in Han China* (1967). A study of economic relations between the Chinese and their neighbors.

High Imperial China (589–1368)

CHAPTER OUTLINE

During the Tang dynasty (618–907), well-to-do families placed glazed pottery figurines in the tombs of their dead. Perhaps they were intended to accompany and amuse the dead in the afterlife. Note the fancy chignon hairstyle of this female flutist, one figure in a musical ensemble. Today collectors around the world seek these figurines.

[Werner Forman/Art Resource, NY]

If Chinese dynasties from the late sixth to the mid-fourteenth centuries were given numbers like those of ancient Egypt, the Sui and Tang dynasties would be called the second empire; the Song, the third; and the Yuan, the fourth. Numbers, however, would not convey the distinct personalities of these dynasties. The Tang (618–907) is everyone's favorite dynasty: open, cosmopolitan, expansionist, exuberant, and creative. It was the example of Tang China that decisively influenced the formation of states and high cultures in Japan, Korea, and Vietnam. Poetry during the Tang attained a peak that has not been equaled since. The Song dynasty (960–1279) rivaled the Tang in the arts; it was China's great age of painting and was the most significant period for philosophy since the Zhou, when Chinese philosophy began. Although not militarily strong, the Song dynasty also witnessed an important commercial revolution. The Yuan (1279–1368) was a short-lived dynasty of rule by Mongols during which China became the most important unit in the largest empire the world has yet seen.

REESTABLISHMENT OF EMPIRE: SUI AND TANG DYNASTIES

In the period corresponding to the European early Middle Ages, the most notable feature of Chinese history was the reunification of China, the recreation of a centralized bureaucratic empire consciously modeled on the earlier Han dynasty (206 B.C.–220 A.D.). Reunification, as usual, began in the north. The first steps were taken by the Northern Wei (386–534), the most enduring of the northern Sino-Turkic states. It moved its court south to Luoyang, made Chinese the language of the court, and adopted Chinese dress and surnames. It also used the leverage of its nomadic cavalry to impose a new land tax, mobilizing resources for state use. The Northern Wei was followed by several short-lived kingdoms. Because the emperors, officials, and military commanders of these kingdoms all came from the same aristocratic stratum, the social distance between them was small, and the throne was often usurped.

The Sui Dynasty

Sui Wendi, the general of mixed Sino-Turkic ancestry, who came to power in 581 and began the Sui dynasty (589–618), was no exception to the above rule. Displaying unusual talent, he unified the north, restored the tax base, reestablished a centralized bureaucratic government, and went on to conquer southern China and unify the country. During his reign, all went well. Huge palaces were built in his Wei valley capital. The Great Wall was rebuilt. The Grand Canal was constructed, linking the Yellow and Yangzi rivers. The canal enabled the northern conquerors to tap the wealth of central and southern China. Peace was maintained with the Turkic tribes along China's northern borders. Eastern Turkic khans (chiefs) were sent Chinese princesses as brides.

The early years of the second Sui emperor were also constructive, but then, Chinese attempts to meddle in steppe politics led to hostilities and wars. The hardships and casualties in campaigns against Korea and along China's northern border produced rising discontent. Natural disasters occurred. The court became bankrupt and demoralized. Rebellions broke out, and once again, there was a free-for-all among the armies of aristocratic military commanders. The winner, and the founder of the Tang dynasty, was a relative of the Sui empress and a Sino-Turkic aristocrat of the same social background as those who had ruled before him.

Chinese historians often compare the short Sui dynasty with that of the Qin (256–206 B.C.). Each brought all of China under a single government after centuries of disunity. Each did too much, fell, and was replaced by a long dynasty. The Tang built on the foundations that had been laid by the Sui, just as the Han had built on those of the Qin.

The Tang Dynasty (618–907)

The first Tang emperor took over the Sui capital, renamed it Chang'an, and made it his own. Within a decade or so, the Tang dynasty had extended its authority over all of China. Government was frugal and tax revenues were adequate to meet government needs and support the military campaigns that would push Chinese borders out further than ever (see Map 3–1). Confucian scholars were employed at the court,

Map 3–1 The Tang empire at its peak during the eighth century. The Tang expansion into Central Asia reopened trade routes to the Middle East and Europe. Students from Bohai, Silla (Korea), and Japan studied in the Tang capital of Chang'an, and then returned, carrying with them Tang books and technology.

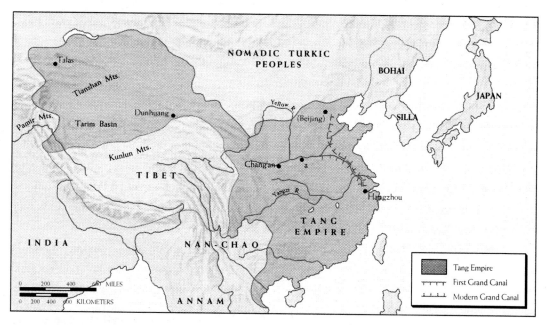

Buddhist temples and monasteries flourished, and peace and order prevailed in the land. The years from 624 to 755 were the good years of the dynasty.

Government The first Tang emperor had been a provincial governor before he became a rebel general. Many of those whom he appointed to posts in his new administration were former Sui officials who had served with him. In building the new administration, he and his successors had to reconcile two conflicting sets of interests. On the one hand, the emperor wanted a bureaucratic government in which authority was centralized in his own person. On the other hand, he had to make concessions to the aristocrats—the dominant elements in Chinese society since the late Han—who staffed his government and continued to dominate early Tang society.

The Dynasties of Imperial China	
589–618	Sui dynasty
618–907	Tang dynasty
960–1279	Song dynasty
1279–1368	Yuan (Mongol) dynasty

The degree to which political authority was centralized was apparent in the formal organization of the bureaucracy. At the highest level were three organs: Military Affairs, the Censorate, and the Council of State. Military Affairs supervised the Tang armies, with the emperor, in effect, the commander-in-chief. The Censorate had watchdog functions: It reported instances of misgovernment directly to the emperor and could also remonstrate with the emperor when it considered his behavior improper. The Council of State was the most important body. It met daily with the emperor and was made up of the heads of the Secretariat, which drafted policies; the Chancellery, which reviewed them; and State Affairs, which carried them out. Beneath State Affairs were the Six Ministries, which continued as the core of the central government down to the twentieth century; beneath them were the several levels of provincial and local administration.

District magistrates were the lowest level of the official hierarchy. Their primary task was to collect taxes and maintain law and order. But they also served as the extension of court authority into local areas. To do their job, they had to contest and diminish the authority of local aristocrats. The district magistrates were, of course, aristocrats themselves, but in time they came to depend more on their official positions than on landholding and kinship ties. Those who served well and rose in the bureaucracy improved the ranking of their clans in the records kept by the central government.

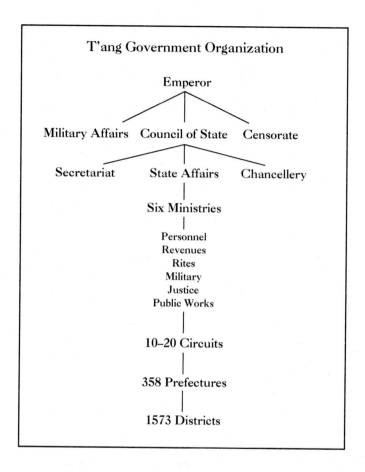

To keep the support of aristocratic families, the court also had to make concessions to them. In the Tang tax system, all land was declared to be the property of the emperor and was then redistributed to able-bodied cultivators, who paid taxes in labor and grain. Because all able-bodied adult males received equal allotments of land (women got less), the land tax system was called the "equal field system." But the system was far from egalitarian. Aristocrats enjoyed special exemptions and grants of "rank" lands that, in effect, confirmed their estate holdings. Those who served the state also received "office" lands that improved their condition.

Aristocrats were also favored in the recruitment of officials. Most officials were recommended for posts or received posts because their fathers had been high officials. They were drawn almost exclusively from the aristocracy, at first from the northwestern aristocratic families that had supported the establishment of the dynasty, and then, in time, from the aristocracies of other areas. Entrance to government schools at Chang'an and the secondary capital at Luoyang was restricted to the sons of nobles and officials. A tiny percentage, however, were recruited by examinations. Those who

A PETTY CLERK THINKS ABOUT HIS CAREER

Han-shan was an eccentric Zen monk of the early Tang dynasty. Details of his life are sparse, but he is credited with writing more than three hundred poems.

What is it about this clerk's lament that seems almost modern?

I'm not so poor at reports and decisions—
Why can't I get ahead in the government?
The rating officials are determined to make
life hard.
All they do is try to expose my faults.
Everything, I guess, is a matter of Fate;
Still, I'll try the exam again this year.

A blind boy aiming at the eye of a sparrow,
Might just accidentally manage a hit.
In vain I slaved to understand the Three
Histories:
Uselessly I pored over the Five Classics.
Until I'm old I'll go on checking census figures;
As in the past, a petty clerk scribbling in tax
ledgers.
When I ask the Book of Changes it says there's
trouble ahead;
All my life is ruled by evil stars.
If only I could be like the tree at the river's edge
Every year turning green again!

From *Cold Mountain: 100 Poems* by the T'ang Poet Han-shan, trans. by B. Watson. Copyright © 1970 by Columbia University Press. Reprinted with permission of the publisher.

---

passed the examinations had the highest prestige and were more likely to have brilliant careers. But as only the sons of well-to-do families could afford the years of study needed to master the Confucian classics and pass the rigorous examinations, even examination bureaucrats were usually the able among the noble.

Empress Wu   Women of the inner court continued to play a role in government. The most striking example is Wu Zhao (626–c. 706). A young concubine of the strong second emperor, she had so entranced his weak heir by her charms that when he succeeded to the throne, she was recalled from the nunnery to which all childless, former wives of deceased emperors were routinely consigned, and was duly installed at the court. She poisoned or otherwise removed her rivals and became his empress. She also had murdered or exiled the statesmen who opposed her growing influence. After the emperor suffered a stroke in 660, she completely dominated the court. After his death in 683, she ruled for seven years as regent and then, deposing her son, became emperor herself, the only woman in Chinese history to hold the title. She moved the court to Luoyang in her native area and proclaimed a new dynasty. A fervent Buddhist with an interest in magic, she saw herself as the incarnation of the Buddha Maitreya and built temples throughout the land. She patronized the White Horse Monastery, appointing one of her favorites as its abbot. Her sexual appetites were prodigious. She ruled China until 705, when at the age of eighty she lost her hold and was deposed. Such, at least, is the story told by Confucian historians of that age, who compared her to "the hen that crowed."

Recent biographers have rehabilitated the empress. Yes, she flourished amid the intrigues of the Tang court, and, yes, she could be ruthless and deserved the name of "iron-hand empress." Nevertheless, she was capable, hardworking, and sagacious, and appointed able officials to key posts. In her struggle for power against the old aristo-crats of northwest China, she turned not to her family but to the products of the examination system and to a group known as the "Scholars of the North Gate," thereby broadening the base of government. The dynamism of a young dynasty may also help explain why court intrigues could be tolerated—without provinces breaking away or military commanders becoming autonomous. Her rule also coincided with the maximal geographical expansion of Tang military power. But after the Empress Wu, no woman ever again became emperor.

The Chang'an of Emperor Xuanzong   Only a few years after Empress Wu was deposed—years filled with further tawdry intrigues—Xuanzong came to the throne. He was a calligrapher, a poet, a musician, a patron of the arts, and a Taoist, and also a man of great personal warmth who maintained good relations with both his family and his official advisors. The new emperor's mother had been executed by Empress Wu on a charge of practicing black magic. To mark a break with Wu's use of examination officials, he appointed special government commissions headed by distinguished aristocrats to reform government finances. Examination bureaucrats lost ground during his reign. The Grand Canal was repaired and extended. A new census extended the tax rolls. Wealth and prosperity returned to the court. Xuanzong's reign (713–756) was also culturally brilliant. Years later, while in exile, the great poet Li Bo (701–762) wrote a verse in which memories of youthful exhilaration merged with the glory of the capital of Xuanzong:

> Long ago, among the flowers and willows,
> We sat drinking together at Ch'ang-an.
> The Five Barons and Seven Grandees were of our company,
> But when some wild stroke was afoot
> It was we who led it, yet boisterous though we were
> In the arts and graces of life we could hold our own
> With any dandy in the town—
> In the days when there was youth in your cheeks
> And I was still not old.
> We galloped to the brothels, cracking our gilded whips,
> We sent in our writings to the palace of the Unicorn,
> Girls sang to us and danced hour by hour on tortoise-shell mats.
> We thought, you and I, that it would be always like this.
> How should we know the grasses would stir and dust rise on the wind?
> Suddenly foreign horsemen were at the Hsien-ku Pass
> Just when the blossom at the palace of Qin was opening on the sunny
>   boughs[1]

[1]A. Waley, *The Poetry and Career of Li Po* (New York: Macmillan, 1950) pp. 87–88.

Chang'an was an imperial city, an administrative city that lived on taxes. It was designed to exhibit the power of the emperor and the majesty of his court. At the far north of the city, the palace faced south. The placement was traditional: Confucius, speaking of Shun, said he had only "to hold himself in a respectful posture and to face due south." In front of the palace was a complex of government offices, from which an imposing 500-foot-wide avenue led to the main southern gate. The city was laid out on a north–south, east–west grid, which one Tang poet compared to a chessboard (see Map 3–2). Each block of the city was administered as a ward with interior streets and gates that were locked at night. Enclosed by great walls, the city covered 30 square miles. Its population was over one million—half within the walls, the other half in suburbs—the largest city in the world. (The population of China in the year 750 was about fifty million—less than 3 percent of its present-day population.) Chang'an was also a trade center from which caravans set out across Central Asia. Merchants from India, Iran, Syria, and Arabia hawked the wares of the Near East and all of Asia in its two government-controlled markets.

Map 3–2 Chang'an. The great city of Chang'an had been a Chinese capital since the Han period. By the eighth century, there were around a million people within the city walls, with the same number close by outside, making it the largest city in the world at the time. The rigorous grid structure accommodated a variety of districts, each with its own function.

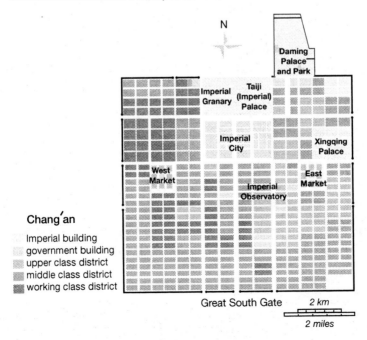

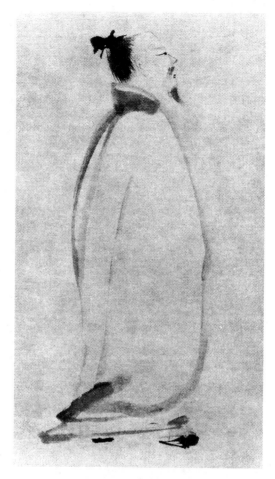

The Tang poet Li Bo as imagined by the great
Song artist Liang Kai.
[Tokyo National Museum/DNP Archives.Com Co., Ltd.]

The Tang Empire A Chinese dynasty is like an accordion, first expanding into the territories of its barbarian neighbors and then contracting back to its original, densely populated core area. The principal threats to the Tang state were from Tibetans in the west, Turks in the northwest and north, and Khitan Mongols in Manchuria.

To protect their borders, the Tang employed a four-tier policy. When nothing else would work, the Tang sent armies. But armies were expensive, and using them against nomads was like sweeping back the waves with a broom. A victory might dissolve a confederation, but a decade or two later, it would reappear under a new tribal leader. For instance, in 630, Tang armies defeated the eastern Turks; in 648, they took the Tarim Basin, opening trade routes to western Asia for almost a century; and in 657, they defeated the western Turks and extended Chinese influence across the Pamir Mountains to petty states near Samarkand. By 698, however, the Turks were back, invading northeastern China, and between 711 and 736, they had complete control of the steppe from the Oxus River to China's northern frontier.

Chinese efforts against Tibet were much the same. From 670, Tibet expanded and threatened China. In 679, it was defeated. In 714, it rose again; wars were fought from 727 to 729; and a settlement was reached in 730. But wars broke out anew. In 752, Tibet entered an alliance with the Thai state of Nan Zhao in Yunnan (today a province in southwestern China that abuts on Tibet). In 763, Tibetan forces captured and looted Chang'an. They were driven out, but it is clear that even during the years of Tang power, no final victory was obtainable.

The human costs of sending armies far afield was detailed in a poem by Li Bo:

Last year we were fighting at the source of the Sang-kan;
This year we are fighting on the Onion River road.
We have washed our swords in the surf of Parthian seas;
We have pastured our horses among the snows of the T'ien Shan,
The King's armies have grown grey and old
Fighting ten thousand leagues away from home.
The Huns have no trade but battle and carnage;
They have no fields or ploughlands,
But only wastes where white bones lie among yellow sands.
Where the House of Ch'in built the great wall that was to keep away the
    Tartars.
There, in its turn, the House of Han lit beacons of war.
The beacons are always alight, fighting and marching never stop.
Men die in the field, slashing sword to sword;
The horses of the conquered neigh piteously to Heaven.
Crows and hawks peck for human guts,
Carry them in their beaks and hang them on the branches of withered trees.
Captains and soldiers are smeared on the bushes and grass;
The General schemed in vain.
Know therefore that the sword is a cursed thing
Which the wise man uses only if he must.[2]

The second tier of Chinese defenses was to use nomads against other nomads. The critical development for the Tang was the rise to power of the Uighur Turks. From 744 to 840, the Uighurs controlled Central Asia and were staunch allies of the Tang. Without their support, the Tang dynasty would have ended sooner.

[2]Waley, pp. 34–35.

The third tier was defenses along China's borders, including the Great Wall. At mid-dynasty, whole frontier provinces in the north and the northwest were put under military commanders who, in time, came to control the provinces' civil governments as well. The bulk of the Tang military was in such frontier commands. At times, their autonomy and potential as rebels were as much a threat to the Tang court as to the nomadic enemy.

Diplomacy is cheaper than war. The fourth tier of defense was to bring the potential enemy into the empire as a tributary. The Tang defined the position of "tributary" with great elasticity. It included principalities truly dependent on China, Central Asian states conquered by China, enemy states such as Tibet or the Thai state of Nan Zhao when they were not actually at war with China, the Korean state Silla, which had unified the peninsula with Tang aid but had then fought Tang armies to a standstill when they attempted to impose Chinese hegemony, and wholly independent states such as Japan. All sent embassies bearing gifts to the Tang court, which housed and fed them and bestowed costly gifts in return.

For some countries, these embassies had a special significance. As the only "developed nation" in East Asia, China was a model for countries still in the throes of forming a state. An embassy gained access to the entire range of Tang culture and technology: its philosophy and writing, governmental and land systems, Buddhism, arts, architecture, and medicine. In 640, there were 8,000 Koreans, mostly students, in Chang'an. Never again would China exert such an influence, for never again would its neighbors be at that formative stage of development.

Rebellion and Decline

From the mid-eighth century, signs of decline began to appear. China's frontiers started to contract. Tribes in Manchuria became unruly. Tibetans threatened China's western border. In 751, an overextended Tang army led by a Korean general was defeated by Arabs near Samarkand in western Asia, shutting down China's caravan trade with the West for more than five centuries. Furthermore, in 755, a Sogdian general, An Lushan, who commanded three Chinese provinces on the northeastern frontier, led 160,000 troops in a rebellion that swept across northern China, capturing Luoyang and then Chang'an. The emperor fled to Sichuan.

The event contained an element of romance. Ten years earlier, the emperor Xuanzong had taken a young woman, Yang Guifei, from the harem of his son (he gave his son another beauty in exchange). So infatuated was he that he neglected not only the other "three thousand beauties of his inner chambers" but the business of government as well. For a while his neglect did not matter because he had an able chief minister, but when the minister died, Xuanzong appointed his concubine's second cousin to the post, initiating a train of events that resulted in the rebellion. En route to Sichuan, his soldiers, blaming Yang Guifei for their plight, strangled her. Her death was later immortalized in a poem that described her "snow-white skin," "flowery face," and "moth eyebrows," as well as the "eternal sorrow" of the emperor, who, in fact, was seventy-two at the time.

After a decade of wars and devastation, a new emperor restored the dynasty with the help of the Uighur Turks, who looted Chang'an as part of their reward. The recovery and the century of relative peace and prosperity that followed illustrate the resilience of Tang institutions. China was smaller, but military governors maintained the diminished frontiers. Provincial governors were more autonomous, but taxes were still sent to the capital. Occasional rebellions were suppressed by imperial armies, sometimes led by eunuchs. Most emperors were weak, but there were three strong emperors who carried out reforms. Edwin O. Reischauer, after translating the diary of a Japanese monk who studied in China during the early ninth century, commented that the "picture of government in operation" that emerges "is amazing for the ninth century, even in China:"

> The remarkable degree of centralized control still existing, the meticulous attention to written instructions from higher authorities, and the tremendous amount of paper work involved in even the smallest matters of administration are all the more striking just because this was a period of dynastic decline.[3]

Of the reforms of this era, none was more important than that of the land. The official census, on which land allotments and taxes were based, showed a drop in population from fifty-three million before the An Lushan rebellion to seventeen million afterward. Unable to put people back on the registers, the government abandoned the equal field system, which was a tax on persons, and replaced it with a tax on land that was collected twice a year. The new twice-a-year tax, begun in 780, lasted until the sixteenth century. Under it, a fixed quota of taxes was levied on each province and then apportioned out to prefectures and districts. But the government revenues from salt and iron nevertheless surpassed those from land.

During the second half of the ninth century, government weakened further. Most provinces became autonomous, often under military commanders, and resisted central control. Wars were fought with the state of Nan Chao in the southwest. Bandits appeared. Droughts led to peasant uprisings. By the 880s, warlords had carved all of China into independent kingdoms, and in 907, the Tang dynasty fell. But within half a century, a new dynasty arose. The fall of the Tang did not lead to centuries of division of the kind that had followed the Han. Something had changed within China.

Tang Culture   The creativity of the Tang period arose from the juxtaposition and interaction of cosmopolitan, medieval Buddhist, and secular elements. The rise of each of these cultural spheres was rooted in the wealth and the social order of the recreated empire.

---

[3]E. O. Reischauer, _Ennin's Travels in T'ang China_ (New York: Ronald Press, 1955) p. 7.

A POEM BY LI BO

The great Tang poet Li Bo (701–762) reputedly wrote 20,000 poems, of which 1,800 have survived.

It has been said that concreteness of imagery is the genius of Chinese poetry. Does this example support that contention?

The River Merchant's Wife: A Letter

> While my hair was still cut straight across my forehead
> I played about the front gate, pulling flowers.
> You came by on bamboo stilts, playing horse,
> You walked about my seat, playing with blue plums.
> And we went on living in the village of Chokan:
> Two small people, without dislike or suspicion.
>
> At fourteen I married My Lord you.
> I never laughed, being bashful.
> Lowering my head, I looked at the wall.
> Called to, a thousand times, I never looked back.
>
> At fifteen I stopped scowling,
> I desired my dust to be mingled with yours

> Forever and forever and forever.
> Why should I climb the look out?
>
> At sixteen you departed,
> You went into far Ku-to-yen, by the river of swirling eddies,
> And you have been gone five months.
> The monkeys make sorrowful noise overhead.
>
> You dragged your feet when you went out.
> By the gate now, the moss is grown, the different mosses,
> Too deep to clear them away!
> The leaves fall early this autumn, in wind.
> The paired butterflies are already yellow with August
> Over the grass in the West garden;
> They hurt me. I grow older.
> If you are coming down through the narrows of the river Kiang,
> Please let me know beforehand,
> And I will come out to meet you
> As far as Cho-fu-Sa.

"The River Merchant's Wife: A Letter" by E. Pound, from *Personae*. Copyright © 1926 by E. Pound. Reprinted by permission of New Directions Publishing Corp.

Tang culture was cosmopolitan not just because of its broad contacts with other cultures and peoples but because of its openness to them. Buddhist pilgrims to India and a flow of Indian art and philosophies to China were a part of it. The voluptuousness of Indian painting and sculpture, for example, helped shape the Tang representation of the *bodhisattva*. Commercial contacts were widespread. Foreign goods were vended in Chang'an marketplaces. Communities of central and western Asians were established in the capital, and Arab and Persian quarters grew up in the seaports of southeastern China. Merchants brought their religions with them. Nestorian Christianity, Zoroastrianism, Manichaeism, Judaism, and Islam entered China at this time. Most would be swept away in the persecutions of the ninth century, but Islam and a few small pockets of Judaism survived until the twentieth century.

Central Asian music and musical instruments entered along the trade routes and became so popular that they almost displaced the native tradition. Tang ladies adopted foreign hairstyles. Foreign dramas and acrobatic performances by western

Caravaneer on a camel. The animal's shaggy mane indicates that it is a Bactrian camel from Central Asia.
[© Réunion des Musées/Art Resource, NY]

Asians could be seen in the streets of the capital. Even among the pottery figurines customarily placed in tombs, there were representations of West Asian traders and Central Asian grooms, along with those of horses, camels, and court ladies that today are avidly sought by collectors and museums around the world. In Tang poetry, too, what was foreign was not shunned but judged on its own merits or even presented as exotically attractive. Of a gallant of Chang'an, Li Bo wrote:

> A young man of Five Barrows suburb east of the Golden Market,
> Silver saddle and white horse cross through wind of spring.
> When fallen flowers are trampled all under, where is it he will roam?
> With a laugh he enters the tavern of a lovely Turkish wench.[4]

[4]S. Owen, *The Great Age of Chinese Poetry: The High T'ang* (New Haven, CT: Yale University Press, 1980), p. 130.

Later in the dynasty, another poet, Li He wrote of service on the frontier:

A Tartar horn tugs at the north wind,
Thistle Gate shines whiter than the stream.
The sky swallows the road to Kokonor.
On the Great Wall, a thousand miles of moonlight.[5]

The Tang dynasty, although slightly less an age of faith than the preceding Six Dynasties, was the golden age of Buddhism in China nonetheless. Patronized by emperors and aristocrats, Buddhist temples acquired vast landholdings and great wealth. Temples and monasteries were constructed throughout China. To gain even an inkling of the beauty and sophistication of the temple architecture, the wooden sculpture, or the paintings on the temple walls, one must view Hōryūji or other old temples at Nara in Japan, for little of note has survived in China. The single exception is the Caves of the Thousand Buddhas at Dunhuang in China's far northwest, which were sealed during the eleventh century for protection from Tibetan raiders and were not rediscovered until the twentieth century. They were found to contain stone sculptures, Buddhist frescoes, and thousands of manuscripts in Chinese and Central Asian languages.

Only during the Tang did China have a "church" establishment that was at all comparable to that of medieval Europe, and even then it was subservient to the far stronger Tang state. Buddhist wealth and learning brought with them secular functions. Tang temples served as schools, inns, or even bathhouses. They lent money. Priests performed funerals and dispensed medicines. Occasionally, the state moved to recapture the revenues monopolized by temples. The severest persecution, which marked a turn in the fortunes of Buddhism in China, occurred from 841 to 845, when an ardently Daoist emperor confiscated millions of acres of tax-exempt lands, returned 260,000 monks and nuns to secular life, and destroyed 4,600 monasteries and 40,000 shrines.

During the early Tang, the principal Buddhist sect was the Tiantai, but after the mid-ninth-century suppression, other sects came to the fore:

1. One devotional sect focused on Maitreya, a Buddha of the future who will appear and create a paradise on earth. Maitreya was a cosmic messiah, not a human figure. The messianic teachings of the sect often furnished the ideology for popular uprisings and rebellions like the White Lotus, which claimed that it was renewing the world in anticipation of Maitreya's coming.

2. Another devotional or faith sect worshiped the Amitabha Buddha, the Lord of the Western Paradise or Pure Land. This sect taught that in the early centuries after the death of the historical Buddha, his teachings had been transmitted properly and people could obtain enlightenment by their own efforts, but that at present, the Buddha's teachings had become so distorted that only by

[5]A. C. Graham, *Poems of the Late T'ang* (Baltimore, MD: Penguin, 1965), p. 9.

reliance on Amitabha could humans obtain salvation. All who called on Amitabha with a pure heart and perfect faith would be saved. Developing a congregational form of worship, this sect became the largest in China and deeply influenced Chinese popular religion.

3. A third sect, and the most influential among Chinese elites, was known in China, where it began, as *Chan*, but is better known in the West by its Japanese name, *Zen*. Chan had no cosmic Buddhas. It taught that the historical Buddha was only a man and exhorted each person to attain enlightenment by his or her own efforts. Although its monks were often the most learned in China, Chan was anti-intellectual in its emphasis on direct intuition into one's own Buddha-nature. Enlightenment was to be obtained by a regimen of physical labor and meditation. To jolt the monk into enlightenment—after he had been readied by long hours of meditation—some Chan sects used little problems not answerable by normal ratiocination: "What was your face before you were conceived?" "If all things return to the One, what does the One return to?" "From the top of a hundred-foot pole, how do you step forward?" The psychological state of the novice attempting to deal with these problems is compared to that of "a rat pursued into a blocked pipe" or "a mosquito biting an iron ball." The discipline of meditation, combined with a Chan view of nature, profoundly influenced the arts in China and subsequently in Korea and Japan as well.

The third characteristic of Tang culture was the reappearance of secular scholarship and letters. The reestablishment of centralized bureaucratic government stimulated the tradition of learning that had been partially interrupted after the fall of the Han dynasty in the third century A.D. A scholarly-bureaucratic complex emerged. Most men of letters were also officials, and most high-ranking officials painted or wrote poems. An anthology of Tang poetry compiled during the Ming period (1368–1644) contained 48,900 poems by almost 2,300 authors. This secular stream of Tang culture was not ideologically anti-Buddhist; officials were often privately sympathetic to Buddhism. But as men involved themselves in the affairs of government, their values became increasingly this-worldly.

Court historians of the Tang revived the Han practice of writing the official history of the previous dynasty. Also, for the first time, scholars wrote comprehensive institutional histories and regional and local gazetteers. They compiled dictionaries and wrote commentaries on the Confucian classics. Other scholars wrote ghost stories or tales of adventure, using the literary language. (Buddhist sermons, in contrast, were often written in the vernacular.) More paintings were Buddhist than secular, but Chinese landscape painting had its origins during the Tang. Nowhere, however, was the growth of a secular culture more evident than in poetry, the greatest achievement of Tang letters.

Whether Li Bo can be called wholly secular is questionable. He might better be called Daoist. But he clearly was not Buddhist. Born in Sichuan, he was exceptional among Tang poets in never having sat for the civil service examinations, although he briefly held an official post at Chang'an, given in recognition of his poetry. Large and muscular, he was a swordsman and a carouser. Of his surviving poems, a fair number have titles like "Bring on the Wine" or "Drinking Alone in the Moonlight." According to legend, he drowned while drunkenly attempting to embrace the reflection of the moon in a lake. His poetry is clear, powerful, passionate, and always sensitive to beauty. It also contains a sense of fantasy, as when he climbed a mountain and saw a star-goddess, "stepping in emptiness, pacing pure ether, her rainbow robes trailed broad sashes." Li Bo, nearer to heaven than to earth, looked down below where:

> Far and wide Tartar troops were speeding,
> And flowing blood mired the wild grasses
> Where wolves and jackals all wore officials' caps.[6]

According to Li Bo, life is brief and the universe is large, but this view did not lead him to renounce the world. His perception of the Way was not quietistic. Rather, he exulted, identifying with the primal flux of *yin* and *yang*:

> I'll wrap this Mighty Mudball of a world all up in a bag
> And be wild and free like Chaos itself![7]

Du Fu (712–770), an equally famous Tang poet, was from a literary family. He failed the metropolitan examination at the age of twenty-three and spent years in wandering and poverty. At thirty-nine, he received an official appointment after presenting his poetry to the court. Four years later, he was appointed to a military post. He fell into rebel hands during the An Lushan rebellion, escaped, and was reappointed to a civil post. But he was then dismissed and suffered further hardships. His poetry is less lyrical and more allusive than Li Bo's. It also reflects more compassion for human suffering: for the mother whose sons have been conscripted and sent to war; for brothers scattered by war; for his own family, to whom he returned after having been given up for dead. Like Li Bo, he felt that humans are short-lived and that nature endures. Visiting the ruins of the palace of the second Tang emperor, he saw "grey rats scuttling over ancient tiles" and "in its shadowed chambers ghost fires green." "Its lovely ladies are the brown soil" and only "tomb horses of stone remain." But his response to this sad scene was to:

> Sing wildly, let the tears cover your open hands.
> Then go ever onward and on the road of your travels,
> Meet none who prolong their fated years.[8]

His response was close to Stoicism, and like that of Li Bo, not the least Buddhist.

[6]Owen, p. 134.
[7]Owen, p. 125.
[8]Owen, pp. 223–224.

SONG DYNASTY (960–1279)

Most traditional Chinese history was written in terms of the dynastic cycle, and for good reason: The pattern of rise and fall, of expansion and contraction, within each dynasty cannot be denied. Certainly, the Song can be viewed from this perspective. It reunified China in 960, establishing its capital at Kaifeng on the Yellow River (see Map 3–3). Mobilizing its resources effectively, it ruled for 170 years. This period is called the Northern Song. Then it weakened. In 1127, it lost the north but continued to rule the south for another 150 years from a new capital at Hangzhou in east-central China. The Southern Song fell before the Mongol onslaught in 1279.

But there is more to Chinese history than the logic of the dynastic cycle. Longer-term changes that cut across dynastic lines were ultimately more important. One such set of changes began during the late Tang and continued on into the Song, affecting its economy, society, state, and culture. Taken together, these changes help to explain why China, after the Tang, did not relapse into centuries of disunity as it had after the Han, and why China would never again experience more than brief intervals of disunity. In this section, we will skip over emperors and empresses, eunuchs and generals, and focus instead on more fundamental transformations.

Map 3–3 The Northern Song and Liao empires (left) and the Southern Song and Jin empires (right).   During the Northern Song, the Mongol Liao dynasty ruled only the extreme northern edge of China. During the Southern Song, in contrast, the Manchurian Jin dynasty ruled half of China.

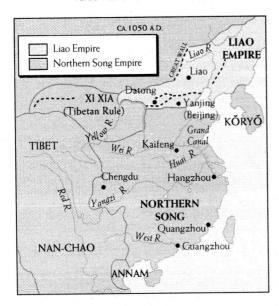
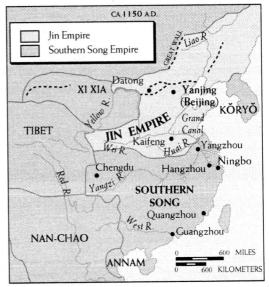

Agricultural Revolution: From Serfs to Free Farmers

Sui and Tang peasants, who tilled their own "equal fields" as well as those of aristocrats, were better off than the serfs of medieval Europe. They had a claim to the soil they tilled, and sometimes mortgaged their lands to moneylenders. European serfs, lacking such a claim, could not. Still, labor service was the heaviest tax, and whether performed on the office or rank lands of aristocrats or on other government lands, it created conditions of social subordination. The tillers, consequently, were not that different from serfs.

The aristocracy weakened, however, over the course of the Tang and after its fall. Estates became smaller as they were divided among male children at each change of generation. Drawn to the capital, the aristocracy became less a landed, and more a metropolitan, elite. After the fall of the Tang, warlords often seized the estates of aristocrats. As the aristocracy declined, the claims of those who worked the soil grew stronger. With the collapse of the equal field system and the rise of the twice-a-year tax (described earlier), farmers could not only mortgage their claims but could buy and sell the land itself. The ownership of land as private property gave the cultivators greater independence; they could move about as they pleased. Taxes paid in grain began to be converted during the Song to taxes in money. The commutation of the labor tax to a money tax gave farmers control over their own time. Conscription, the cruelest and heaviest labor tax of all, disappeared as the conscript armies of the early and middle Tang gave way to a professional soldiery.

Changes in technology also benefited the cultivator. New strains of an early-ripening rice permitted double-cropping. In the Yangzi region, extensive water-control projects were carried out, and more fertilizers were used. New commercial crops were developed. Tea, which had been introduced during the Six Dynasties as a medicine and had been drunk by monks during the Tang, became widely cultivated; cotton also became a common crop. Because taxes paid in money tended to become fixed, much of the increased productivity accrued to the cultivator. Of course, landlords benefitted more than independent small farmers, and landless tenant farmers benefited not at all.

With aristocrats and their interference in local affairs gone, the district magistrate's authority increased. He became the sole representative of imperial authority in local society. But there were too many villages in a district for him to be involved regularly in their internal affairs. When taxes were paid and order was maintained, the governance of the village was left to the village elites. As a result, the Song farmer not only was freer and more affluent but also enjoyed a substantial measure of self-government.

A scholar-gentry class also began to appear during the Song, though it became vastly more important later on. A typical gentry family lived in a village, or, it might move to a district seat or market town. Because of a more inclusive conception of lineage, most gentry families had at least one member who had passed the prefectural civil service examination. Socially and culturally, these gentry were more like magistrates than villagers. But even those who lived in towns owned village lands and had common interests with local landholders. Although far less powerful than the former local aristocrats, the gentry participated in local affairs and acted as a buffer between village and magistrate.

Commercial Revolution

During the Song dynasty a variety of interacting factors propelled the economy to a new level of prosperity: movements of people, new technologies, the growth of cities, the spread of money, and rising trade.

China's center of gravity moved south. During the Tang, the north had been the most populous and productive region of China. But from the late ninth century, the weight of China's population, agriculture, and culture shifted to the lower and eastern Yangzi basin. Between 800 and 1100, China's total population rose to about 100 million, but the population of the Yangzi basin tripled. Yangzi rice paddies yielded more per acre than the wheat or millet fields of the north, and its rice became the tax base of the empire. The new wealth led to the establishment of so many new schools that the government had to set regional quotas for the examination system to prevent the Yangzi region from dominating all of China. For strategic reasons, the Northern Song capital itself was kept in the north, but it was situated at Kaifeng, further east than Luoyang, at the point where the Grand Canal, which carried tax rice from the south, joined the Yellow River.

Technology and Money   New inventions fed the Song economy. Iron-smelting in north China was the most advanced in the world. It used coke and bellows to heat furnaces to the temperatures required for carbonized steel. These smelters provided China with better tools and weapons. Printing had begun earlier with carved seals; the earliest woodblock texts, mostly on Buddhist subjects, appeared in the seventh century; by the tenth century, a complete edition of the classics had been published; and by mid-Song, books printed with movable type were fairly common. Other Song inventions were the abacus, grenades and projectiles containing gunpowder, and finer textiles and porcelains.

Exchange during the Tang had been based on silk. Coins had been issued, but a weak demand limited their circulation. During the Northern Song, large amounts of copper cash were coined, and demand outstripped supply. Coins were minted with holes in the center, and a string of 1,000 coins was the unit for large transactions. Beginning in the Southern Song, silver was minted to complement copper, ten times more silver in the late twelfth century than in the early eleventh century. Merchants also used letters of credit and various kinds of paper money. Money spread from the cities to penetrate the village economy: by 1065, tax receipts paid in money had risen to thirty-eight million strings of cash—in comparison to two million in mid-Tang.

Trade   Tang cities were administrative. They lived on taxes drawn from a non-commercial hinterland. They became commercial as official salaries and governmental expenditures created a demand for commodities and services, and artisans and merchants arose to provide them. The Tang pattern continued in most regions during the Song. But in the capital and in economically advanced regions along the Yangzi, regional commercial networks spread from cities to district seats and market towns, and to village markets beneath them. As commerce grew, cities of more than 100,000 households almost quadrupled in number. Kaifeng, the Northern Song capital, had 260,000 households, probably more than one million inhabitants. Hangzhou, the Southern Song capital, had 391,000 households. Compare these to the cities of medieval Europe: London during the Northern Song had a population of 18,000; Rome during the Southern Song had 35,000; and Paris, a century later, fewer than 60,000.

Moreover, unlike Chang'an with walled wards that closed at night, these Song capitals were open within and spread beyond their outer walls. Their main avenues were lined with shops, as in present-day Chinese cities. Their marketplaces were managed by merchant guilds, not government officials. A taste for luxury and an increasingly secular lifestyle accompanied the growing wealth. Restaurants, theaters, wine shops, and brothels abounded. Entertainment quarters sprang up, with fortune tellers, jugglers, chess masters, acrobats, and puppeteers. Such professions had not been absent from Chang'an, but during the Song, their numbers increased, and they catered to traders and rich merchants as well as to officials.

Trade between regions during the Song was limited to luxury goods like silk, lacquerware, medicinal herbs, and porcelains. Only where transport was cheap—along rivers, canals, or the coast—was interregional trade in bulk commodities economical, and even then, it was usually carried on only to make up for periodic shortages.

Foreign trade also flourished. From the Han to the Tang, Chinese ships had sailed along the coast, from one landmark to another. A journey to Malaya took five months. In the Song, however, ocean routes replaced coastal shipping. Ships equipped with watertight compartments, sails not wholly dependent on tailwinds, better rudders, the compass, and a deeper understanding of monsoon winds made this possible. Chinese captains, navigating with the aid of the compass, dominated the sea routes to Malaya and Sumatra, and occasionally ventured into the Indian Ocean. New Chinese trader communities dotted the cities of Southeast Asia. Arabs dominated Indian Ocean routes from the Near East to Southeast Asia, and Arab and Persian communities were established in Chinese ports. The content of the overseas trade reflected China's advanced economy: It exported finished goods and imported raw materials. Porcelains were sent to Southeast Asia and then were carried by Arab ships to medieval trading centers on the Persian Gulf and down the coast of East Africa as far south as Zanzibar.

Foreign trade continued as usual along China's northern and western borders. Chinese merchants bought horses from Tibetan, Turkic, and Mongol traders, and sold silks, tea, and rhubarb. Then, during the Yuan, Mongol unity revived the Silk

"CHASTE WOMAN" SHI

Hong Mai (1123–1202 A.D.) was a collector of stories—fantastic, folkloric, and factual. Unlike the usual Confucian homilies on the proper virtues of women, his stories, and those told by other Song storytellers, contained broader perspectives. They reflected the actual diversity of Chinese society. In this story the Chinese belief in ghosts enables the wronged Ning to have a hand in the villain's downfall.

Is the moral of this tale simply that justice ultimately prevails? Can a more complex interpretation be made? What does it say about the dynamics of Song society?

Ning Six of South Meadow village, in the southern suburbs of Jianchang, was a simple-minded man who concentrated on his farming. His younger brother's wife, Miss Shi, was a little sleeker than her peers. She was also ruthless and licentious, and had an adulterous affair with a youth who lived there. Whenever Ning looked askance at her she would scold him and there was not much he could do.

Once Miss Shi took a chicken, wanting to cook it. When Ning learned of it, he went into her room, demanded that she give it to him, then left with it. Miss Shi quickly cut her arm with a knife, then went to the neighbors screaming, "Because my husband is not home, brother-in-law offered me a chicken and tried to force me to have sex with him. I resisted, threatening to kill myself with the knife I was holding, and so just managed to escape."

Ning at that time had no wife, so the neighbors thought she might be telling the truth. They took them to the village headman, then the county jail. The clerks at the jail reviewed the evidence and demanded 10,000 cash to set things right. Ning was poor and stingy, and moreover, knew himself to be in the right, so stubbornly refused. The clerks sent up the dossier to the prefect Dai Qi. Dai was unable to examine it but noted that it involved an ordinary village wife who was able to protect her virtue and her body and not be violated. The administrative supervisor, Zhao Shiqing, concurred with Qi, and they sent up the case making Ning look guilty. Ning received the death penalty and Miss Shi was granted 100,000 cash, regular visits from the local officials, and a banner honoring her for her chastity. From this, she acquired a reputation as a chaste wife. The local people all realized Ning had been wronged and resented how overboard she had gone.

In the end Miss Shi had an affair with a monk at the nearby Lintian temple. Charges were brought and she received a beating and soon became ill. She saw Ning as a vengeful demon and then died. The date was the sixth month of 1177.

Road, and overland routes again competed with the equally perilous sea routes. After 1600, except along the border, China's foreign trade was predominantly a matter of oceanic commerce.

Government: From Aristocracy to Autocracy

Historians debate the nature of government during the millennium after the Tang. One school calls this the age of autocracy or China's age of absolute monarchy. Earlier emperors, as noted, were often personally powerful, but beginning with the Song, changes occurred that made it easier for emperors to be autocrats. Examples of such autocrats are not few in number. A second school argues that "autocracy" is the wrong word. Even if the potential for despotic behavior was there, most emperors were content to oversee the regular workings of bureaucratic government. It was the existence of a non-aristocratic, centralized bureaucracy of talent that made China so different from Europe in its age of absolute monarchy. Both arguments have some merit.

One change was that Song emperors had direct personal control over more offices than their Tang predecessors. For example, the Board of Academicians, an advisory office or "kitchen cabinet," presented the emperor with policy options separate from those presented by the Secretariat-Chancellery. By using the one against the other, the emperor kept power in his own hands and prevented bureaucrats in the Secretariat-Chancellery from dominating the government.

The second change was that the central government was better funded than previously. Revenues in 1100 were three times the peak revenues of the Tang, partly a result of the growth of population and agricultural wealth, and partly a result of the establishment of government monopolies on salt, wine, and tea, and various duties, fees, and taxes levied on domestic and foreign trade. During the Northern Song, these commercial revenues rivaled the land tax; during the Southern Song, they surpassed it. As a matter of ideology, Confucian officials continued to stress the primacy of land, but throughout late imperial China, commerce tended to be more important.

The third change that strengthened emperors was the disappearance of the aristocracy. During the Tang, the emperor had come from the same Sino-Turkic aristocracy of northwestern China as most of his principal ministers, and he was, essentially, the organ of a state that ruled on behalf of this aristocracy. Aristocrats monopolized the high posts of government. They married among themselves and with the imperial family. They called the emperor the Son of Heaven, but they knew he was one of them. During the Song, in contrast, the highest government officials were commoners, mostly products of the examination system. They were separated from the emperor by an enormous social gulf and saw him as a person apart. Able emperors took advantage of this.

The Tang officialdom had been largely self-perpetuating: The sons of officials were favored and officials were mainly drawn from the aristocracy. Only 10 percent were exam-passers. During the Northern Song, the figure rose to 57 percent and exam-passers held the highest official posts. By the Southern Song, the number of exam-passers became so large that the percentage obtaining official positions declined. For the sons of wealthy and powerful families, passing the highest examination became a certification of family status in local society.

Examinations were given at three levels. At each, only a tiny percentage of candidates were passed. Elaborate precautions were taken to prevent cheating or favoritism. Before entering the walled examination cubicles, candidates were searched. Completed examinations were copied by clerks and numbered so that the grading officials could not identify candidates by name or calligraphy. A few took the examinations over and over into late middle-age, but the average passer was in his mid-thirties.

To pass the examinations, the candidate had to memorize the Confucian classics, interpret selected passages, write in the literary style, compose poems on themes given by the examiners, and propose solutions to contemporary problems in terms of Confucian philosophy. The quality of the officials produced by the Song system was impressive. A parallel might be drawn with nineteenth century Britain, where students in the classics at Oxford and Cambridge went on to become generalist bureaucrats. The Chinese examination system that flourished during the Song continued, with some interruptions, into the twentieth century. The continuity of Chinese government during this millennium rested on the examination elite, with its common culture and values.

The social base of this examination meritocracy was triangular, consisting of land, education, and office. Landed wealth paid the costs of education. A good education led to examination success. Passing examinations led to office. Office-holding enabled a family to preserve its wealth. (The perks of office were substantial enough to overcome the division of the family property at each change of generation.) The majority of the population was outside of this meritocracy: A poor peasant or city dweller could not afford the years of study needed to pass the examinations and could not hope to attain an official position. Within the meritocracy, some families passed the examinations for several generations running. More often, the sons of well-to-do officials did not study as hard as those with bare means. The adage "shirt sleeves to shirt sleeves in three generations" is not inappropriate to the Song and later dynasties. In China's extended-family system (sometimes called lineages or clans), a wealthy official often provided education for the bright children of poor relations.

How the merchants related to this system is less clear. They had wealth but were despised by scholar-officials as grubby profit seekers and were barred from taking the examinations. Some merchants avoided the system altogether—a thorough education in the Confucian classics did little to fit a merchant's son for a career in commerce. Others bought land for status and security, and their sons or grandsons took the exams. Similarly, a small peasant might build up his holdings, become a landlord, and educate a son or grandson. The system was steeply hierarchical, but it was not closed nor did it produce a new, self-perpetuating elite.

Song Culture

As society and government changed during the Tang–Song transition, so too did culture. Song culture retained some of the energy of the Tang while becoming more intensely and perhaps more narrowly Chinese. The preconditions for the rich Song culture were a rising economy, an increase in the number of schools and higher literacy, and the spread of printing. Song culture was less aristocratic, less cosmopolitan, and more closely associated with the officials and the scholar-gentry, who were both its practitioners and its patrons. It is often said to have been somewhat less Buddhist than the Tang, though recent scholarship has called this into question. Certainly, the Chan (Zen) sect kept its vitality; but it is also true that some Confucians became outspokenly anti-Buddhist and anti-Taoist. Within high culture, as defined by civil service examinations, the sidestream of Tang secularism broadened and became mainstream during the Song.

Chinese consider the Song dynasty as the peak of their traditional culture. It was, for example, China's greatest age of pottery and porcelains. High-firing techniques were developed, and kilns were established in every area. Glazes were varied and shapes were restrained and graceful. Song pottery, like nothing produced in the world before it, made ceramics a major art form in East Asia. The Song was also an age of great historians. Sima Guang (1019–1086) wrote *A Comprehensive Mirror for Aid in Government*, which treated not a single dynasty but all Chinese history. His work was more sophisticated than previous histories in that it included a discussion of documentary sources and an explanation of why he chose one source rather than another. The greatest achievements of the Song, however, were in philosophy, poetry, and painting.

Philosophy   The Song dynasty was second only to the Zhou as a creative age in philosophy. Its intellectual vitality was a consequence of struggles between ideas.

During the later Northern Song, the school of Wang Anshi (1021–1086) held power at the court. Wang had carefully studied the Confucian classics and had rediscovered, he felt, the values of the ideal Zhou society. This discovery made him, in his own eyes at least, the true successor to Confucius. The key to his teachings was that proper institutions would make society moral and prosperous.

Concretely, Wang's "new policies" held that government should do more: State trading offices, not private merchants, should handle large-scale commerce; government offices, not large landowners, should make loans to poor farmers; local offices, not wealthy individuals, should establish moral authority in a community; government schools, not private academies, should be responsible for education in prefectures and counties. Wang also advocated military expansion. Officials of his school lost power in 1126 when the (Manchu) state of Jin defeated Song armies and overthrew the Northern Song.

The opposition to Wang was the "conservatives," who built a base during the Northern Song, dominated the court during the Southern Song, and were acknowledged as orthodox after 1315, when their interpretation of Confucianism became the standard for the civil service examinations. They argued, essentially, that government should do less. They criticized Wang's emphasis on institutions as "Legalist."

The most important in a series of "conservative" thinkers was Zhu Xi (1130–1200), whose thought, with ups and downs, remained the standard into the early twentieth century. Zhu studied Daoism and Buddhism, along with Confucianism, as a youth. A prodigy, he passed the metropolitan examination at the age of eighteen. He then became famous as a teacher at the White Deer Grotto Academy. He made Confucianism a more

Song dynasty philosopher Zhu Xi (1130–1200). His Neo-Confucian ideas remained central down to the twentieth century.
[Photo Credit: Imagemore/Glow Images]

personal philosophy by incorporating Buddhist elements and by emphasizing the Four Books—*Analects, Mencius, Doctrine of the Mean, and Greater Learning.* As a consequence, his teachings became a viable alternative to Buddhism among Chinese intellectuals. The reach of his ideas was multiplied during the Southern Song and later by the rapid spread of printing and by the greater numbers passing the state examinations.

Zhu taught that human nature is a part of the larger cosmos and contains moral principles that can be grasped by study and by meditation. Apprehending these inner moral principles leads to an ethical transformation by which the scholar becomes a moral exemplar for all of society. Such men, and not government institutions, were the key to morality and social order. Their moral presence made an overelaborate array of government institutions intrusive and unnecessary. It is difficult to think of the scholar-gentry class and the role it played in Ming and Qing society apart from this philosophy.

If we search for comparable figures in other traditions, we might pick Thomas Aquinas (1224–1274) of medieval Europe or the Islamic theologian al-Ghazali (1058–1111), each of whom produced a new philosophical synthesis that lasted for centuries. Aquinas combined church theology with Aristotle, just as Zhu Xi joined Confucian teachings with Buddhist metaphysical notions. Because Zhu Xi spoke of the "great ultimate" and because he emphasized Chan-like meditation, later critics attacked him as a Buddhist wolf in the clothing of a Confucian sheep. This was unfair. Where Aquinas made philosophy serve religion, Zhu Xi made religion serve philosophy. In his hands, the great ultimate (also known as principle or *li*) lost its otherworldly character and became the basis of morality and of all things in the universe. Zhu reaffirmed the positive ethical truths enunciated by Confucius over a thousand years earlier.

Historians argue, probably correctly, that Zhu Xi's teachings were a bulwark for the stability of late imperial China. Like the exam system, the bureaucracy, the imperial institution, the scholar-gentry class, and the land system, his interpretation contributed to continuity and impeded change. A few go further and say the Zhu Xi orthodoxy stifled change during the later dynasties. While not entirely untrue, this may overstate since there were always competing systems of thought.

Poetry Song poets were in awe of those of the Tang, yet Song poets were also among China's best. A Japanese scholar of Chinese literature wrote:

> Tang poetry could be likened to wine, and Song poetry to tea. Wine has great power to stimulate, but one cannot drink it constantly. Tea is less stimulating, bringing to the drinker a quieter pleasure, but one which can be enjoyed more continuously.[9]

The most famous poet of the Northern Song was Su Dungpo (1037–1101), a man who participated in the full range of the culture of his age: He was a painter and calligrapher, particularly knowledgeable about inks; he practiced Chan (Zen) and wrote commentaries on the Confucian classics; he superintended engineering projects; and he was

---

SU DUNGPO REMEMBERED BY A DISCIPLE

After Su's death, a disciple wrote these lines.

How does the sentiment in this poem relate to the Confucian humanism encountered in the document in Chapter 2?

When with tall hat and firm baton he stood in council,

The crowds were awed at the dignity of the statesman in him.
But when in cloth cap he strolled with cane and sandals,
He greeted little children with gentle smiles.

From *An Introduction to Sung Poetry*, by K. Yoshikawa, trans. by B. Watson. Cambridge, MA: Harvard University Press, p. 122. Copyright © 1967 by the Harvard-Yenching Institute Monograph Series. Reprinted by permission of the publisher.

---

[9]K. Yoshikawa, *An Introduction to Song Poetry*, trans. by B. Watson (Cambridge, MA: Harvard University Press, Harvard-Yenching Institute Monograph Series, 1967), p. 37.

a connoisseur of cooking and wine. His life was shaped by politics. He was a conservative, believing in a limited role for government and social control through morality.

Passing the metropolitan examination, Su rose through a succession of posts to
become the governor of a province—a position of immense power. While considering
death sentences, which could not be carried over into the new year, he wrote:

> New Year's Eve—you'd think I could go home early
> But official business keeps me.
> I hold the brush and face them with tears:
> Pitiful convicts in chains,
> Little men who tried to fill their bellies,
> Fell into the law's net, don't understand disgrace.
> And I? In love with a meager stipend
> I hold on to my job and miss the chance to retire.
> Do not ask who is foolish or wise;
> All of us alike scheme for a meal.
> The ancients would have freed them a while at New Year's—
> Would I dare do likewise? I am silent with shame.[10]

Eight years later, when the reformers came to power, Su himself was arrested
and spent 100 days in prison, awaiting execution on a charge of slandering the
emperor. Instead, he was released but exiled. He wrote, "Out the gate, I do a dance,
wind blows in my face; our galloping horses race along as magpies cheer."[11] Arriving at
his place of exile, he reflected:

> Between heaven and earth I live,
> One ant on a giant grindstone,
> Trying in my petty way to walk to the right
> While the turning of the mill wheel takes me endlessly left.
> Though I go the way of benevolence and duty,
> I can't escape from hunger and cold.[12]

But exile was soon turned to art. He farmed a plot of land at the "eastern slope,"
from which he took his literary name, Dungpo. Of his work there, he wrote:

> A good farmer hates to wear out the land;
> I'm lucky this plot was ten years fallow.
> It's too soon to count on mulberries;

[10]Yoshikawa, p. 119.
[11]Yoshikawa, p. 117.
[12]Yoshikawa, p. 105.

My best bet is a crop of wheat.
I planted seed and within the month
Dirt on the rows was showing green.
An old farmer warned me,
Don't let seedlings shoot up too fast!
If you want plenty of dumpling flour
Turn a cow or sheep in here to graze.
Good advice—I bowed my thanks;
I won't forget you when my belly's full.[13]

After 1086, the conservatives regained control of the government, and Su resumed his official career. In 1094, another shift occurred and Su was again sent into exile on the distant southern island of Hainan. After still another shift, Su was on his way back to the capital when he died in 1101.

Painting   In the West, penmanship and painting are quite separate, one merely a skill, the other esteemed as an art. In China, calligraphy and painting were equally appreciated and were seen as related. A scholar spent his life with brush in hand. Each stroke of the brush on silk or paper was final. Mistakes could not be covered up. The same qualities of line, balance, and strength needed for calligraphy carried over to painting. Chinese calligraphy is immensely pleasing even to the untutored Western eye, and it is not difficult to distinguish between the elegant strokes of Huineng, the last emperor of the Northern Song, and the powerful brushwork of the Chan (Zen) monk Zhang Zizhi.

Song painting was varied—of birds and flowers; of fish and insects; of horses, monkeys, and water buffalo; of scholars, emperors, Buddhas, or Taoist immortals. But its crowning achievement was landscapes. Song landscapes are quite unlike those of the West. Each element of a painting was presented in its most pleasing aspect; the painting was not constrained by single-point perspective. Paintings had no single source of illumination with light and shadow but an overall diffusion of light. Space was an integral part of the painting. A typical painting might have craggy rocks or twisted pine trees in the foreground, then mist or clouds or rain to create distance, and in the background the outlines of mountains or cliffs fading into space. If the painting contained human figures at all, they were small in a natural universe that was very large. Chinese painting thus reflected the same worldview as Chinese philosophy or poetry. The goal of the painter was to depict the inner reality of the scene and not to be bound up in surface details. But since the same subject matter was painted by all, the difference between a master and a second-rate painter lay in the skillfulness of the brushwork.

In paintings by monks or masters of the Chan school, the presentation of an intuitive vision of an inner reality became even more pronounced. Paintings of Bodhidharma, the legendary founder of the Chan sect, are often dominated by a single

[13]Yoshikawa, pp. 119–120.

powerful downstroke of the brush, defining the edge of his robe. Paintings of patriarchs tearing up sutras or sweeping dust with a broom from the mirror of the mind are almost as calligraphic as paintings of bamboo. A Yuan dynasty painting in the style of Shi Ke shows the figure of a monk or sage who is dozing or meditating. A Chan "broken ink" landscape might contain rocks, water, mountains, and clouds, each represented by a few explosive strokes of the brush.

YUAN DYNASTY (1279–1368): CHINA IN THE MONGOL WORLD EMPIRE

The Mongols created the greatest empire in the history of the world. It extended from the Caspian Sea to the Pacific Ocean; from Russia, Siberia, and Korea in the north to Persia and Burma in the south (see Map 3–4). Invasion fleets were even sent to Java and Japan, although without success. Mongol rule in China is one chapter of this larger story.

Rise of the Mongol Empire

A nomadic people, the Mongols lived to the north of China on grasslands where they raised horses and herded sheep. They lived in felt tents called yurts—they sometimes called themselves "the people of the felt tents." Women performed much of the work

Map 3–4 The Mongol empire in the late thirteenth century. Note the four khanates: the Golden Horde in Russia, the Ilkhanate in Persia, Chagatai in Central Asia, and the Great Khanate extending from Mongolia to southern China. China became one state in a multistate system.

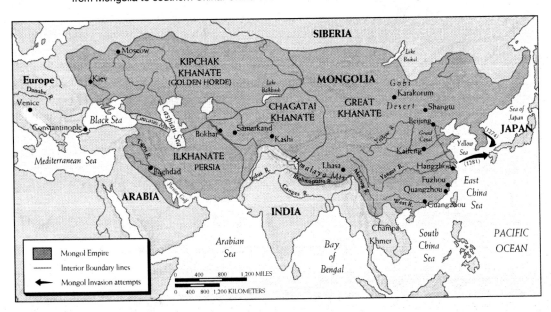

and were freer and more easygoing than women in China. Families belonged to clans, and related clans to tribes. Tribes would gather during the annual migration from summer plains to winter pasturage. Chiefs were elected, most often from noble lineages, for their courage, military prowess, judgment, and leadership. Like Manchu or Turkic, the Mongol tongue was Altaic.

The Mongols believed in nature deities and in the sky god above all others. Sky blue was their sacred color. They communicated with their gods through religious specialists called *shamans*. Politically divided, they traded and warred among themselves and with settled peoples on the borders of their vast grassland domains.

The founder of the Mongol empire, Temujin, was born in 1167, the son of a tribal chief. While Temujin was still a child, his father was poisoned. He fled, and after wandering for some years, he returned to the tribe, avenged his father, and in time became chief himself. Through his shrewd policy of alliances and remarkable survival qualities, by the time he was forty he had united all Mongol tribes and had been elected their great khan, or ruler. It is by the title *Genghis* (also spelled *Jenghiz* or *Chinggis*) *Khan* that he is known to history. Genghis possessed an extraordinary charisma, and his sons and grandsons also became wise and talented leaders. Why the Mongol tribes, almost untouched by the higher civilizations of the world, should have produced such leaders at this point in history is difficult to explain.

A second conundrum is how the Mongols, who numbered only about a million and a half, created the army that conquered vastly denser populations. Part of the answer is institutional. Genghis organized his armies into "myriads" of 10,000 troops, with decimal subdivisions of 1,000, 100, and 10. Elaborate signals were devised so that, in battle, even large units could be manipulated like the fingers of a hand. Mongol tactics were superb: Units would retreat, turn, flank, and destroy their enemies. The historical record makes amply clear that Genghis's nomadic cavalry had a paralytic effect on the peoples they encountered. The Mongols were peerless horsemen and their most dreaded weapon was the compound bow, short enough to be used from the saddle yet more powerful than the English longbow (a 150-pound pull versus a 100-pound pull).

They were astonishingly mobile. Each man carried his own supplies. Trailing remounts, they covered vast distances quickly. In 1241, for example, a Mongol army had reached Hungary, Poland, and the shore of the Adriatic and was poised for a further advance into western Europe. But when word arrived of the death of the great khan, the army turned and galloped back to Mongolia to help choose his successor.

When this army encountered walled cities, it learned the use of siege weapons from the enemies it had conquered. Chinese engineers were used in campaigns in Persia. The Mongols also used terror as a weapon. Inhabitants of cities that refused to surrender in the Near East and China were put to the sword. Large areas in north China and Sichuan were devastated and depopulated in the process of conquest. Descriptions of the Mongols by those whom they conquered dwell on their physical toughness and pitiless cruelty.

But the Mongols had strengths that went beyond the strictly military. Genghis opened his armies to other nomadic peoples of the steppe. As long as they complied with the military discipline demanded of his forces, they could participate in his triumphs. In 1206, Genghis promulgated laws designed to prevent the normal wrangling and warring between tribes that would undermine his empire. Genghis also obtained thousands of pledges of personal loyalty from his followers, and he appointed these "vassals" to command his armies and staff his government. This policy gave to his forces an inner coherence that countered the divisive effect of tribal loyalties.

The Mongol conquests were all the more impressive in that, unlike the earlier Arab expansion, they lacked the unifying force of religious zeal. To be sure, at an assembly of chiefs in 1206, an influential shaman revealed that it was the sky god's will that Genghis conquer the world. Yet other unabashedly frank words attributed to Genghis may reveal a truer image of what lay behind the Mongol drive to conquest: "Man's highest joy is in victory: to conquer one's enemies, to pursue them, to deprive them of their possessions, to make their beloved weep, to ride on their horses, and to embrace their wives and daughters."[14]

Genghis divided his far-flung empire among his four sons, who, aided by their sons, completed the conquest. Trade and communications were maintained within the empire, but over several generations, each of the four khanates became independent. The khanate of Chagatai in Central Asia remained purely nomadic. A second khanate of the Golden Horde ruled Russia from the lower Volga. The third was in Persia. The fourth, led by those who succeeded Genghis as great khans, centered first on Mongolia and then China.

Mongol Rule in China

The standard theory used in explaining Chinese history is the dynastic cycle. A second theory explains the history in terms of the interaction between the settled people of China and nomads of the steppe. When strong states emerged in China, their wealth and population enabled them to expand militarily onto the steppe. But when China was weak, as was often the case, steppe peoples overran China. To review briefly:

1. During the Han dynasty (206 B.C.–220 A.D.), the most pressing problem in foreign relations was the Xiong Nu empire to the north.

2. During the centuries that followed the Han, various nomadic peoples invaded and ruled northern China.

3. The energy and institutions of the Sino-Turkic rulers of the northern dynasties shaped China's reunification during the Sui (581–618) and Tang (618–907) dynasties. The Uighur Turks also played an ongoing role in Tang defense policy.

[14]J. K. Fairbank, E. O. Reischauer, and A. M. Craig, *East Asia: Tradition and Transformation* (Boston, MA: Houghton Mifflin, 1989), p. 164.

4. Northern border states became even more important during the Song. The Northern Song (960–1126) bought peace with payments of gold and silver to the Liao. The Southern Song (1126–1279), for all of its cultural brilliance, was little more than a tributary state of the Jin, which had expanded into northern China.

From the very start of the Mongol pursuit of world hegemony, China's riches were a target. But Genghis proceeded cautiously, determined to leave no enemy at his back. He first disposed of the Tibetan state to the northwest of China and then of the Manchu state of Jin that ruled north China. Mongol forces took Beijing in 1227, the year Genghis died. They went on to take Luoyang and the southern reaches of the Yellow River in 1234, and all of north China by 1241. During this time, the Mongols were interested mainly in loot. Only later did Chinese advisers persuade them that more wealth could be obtained by taxation.

Kublai (1216–1294), a grandson of Genghis, was chosen as the great khan in 1260. In 1264, he moved his capital from Karakorum in Mongolia to Beijing, and in 1271,

Kublai Khan (1216–1294)
[Picture Desk, Inc./Kobal Collection]

he adopted a Chinese dynastic name, the Yuan. Then, as the ruler of a Chinese dynasty, he went to war with the Southern Song. Once the decision was made, the Mongols swept across southern China. The last Song stronghold fell in 1279.

Kublai Khan's rule in Beijing reflected the mixture of cultural elements in Mongol China. From Beijing, Kublai could rule as a Chinese emperor, which would not have been possible in Karakorum. He adopted the Chinese custom of hereditary succession. He rebuilt Beijing as a walled city in the Chinese style. But Beijing was far to the north of any previous Chinese capital, away from centers of wealth and population; to provision it, the Grand Canal had to be extended. From Beijing, Kublai could look out onto Manchuria and Mongolia and maintain ties with the other khanates. The city proper was for the Mongols. It was known to the West as *Cambulac*, "the city (*baliq*) of the khan." Chinese were segregated in an adjoining walled city. The palace of the khan was designed by an Arab architect; its rooms were Central Asian in style. Kublai also maintained a summer palace at Shangtu (the "Xanadu" of Samuel Taylor Coleridge's poem) in Inner Mongolia, where he could hawk and ride and hunt in Mongol style.

Early Mongol rule in north China was rapacious and exploitative, but it later shifted toward Chinese forms of government and taxation, especially in the south and at the local level. Because it was a foreign military occupation, civil administration was highly centralized. Under the emperor was a Central Secretariat, and beneath it were ten "Moving Secretariats," which became the provinces of later dynasties. These highly centralized institutions and the arbitrary style of Mongol decision-making accelerated the trend toward absolutism that had started during the previous dynasty.

About 400,000 Mongols lived in China during the Yuan period. For such a tiny minority to control the Chinese majority, it had to stay separate. One measure was to make military service a monopoly of Mongols and their nomadic allies. Garrisons were established throughout China, with a strategic reserve on the steppe. Military officers were always regarded as more important than civil officials. The second measure was to use ethnic classifications in appointing civil officials. The highest category was the Mongols, who held the top civil and military posts. The second category included Persians, Turks, and other non-Chinese, who were given high civil posts. The third category was northern Chinese, including Manchus and other border peoples, and the fourth was southern Chinese. Even when the examination system was sporadically revived after 1315, the Mongols and their allies took an easier examination; their quota was as large as that for Chinese; and they were appointed to higher offices.

The net result was an uneasy symbiosis. Chinese officials directly governed the Chinese populace, collecting taxes, settling disputes, and maintaining the local order. Few of these officials ever learned to speak Mongolian, yet without their positive cooperation, Mongol rule in China would have been impossible. The Mongols, concentrated in Beijing, large cities, and in garrisons, spoke Mongolian among themselves and usually did not bother to learn Chinese. A few exceptions wrote poetry in Chinese and painted in the Chinese style. Communication was through interpreters. When a

MARCO POLO DESCRIBES THE CITY OF HANGZHOU

Marco Polo was a Venetian. In 1300, Venice had a population of more than 100,000 and was one of the wealthiest of Mediterranean city-states. But Polo was nonetheless unprepared for what he saw in China. Commenting on Hangzhou, China's capital during the Southern Song, he first noted its size (ten or twelve times larger than Venice), then its many canals and bridges, its streets "paved with stones and bricks," and its location between "a lake of fresh and very clear water" and "a river of great magnitude." He spoke of "the prodigious concourse of people" frequenting its ten great marketplaces and of its "capacious warehouses built of stone for the accommodation of merchants who arrive from India and other parts." He then described the life of its people.

Europeans who read Marco Polo's account of China thought it was too good to be true. Would you agree?

Each of the ten market-squares is surrounded with high dwelling-houses, in the lower part of which are shops, where every kind of manufacture is carried on, and every article of trade is sold; such, amongst others, as spices, drugs, trinkets, and pearls. In certain shops nothing is vended but the wine of the country, which they are continually brewing, and serve out fresh to their customers at a moderate price. The streets connected with the market-squares are numerous, and in some of them are many cold baths, attended by servants of both sexes, to perform the offices of ablution for the men and women who frequent them, and who from their childhood have been accustomed at all times to wash in cold water, which they reckon highly conducive to health. At these bathing places, however, they have apartments provided with warm water, for the use of strangers, who from not being habituated to it, cannot bear the shock of the cold. All are in the daily practice of washing their persons, and especially before their meals.

In other streets are the habitations of the courtesans, who are here in such numbers as I dare not venture to report; and not only near the squares, which is the situation usually appropriated for their residence, but in every part of the city they are to be found, adorned with much finery, highly perfumed, occupying well-furnished houses, and attended by many female domestics. These women are accomplished, and are perfect in the arts of blandishment and dalliance, which they accompany with expressions adapted to every description of person, insomuch that strangers who have once become so enchanted by their meretricious arts, that they can never divest themselves of the impression. Thus intoxicated with sensual pleasures, when they return to their homes they report that they have been in Kin-sai [Hangzhou], or the celestial city, and pant for the time when they may be enabled to revisit paradise.

The inhabitants of the city are idolaters, and they use paper money as currency. The men as well as the women have fair complexions, and are handsome. The greater part of them are always clothed in silk, in consequence of the vast quantity of that material produced in the territory of Kin-sai, exclusively of what the merchants import from other provinces. Amongst the handicraft trades exercised in the place, there are twelve considered to be superior to the rest, as being more generally useful; for each of which there are a thousand workshops, and each shop furnishes employment for ten, fifteen, or twenty workmen, and in a few instances as many as forty, under their respective masters. The natural disposition of the native inhabitants of Kin-sai is pacific, and by the example of their former kings, who were themselves unwarlike, they have been accustomed to habits of tranquility. The management of arms is unknown to them, nor do they keep any in their houses. Contentious broils are never heard among them. They conduct their mercantile and manufacturing concerns with perfect candour and probity. They are friendly towards each other, and persons who inhabit the same street, both men and women, from the mere circumstance of neighbourhood, appear like one family. In their domestic manners they are free from jealousy or suspicion of their wives, to whom great respect is shown, and any man would be accounted infamous who should presume to use indecent expressions to a married woman. To strangers also, who visit their city in the way of commerce, they give proofs of cordiality, inviting them freely to their houses, showing them hospitable attention, and furnishing them with the best advice and assistance in their mercantile transactions. On the other hand, they dislike the sight of soldiery, not excepting the guards of the grand khan, as they preserve the recollection that by them they were deprived of the government of their native kings and rulers.

Excerpt from *The Travels of Marco Polo*, 1908, from Everyman's Library. Reprinted by permission of David Campbell Publishers, London, pp. 290–301.

Chinese district magistrate sent a query to the court, the ruling was made in Mongolian. (The Mongols had borrowed the alphabet of the Uighurs to transcribe their tongue.) A word-for-word translation in Chinese was written below the Mongolian and passed back down to the magistrate. As the two languages are syntactically very different, the resulting Chinese was grotesque.

Foreign Contacts and Chinese Culture

Diplomacy and trade through the greater Mongol empire brought China into contact with other higher civilizations for the first time since the Tang. Persia and the Arab world were especially important. Merchants, missionaries, and diplomats voyaged from the Persian Gulf and across the Indian Ocean to seaports in southeastern China. The Arab communities in Guangzhou (Canton) and other ports were larger than they had been during the Song. Camel caravans carrying silks and ceramics left Beijing to pass through the Central Asian oases and on to Baghdad. Although the Mongols did not favor Chinese merchants and most trade was in other hands, Chinese trade also expanded. Chinese communities became established in Tabriz, the center of trading in western Asia, and in Moscow and Novgorod. It was during this period that knowledge of printing, gunpowder, and Chinese medicine spread to western Asia. Chinese ceramics influenced those of Persia as Chinese painting influenced Persian miniatures.

In Europe, knowledge of China was transmitted by the Venetian trader Marco Polo, who said he had served Kublai as an official between 1275 and 1292. His book, *A Description of the World*, was translated into most European languages. Many readers doubted that a land of such wealth and culture could exist so far from Europe, but the book excited an interest in geography. When Christopher Columbus set sail in 1492, his goal was to reach Polo's Zipangu (Japan).

The greatest of all Muslim travelers, the Moroccan Ibn Battuta (1304–1370), traveled throughout much of the Mongol world in the fourteenth century. His observations are a rich source of information about the societies he visited. Ever curious, he had a sharp eye for detail. "The Chinese infidels eat the flesh of swine and dogs, and sell it in their markets. They are wealthy folk and well-to-do, but they make no display either in their food or their clothes."

Other cultural contacts were fostered by the Mongol toleration or encouragement of religion. Nestorian Christianity, spreading from Persia to Central Asia, reentered China during the Mongol era. The mother of Kublai Khan was a Christian of this sect. Churches were built in main cities. Several papal missions were sent from Rome to the Mongol court. An archbishopric was established in Beijing; a church was built, sermons were preached in Turkish or Mongolian, and choirboys sang hymns. Kublai sent Marco Polo's father and uncle with a letter to the pope asking for 100 intelligent men acquainted with the seven arts.

Tibetan Buddhism with its magical doctrines and elaborate rites was the religion most favored by the Mongols, but Chinese Buddhism also flourished. Priests and monks of all religions were given tax exemptions. It is estimated that half a million Chinese became Buddhist monks during the Mongol century. The foreign religion that made the greatest gains was Islam, which became permanently established in Central Asia and western China. Mosques were built in the Islamic areas, in Beijing, and in southeastern port cities. Even Confucianism was regarded as a religion by the Mongols, and its teachers were exempted from taxes. But as scholar-gentry rarely obtained important offices, they saw the Mongol era as a time of hardship.

Despite these wide contacts with other peoples and religions, the high culture of China appears to have been influenced almost not at all—partly because China had little to learn from other areas, and partly because the centers of Chinese culture were in the south, the last area to be conquered and the area least affected by Mongol rule. Also, in reaction to the Mongol conquest, Chinese culture became conservative and turned in on itself. Scholars wrote poetry in the style of the Song. New schools of painting developed, but the developments were from within the Chinese tradition, and the best of Yuan paintings continued the style of the Song. Yuan historians, as usual, wrote the official history of the dynasty that preceded it. The head of the court bureau of historiography was a Mongol, but the histories produced by his Chinese staff were in the traditional mold. As the dynasty waned, unemployed scholars wrote essays expressing loyalty toward the Song and satirizing the Mongols. Their writings were not censored: The Mongols could not read them, did not read them, or did not care.

The major contribution to Chinese arts during the Yuan was by dramatists, who combined poetic arias with vaudeville theater to produce a new operatic drama. Performed by traveling troupes, the operas used few stage props. They relied for effect on makeup, costumes, pantomime, and stylized gestures. Women's roles were usually played by men. Except for the arias—the highlights of the performance—the dramas used vernacular Chinese, appealing to a popular audience. The unemployed scholars who wrote the scripts drew on the entire repertoire of the Song storyteller. Among stock figures of the operas were a Robin Hood-like bandit; a famous detective-judge; the Tang monk who traveled to India; warriors and statesmen of the Three Kingdoms; and romantic heroes, villains, and ghosts. Justice always triumphed, and the dramas usually ended happily. In several famous plays, the hero gets the girl, despite objections by her parents and seemingly insurmountable obstacles, by passing the civil service examinations in first place. As the examinations were not held during most of the Yuan, this resolution of the hero's predicament looked back to the Song. Yuan drama continued almost unchanged in later dynasties, and during the nineteenth century, it merged with a form of southern Chinese theater to become today's Beijing Opera.

Last Years of the Yuan

Despite the Mongol military domination of China and the highly centralized institutions of the Mongol court, the Yuan was the shortest of China's major dynasties. Little more than a century elapsed between Kublai's move to Beijing in 1264 and the dynasty's collapse in 1368. The rule of Kublai and his successor had been effective, but thereafter a decline set in. By then, the Mongol empire as a whole no longer lent strength to its parts. The khanates became separated by religion and culture as well as by distance. Even tribesmen in Mongolia rebelled now and then against the great khans in Beijing, who, in their eyes, had become too Chinese. The court at Beijing, too, had never really gained legitimacy. Some Chinese officials served it loyally to the end, but most Chinese saw the government as carpetbaggers and saw Mongol rule as a military occupation. When succession disputes, bureaucratic factionalism, and pitched battles between Mongol generals broke out, Chinese showed little inclination to rally in support of the dynasty.

Problems also arose in the countryside. Taxes were heavy and some local officials corrupt. The government issued excessive paper money and then refused to accept it in payment for taxes. The Yellow River changed its course, flooding the canals that carried grain to the capital. At great cost and suffering, a labor force of 150,000 workers and 20,000 soldiers rerouted the river to the south of the Shandong peninsula. Further natural disasters during the 1350s led to popular uprisings. The White Lotus sect preached the coming of Maitreya. Regional military commanders, suppressing the rebellions, became independent of central control. Warlords arose. The warlord who ruled Sichuan was infamous for his cruelty. Important economic regions were devastated and in part depopulated by rebellions. At the end, a rebel army threatened Beijing, and the last Mongol emperor and his court fled on horses to Shangdu. When that fell, they fled still deeper into the plains of Mongolia.

IMPERIAL CHINA IN HISTORICAL PERSPECTIVE

Rough parallels between China and Europe persisted until the sixth century A.D. Both saw the rise and fall of great empires. At first glance, the three-and-one-half centuries that followed the Han dynasty appear remarkably similar to the comparable period after the collapse of the Roman empire: Central authority broke down, private armies arose, and aristocratic estates were established. Barbarian tribes once allied to the empires invaded and pillaged large areas. Otherworldly religions entered to challenge earlier official worldviews. In China, Neo-Daoism and then Buddhism challenged Confucianism, just as Christianity challenged Roman conceptions of the sociopolitical order.

But from the late sixth century, a fundamental divergence occurred. Europe tailed off into centuries of feudal disunity and backwardness. A ghost of empire lingered in the European memory. But the reality, even after centuries had passed, was that tiny areas like France (1/17th the size of China), Italy (1/32nd) or Germany (1/27th) found it difficult to establish an internal unity, much less recreate a pan-European or pan-Mediterranean empire. In contrast, China, which is about the size of Europe and geographically no more natural a political unit, put a unified empire back together again, attaining a new level of wealth, power, and culture, and unified rule that has continued until the present. What explains the difference?

One reason the empire was reconstituted in China was that the victory of Buddhism in China was less complete than that of Christianity in Europe. Confucianism, and its conception of a unified empire, survived within the aristocratic families and at the courts of the Six Dynasties. It is difficult even to think of Confucianism apart from the idea of a universal ruler, aided by men of virtue and ability, ruling and "all under Heaven" according to Heaven's Mandate. In contrast, Roman concepts of political order were not maintained after the fall of Rome. Empire was never a critical element in Christian thought—except perhaps in Byzantium, where empire lasted longer than it did in western Europe. The notion of a "Christian king" did appear in the West, but basically, the kingdom sought by Jesus was not of this world.

The second consideration was China's greater cultural homogeneity. It had a common written language that was fairly close to all varieties of spoken Chinese. Minority peoples and even barbarian conquerors—apart from the Mongols—were rapidly Sinicized. In contrast, after Rome, the Mediterranean fell apart into its component cultures. Latin became the universal language of the Western church, but for most Christians, it was a foreign language and a part of the mystery of the Mass, and even in Italy, it became an artificial language, separate from the living tongue. European languages and cultures were divisive forces.

The third factor was the combination in the post-Han, northern Chinese states of economic strength based on Chinese agriculture with the military striking force of a nomadic cavalry. There was nothing like it in Europe. Such a northern state reunified China in 589.

The fourth and perhaps critical factor was China's population density. The province (called a *circuit* at the time) of Hubei had a registered population of 10,559,728 during the eighth century. Hubei was about one-third the size of France, which in the eleventh century had a population of about two million. That is to say, even comparing China with France three centuries later, China's population density was fifteen times greater. (This comparison, it should be noted, is with a nonrice-producing area of China. Rice producing areas were even more densely populated.) Greater population density resulted in a different kind of history.

Population density also helps explain why the Chinese could absorb barbarian conquerors so much more quickly than could Europe. More cultivators provided a larger agricultural surplus to the northern kingdoms than that enjoyed by comparable kingdoms in Europe. Greater numbers of people also meant better communications and a better base for commerce. To be sure, the centuries that followed the Han saw a decline in commerce and cities. In some areas, money went out of use to be replaced by barter or the use of silk as currency. But the economic level remained higher than in early medieval Europe.

Several of the factors that explain the Sui–Tang regeneration of a unified empire apply equally well or better to the Song and subsequent dynasties. As more schools were established and literacy rose, Confucianism and the ideal of a unified China became more widely accepted. Chinese culture was more homogeneous and less open to outside influences in the tenth century than it had been four centuries earlier. The population had also grown, with the Yangzi basin emerging as a new center of gravity.

The cyclical regeneration of centralized bureaucratic government—even under outside conquerors—may also be explained in terms of the interests it served. For the military leader who established the dynasty, the bureaucratic state was a huge tax machine that supported his armies and bestowed on him revenues beyond the imaginings of contemporary European monarchs. Government by civil officials also offered some promise of security for his progeny by acting as a counterweight against ambitious army generals. For the scholar-gentry class, service to the state was the means to maintain family wealth, power, and status. Nothing mattered more. For merchants, a strong state was not an unmixed blessing: It might tax their profits or establish monopolies on the commodities they traded, but it also provided order and stability. More often than not, commerce expanded during such periods. For farmers, the picture was also unclear: Taxation was often exploitative, but orderly exploitation was usually preferable to rapacious warlords, bandits, or marauding armies.

Comparisons across continents are difficult, but it seems likely that Tang and Song China had longer stretches of good government than any other part of their contemporary world. Not until the nineteenth century would comparable bureaucracies of talent and virtue appear in the West.

REVIEW QUESTIONS

1. How could China recreate its empire—just 400 years after the fall of the Han—when Rome could not? Are there similarities between the Qin–Han transition and that of the Sui–Tang? Between Han and Tang expansion and contraction?

2. How did the Chinese economy change between the Tang, the Northern Song, and the Southern Song? The polity? China's relationships to surrounding states?

3. What do Chinese poetry and art tell us about Chinese society? About women? About war?

4. What drove the Mongols to conquer most of the known world? How could their military accomplish the task? Once they had conquered China, how did they rule it? What was the Chinese response to Mongol rule?

SUGGESTED READINGS

General

BOL, P. K. *The Culture of Ours* (1992). A most insightful intellectual history of the Tang through the Song dynasties.

CAHILL, J. *Chinese Painting* (1960). An excellent survey.

FAIRBANK, J.K., AND TWITCHETT, D., EDS. *Cambridge History of China*. Volume 3 (1979) treats "*Sui and T'ang China, 589–906;*" Volume 6 (1994) treats "*Alien Regimes and Border States, 710–1368,*" which includes the era of Mongol rule.

KIERMAN, F. A. JR., AND FAIRBANK, J. K., EDS. *Chinese Ways in Warfare* (1974). Chapters by different authors on the Chinese military from the Zhou to the Ming.

OWEN, S., TRANS. AND ED. *An Anthology of Chinese Literature: Beginnings to 1911* (1996). Read together with other chapters as well.

Sui and Tang

ADSHEAD, S.A.M. *T'ang China: The Rise of the East in World History* (2004).

EBREY, P. B. *Women and the Family in Chinese History* (2003).

EBREY, P. B. *The Aristocratic Families of Early Imperial China* (1978).

McMULLEN, D. *State and Scholars in Tang China* (1988).

OWEN, S. *The Great Age of Chinese Poetry: The High T'ang* (1980).

PULLEYBLANK, E. G. *The Background of the Rebellion of An Lu-shan* (1955). A study of the 755 rebellion that weakened the central authority of the Tang dynasty.

REISCHAUER, E. O. *Ennin's Travels in T'ang China* (1955). China as seen through the eyes of a ninth-century Japanese Marco Polo.

SCHAFER, E. H. *The Golden Peaches of Samarkand* (1963). A study of Tang imagery.

TEISER, S. *The Ghost Festival in Medieval China* (1988). On Tang popular religion.

WANG, G. W. *The Structure of Power in North China during the Five Dynasties* (1963). A study of the interim period between the Tang and the Song dynasties.

WRIGHT, A. F. *The Sui Dynasty* (1978).

Song

BOL, P. *Neo-Confucianism in History* (2008).

CHANG, C. S., AND SMYTHE, J. *South China in the Twelfth Century* (1981). China as seen through the eyes of a twelfth-century Chinese poet, historian, and statesman.

DAVIS, E. I. *Society and the Supernatural in Song China* (2001).

GERNET, J. *Daily Life in China on the Eve of the Mongol Invasion* (1962).

HAEGER, J. W., ED. *Crisis and Prosperity in Sung China* (1975).

HYMES, R. *Way and Byway: Taoism, Local Religion, and Models of Divinity in Sung and Modern China* (2002).

HYMES, R. *Statesmen and Gentlemen* (1987). On the transformation of officials into a local gentry elite during the twelfth and thirteenth centuries.

ROSSABI, M. *China among Equals* (1983). A study of the Liao, Jin, and Song empires and their relations.

TAO, J. S. *The Jurchen in Twelfth Century China: A Study of Sinicization* (1977).

TU, W. M. *Confucian Thought: Selfhood as Creative Transformation* (1985).

YOSHIKAWA, K. *An Introduction to Sung Poetry*, trans. by B. Watson (1967).

Yuan

ALLSEN, T. T. *Mongol Imperialism* (1987).

BIRGE, B. *Women, Property, and Confucian Reaction in Sung and Yuan China* (2002). On the decline of women's property rights in post-Song China.

DARDESS, J. W. *Conquerors and Confucians: Aspects of Political Change in Late Yuan China* (1973).

DE RACHEWILTZ. TRANS. *The Secret History of the Mongols* (2003). On the rise of Genghis to power.

LANGLOIS, J. D. *China under Mongol Rule* (1981).

MARTIN, H. D. *The Rise of Chingis Khan and His Conquest of North China* (1981).

MORGAN, D. *The Mongol Empire and its Legacy* (1999). Genghis, the several khanates, and the aftermath of empire.

ROSSABI, M. *Khubilai Khan: His Life and Times* (2005).

RATCHNEVSKY, P. *Genghis Khan: His Life and Legacy* (1992).

WEST, E. E. *Mongolian Rule in China* (1989)

CHAPTER FOUR

Late Imperial China: The Ming (1368–1644) and Qing (1644–1912) Dynasties

Fisherman on an Autumn River, a Ming dynasty scroll painting by Dai Qin (1390–1460).
Painting. Ink and color on paper. 18-1/8 x 291-1/4 in. (46 x 740 cm). Courtesy of the Freer Gallery of Art, Smithsonian Institution, Washington, DC]

CHAPTER OUTLINE

The Ming and the Qing were China's last dynasties. The Ming was Chinese, the Qing (pronounced ching), a dynasty of conquest in which the ruling house and an important segment of the military were non-Chinese Manchus. The two dynasties were nevertheless sufficiently similar in their institutions and pattern of rule that historians once spoke of "Ming–Qing despotism" as if it were a single system. In one respect, the Ming and Qing were just the last in the long parade of the centralized bureaucratic regimes of imperial China. In the Tang recreation of centralized empire, the Chinese had forged a form of government so efficient, and so closely geared to the deeper familial and educational constitution of the society, that thereafter they rebuilt such a government after each dynastic breakdown. Even dynasties of conquest adopted large parts of the pattern. This pattern clearly continued during the Ming and Qing, giving these dynasties' histories a recognizable cyclical cast.

But noncyclical trends that cut across dynastic lines may have been more important. China's population had been stable within a narrow range for over a millennium from the Han to the Song, but broke out of that range during the Ming and experienced unprecedented growth during the Qing. In this regard, the Ming–Qing set China on the path to becoming what it is today. Commerce reached higher levels than ever before. The diaspora of Chinese to Southeast Asia and the world beyond that started in the eighteenth century and spurted in the nineteenth, while beyond the scope of this volume, was a consequence of both population pressure and export institutions. Another critical change occurred in the balance of power between China and the steppe, which had been a fundamental dimension of all Chinese history down to the nineteenth century. Simply put, firearms initially gave Europe only a small advantage in the interior of China but, by the late Qing, gave China a tremendous edge against steppe cavalry. The result was the Chinese subjugation of the non-Chinese populations of Tibet, Central Asia, and a part of Mongolia. Chinese control of these areas today is in large part a gift from the Manchus.

This chapter emphasizes the dynamism of China during these late centuries. If we refer to the Ming–Qing as "late imperial China" or as a "late traditional society," it is to avoid labels such as "medieval" or "early modern," which, unwisely, attempt to locate China somewhere along the continuum of European history. But "late imperial" and "late traditional" should not be read to mean "late static." For in China, the economy grew, the society became more integrated, and the apparatus of government became more sophisticated than ever before. These advances positively shaped China's response to Europe during the nineteenth century. But we must also note that Europe's transformation during these centuries was even more sweeping. In fact, Greece and Rome apart, most of what seems important in European history—the Renaissance, the Reformation, the scientific revolution, the formation of nation-states, the industrial revolution, the Enlightenment, and the democratic revolution—happened during the Ming and the Qing dynasties. As we view China from the perspective of Europe, China appears to have been caught in a tar pit of slow motion. But such was not the case; it was actually the West that had accelerated.

ECONOMIC REGIONS

No historian would write of Europe without distinguishing between England, France, and Germany. China's geographical diversity is no less than that of Europe, but is often masked by its political and cultural unity. Excluding the Tibetan massif and the Himalayas, the parched oasis-strewn deserts of Central Asia, the grasslands of the Mongolian steppe, and the forests of Manchuria, China's heartland consists of three tiers, each with two or three economic regions (see Map 4–1).

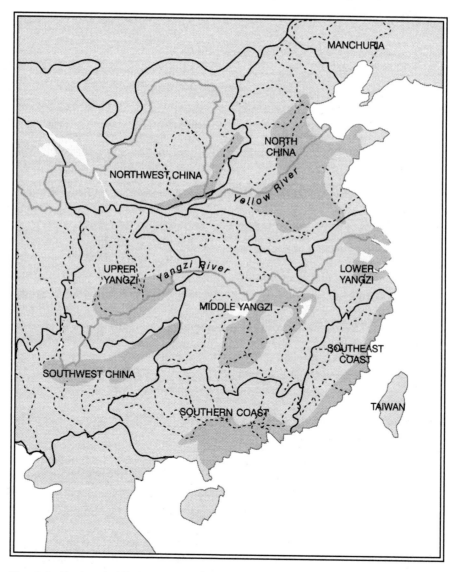

Map 4–1 Regions in Ming–Qing China.

The northernmost tier, along the Yellow River, contains north China and northwest China. North China is flat and prone to floods when the silted Yellow River overflows its banks. Farmers grew sorghum, wheat, millet, and barley on its dry fields. Politically it was the most important region of China because it contained the capital, Beijing. Because of propinquity, it was the first area conquered by the Manchus. Northwest China is semiarid, lightly populated, poor, and separated from the rest of China by mountains in the south and east. The door to trade with central Asia and the steppe beyond, its population included Mongols, Tibetans, and Chinese Muslims, as well as Han Chinese.

The second tier also follows the course of a river; its regions are the Lower, Middle, and Upper Yangzi. Of all China, the Lower Yangzi, consisting of the delta and lower reaches of that river, had the densest population, the best irrigation, the most commercialized agriculture, the most urbanization, and the highest level of education. This region alone paid one-quarter of the Qing land tax. In modern times, the delta city of Shanghai extends its sway over much of the region. The Middle Yangzi was also rich, with rice paddies and a thriving commerce. The Upper Yangzi, mainly Sichuan Province, was agriculturally fertile, but cut off from the rest of China by mountains. It was the region from which both the Zhou and Qin had emerged to conquer China in ancient times.

The third, southern tier also has three regions. One is the mountainous southeast coast opposite Taiwan. Farmers in its scattered and terraced valleys grew tea and other crops, spoke a variety of dialects, and engaged in coastal trade. Emigrants from the region peopled the Chinatowns of Southeast Asia during the nineteenth century. Further south was the southern coastal region centered on Guangzhou (Canton) and its hinterland, a region drained by the East, West, and North Rivers. A hub of oversea trade during the eighteenth and nineteenth centuries, it also became a focus for emigration (until recently, most Chinese in the United States spoke Cantonese). This was the area where Sun Zhongshan (Sun Yatsen) began his revolution in the early twentieth century. Last was southwest China, a mountainous, landlocked, lightly populated, fringe area of the Chinese heartland. It had both mines and agriculture. Before the modern era, half of its population was made up of Tibetan and other non-Han ethnic groups.

PEOPLE

China's population rose from about 60 or 90 million in 1368 at the start of the Ming dynasty to about 125 million at its end in 1644. The population then soared during the early and middle Qing dynasty, reaching more than 410 million several decades into the nineteenth century. The denser population stimulated commercial growth and gave new prominence to the role of the scholar-gentry class in local society. More than ever, they mediated between the district offices and the populous villages.

An increase in food supply undergirded population growth. During the Ming, the spread of the best Song agricultural technology and new strains of rice accounted for 40 percent of the higher yields, and newly cultivated lands accounted for the rest. During the Qing, half the increased food supply was due to new lands and the other half to better seeds, fertilizers, and irrigation. New crops introduced from America during the late Ming, such as maize, sweet potatoes, and peanuts (which could be planted on dry sandy uplands and did not compete with rice) also bolstered the food supply. By the nineteenth century, maize was grown in all parts of China.

In north China, the population had declined from thirty-two million to eleven million during the Mongol conquests. The Ming government repopulated its open lands, resettling villages, building water-control systems, and reopening the Grand Canal in 1415. The movement of people north continued until the nineteenth century. In the north, most farmers owned the land they worked, though at times they used hired labor.

South and southwest China also saw an influx of migrants from the densely populated middle Yangzi region, many settling in hilly or mountainous border areas that were agriculturally marginal. The White Lotus Rebellion of 1796–1804 occurred in such a recently settled area far from centers of governmental authority. The Miao wars of the late eighteenth century also were precipitated by movements of Chinese settlers into southwestern uplands previously left to the slash-and-burn agriculture of the Miao tribes. Other Chinese crossed over to the island of Taiwan or emigrated overseas. During the Qing dynasty, sizeable Chinese mercantile communities became established in Southeast Asia—though emigration during the nineteenth century was far greater.

The Yangzi basin, meanwhile, became even more densely populated. The lower Yangzi region and the delta, well supplied with waterways, had long been the rice basket of China, but from the late Ming, agricultural cash crops such as silk and cotton came to predominate. Cotton was so widely grown in the delta that by the early nineteenth century food had to be brought in from other areas. In the lower Yangzi, absentee landlords owned almost nine-tenths of the land. A rich landlord's holdings might be subdivided among tenants, who paid fixed rents in kind. South coastal China also had extensive absentee landlords, but clans owned more land, managing it collectively and distributing rents among their members.

There are many unanswered questions regarding population growth during these six centuries. Was there a decline in the death rate and, if so, why? Did new lands and technology simply raise the limit on the number of mouths that could be fed? Did population oblige by promptly increasing? Certainly the Ming–Qing era was the longest continuous period of effective government in Chinese history. The years of Ming rule over outlying provinces were longer than such periods in earlier dynasties, and the transition to Qing rule was quicker and less destructive. How much did these long periods of peace contribute to population growth? Epidemics were not absent. In the great plagues from 1586 to 1589 and from 1639 to 1644, as many as 20 to 30 percent of the people died in the most populous regions of China, and in specific counties and villages, the figure was higher. Another epidemic occurred in 1756 and a cholera epidemic from 1820 to 1822. But population growth soon overcame such losses. Most historians view the eighteenth century as the most prosperous in Chinese history. But by the early decades of the nineteenth century, Chinese living standards had begun to decline. An ever-increasing population was no blessing.

CHINA'S THIRD COMMERCIAL REVOLUTION

Commerce in China flourished between 300 B.C. and 220 A.D. (the late Zhou through the Han dynasties), only to decline in the centuries of disunity that followed. Chapter 2 gave Sima Qian's description of wealthy Han merchants. Commerce again surged between 850 and 1250 (late Tang through Song), only to contract again during the Mongol conquest. At the end of the Mongol dynasty, warlords confiscated merchant wealth. Early Ming emperors also set their faces against commerce. Isolationist and agrarian in orientation, they restricted the use of foreign goods, required licenses for junks, and attempted to encase foreign trade within the constraints of the tribute system—a system by which neighboring countries paid tribute to China in return for peace and trading opportunities. They overissued paper money that became worthless. They established government monopolies with restrictions on maritime trade and shipping that stifled enterprise and depressed the southeastern coastal region. But then, in the mid-sixteenth century, commerce again began to grow, buoyed by rising population and agriculture and aided by a relaxation of government controls. This new growth was overwhelmingly in private hands.

If the Han and Song growth may be called, respectively, China's first and second commercial revolutions, then the expansion between 1500 and 1800 was the third. This revolution was partly the extension to other parts of China of changes begun earlier in the Yangzi area, but it had new features as well. By the early nineteenth century, if not earlier, China was the most highly commercialized nonindustrial society in the world.

One stimulus to commerce was imported silver, which played the role in the Ming–Qing economy that copper cash had played during the Song. The Chinese balance of trade was favorable. Beginning in the mid-sixteenth century, silver from mines in western Japan entered China, and from the 1570s, Spanish galleons sailing from Acapulco to China via Manila brought in Mexican and Peruvian silver. In exchange, Chinese silks and porcelains were vended in the shops of Mexico City. The late Ming court also opened silver mines in the southwestern provinces of Guizhou and Yunnan. In the eighteenth century, copper mines were opened in south China. Also, private "Shanxi banks" opened branches throughout China to facilitate the transfer of funds from one area to another and extend credit for trade. Eventually, they opened offices in Singapore, Japan, and Russia, as well.

As in Europe, so in China did the influx of silver and increased liquidity lead to inflation and commercial growth. The price of land rose steadily. During the sixteenth century, the thirty or forty early Ming taxes on land that were payable in grain, labor service, and cash were consolidated into one tax payable in silver, the so-called Single Whip Reform. To obtain the silver, farmers sold their grain in the market, prompting some to switch from grain to more profitable cash crops. Moreover, by the early nineteenth century, there were six times as many farm families as in the mid-fourteenth century.

Urban growth between 1500 and 1800, responding to flourishing local markets, occurred mainly at the level of intermediate market towns. These towns grew more rapidly than the population as a whole and provided the ties between local markets and larger provincial capitals and cities such as Beijing, Hangzhou, and Guangzhou (Canton). The commercial linkage of local, intermediate, and large cities was not entirely new, having occurred during the Song dynasty in the lower Yangzi region. But now, it spread over most of China. In the silk and cotton trade, merchants capitalists in the cities often organized and financed each stage of production from fiber to dyed cloth—like the "putting out" system of seventeenth-century Europe.

Interregional trade also gained. Whereas Song trade between regions was mainly in luxury goods such as silk, lacquerware, porcelains, medicines, and paintings, early Qing traders also dealt in staples such as grain, timber, salt, iron, and cotton. Not that China developed a national economy. Its regional economies, each the size of a large European nation, were still the focus for most economic activity. But a new level of trade developed among them, especially where water transport made such trade economical. Foreign trade also flourished. The Song sea routes to Southeast Asia and beyond were revived and further stimulated commerce within China.

Women in the Commercial Revolution

The Confucian family ideal changed little during the Ming and Qing dynasties. A woman was expected to obey first her parents, then her husband, and finally her son—when he became the new family head. Physically, women became more constricted. Footbinding, which had begun among the elite during the Song dynasty, spread through the upper classes during the Ming and to many commoners during the mid-to-late Qing. Most girls were subjected to this cruel and deforming procedure. Even in villages, women with big—that is to say, normal—feet were sometimes considered unmarriageable. An exception to the rule was the Hakka people of south China. Hakka women with unbound feet worked in the fields alongside their male kinsmen. Another exception was the Manchus. One Manchu (Qing) emperor issued an edict banning footbinding among the Chinese, but the Chinese ignored it.

THE THIN HORSE MARKET[1]

In China, ancestors, without descendants to perform the rites, ran the danger of becoming hungry ghosts or wandering spirits. Consequently, having a son who would continue the family line was an act of filial piety. If a wife failed to produce an heir, an official, a merchant, or a wealthy landowner might take a concubine and try again. Or he might do so simply because he was able to, because it gave him pleasure, and because it was socially acceptable. For a poor peasant household, after a bad harvest and faced with high taxes, the sale of a comely daughter often seemed preferable to the sale of ancestral land.

Concubines usually had no choice in the matter. But neither did many brides in premodern China. Was a woman better off as the wife of a poor peasant, experiencing hardship, hunger, and want, or as the concubine in a wealthy household with servants, good food, and the likelihood that her children would receive an education? What does the following passage tell us about attitudes toward women in premodern China?

Upwards of a hundred people in Yangzhou earn a living in the "thin horse" business. If someone shows an interest in taking a concubine, a team of a broker, a drudge, and a scout stick to him like flies. Early in the morning, the teams gather to wait outside the doors of potential customers, who usually give their business to the first team to arrive. Any teams coming late have to wait for the next opportunity. The winning team then leads their customer to the broker's house. The customer is then served tea and seated to wait for the women. The broker leads out each of them, who do what the matchmaker tells them to do. After each of her short commands, the woman bows to the customer, walks forward, turns toward the light so the customer can see her face clearly, draws back her sleeves to show him her hands, glances shyly at him to show him her eyes, says her age so he can hear her voice, and finally lifts her skirt to reveal whether her feet are bound. An experienced customer could figure out the size of her feet by listening to the noise she made as she entered the room. If her skirt made noise when she walked in, she had to have a pair of big feet under her skirt. As one woman finishes, another comes out, each house having at least five or six. If the customer finds a woman to his liking, he puts a gold hairpin in her hair at the temple, a procedure called "inserting the ornament." If no one satisfies him, he gives a few hundred cash to the broker or the servants.

If the first broker gets tired, others will willingly take his place. Even if a customer has the stamina to keep looking for four or five days, he cannot finish visiting all the houses. Nevertheless, after seeing fifty to sixty white-faced, red-dressed women, they all begin to look alike and he cannot decide which are pretty or ugly. It is like the difficulty of recognizing a character after writing it hundreds or thousands of times. Therefore, the customer usually chooses someone once his mind and eyes can no longer discriminate. The owner of the woman brings out a piece of red paper on which are listed the "betrothal presents," including gold jewelry and cloth. Once he agrees to the deal, he is sent home. Before he even arrives back at his lodgings, a band and a load of food and wine are already waiting there. Before long, presents he was to send are prepared and sent back with the band. Then a sedan chair and all the trimmings—colorful lanterns, happy candles, attendants, sacrificial foods—wait outside for the customer's arrangement. The cooks and the entertainer for the wedding celebration also arrive together with foods, wine, candy, tables, chairs, and tableware. Without the customer's order, the colorful sedan chair for the girl and the small sedan chair for her companion are dispatched to get the girl. The new concubine performs the bowing ceremony with music and singing and considerable clamor. The next morning before noon the laborers ask for rewards from the man, then leave to prepare another wedding for another customer in the same manner.

[1]A horse market is for the sale of horses. A "thin horse" market is the market for concubines. The name implies a measure of criticism.

Reprinted with permission of The Free Press, a division of Simon & Schuster, Inc. from *Chinese Civilization: A Sourcebook* by P. B. Ebrey. Copyright © 1993 by P. B. Ebrey.

As population grew and the size of the average farm shrank, growing numbers of women worked at home, spinning, weaving, and making other products for burgeoning commercial markets. As the woman's contribution to the household income grew, her voice in household decisions often became larger than Confucian doctrines might deem proper. But at the same time, women's legal rights—to inheritance and control of dowries—became more limited than in previous dynasties. Furthermore, the commercial revolution also increased the number of rich townsmen who could afford concubines and patronize teahouses, restaurants, and brothels.

THE PATTERN OF MING RULE

One might expect the massive demographic and economic changes of the Ming–Qing eras to have produced, if not a bourgeois revolution, at least some profound alteration in the political superstructure of China. They did not. Ming and Qing government was much like that of the Song and Yuan, only improved and stronger. Historians sometimes speak of this late imperial system as "perfected." It was able to contain and use the kind of new commercial energies that had wrought immense changes within the late-feudal monarchies of Europe. What institutions were the that made this possible?

Emperors

One institution was emperorship. At a time of famine and peasant rebellions, the man who would become the first Ming emperor (r. 1368–1398) rose as a rebel leader against the crumbling Mongol state. He consolidated a military base in the Yangzi valley, established his capital at Nanjing in 1368, and pursued the remaining Mongol forces. The last Mongol stronghold in the remote southwestern province of Yunnan fell in 1382. Known by his posthumous name of Hongwu, meaning "vast military," the first Ming emperor has been described by Chinese historians as bold, shrewd, and visionary, but also as cruel, suspicious, and paranoid during his last years. His thirty years of rule to 1398, nonetheless, had the vigor characteristic of dynastic founders. He looked to the Tang for inspiration but in many respects followed Mongol precedents.

Hongwu was an autocrat. He abolished the Secretariat of high officials that had coordinated important matters within the Song and Yuan governments, and personally made all decisions. One historian noted that in one eight-day period Hongwu received

The first Ming emperor, Hongwu (r. 1368–1398).
[National Palace Museum, Taipei, Taiwan/The Bridgeman Art Library]

1,600 memorials dealing with 3,391 issues. Another observed that "at the rate of 200 documents in a 10-hour day, each document could get on average three minutes' consideration."[1] Since weighty issues were considered, during the late fourteenth and fifteenth centuries the emperor was the "bottleneck" official without whose active participation, the business of government would bog down.

He was a despot. Hongwu, and his successors as well, had their own secret police and prisons where those who gave even minor offense were cruelly tortured. Even high officials might suffer the humiliating and sometimes fatal punishment of having their bared buttocks beaten with bamboo rods at court—a practice inherited from the Mongols. The dedication and loyalty even of officials who were cruelly mistreated attest to the depth of their Confucian ethical formation. Toward the end of the dynasty, a censor who had served three emperors ran afoul of a powerful eunuch. The eunuch obtained an imperial order and had the official tortured to death in 1625.

[1]J. Fairbank and M. Goldman, *China: A New History* (1998), p. 130

In his deathbed notes to his sons, the official blamed the villain for his agonies but wrote that he welcomed death because his body belonged to his "ruler-father." An earlier mid-sixteenth-century incident involved Hai Rui, the most famous censor of the Ming period:

> Hai presented himself at the palace gate to submit a memorial denouncing some of the emperor's notorious idiosyncrasies. The emperor flew into a rage and ordered that Hai not be permitted to escape. "Never fear, sire," the eunuch go-between told the emperor. "He has said goodbye to his family, has brought his coffin with him, and waits at the gate!" Shih-tsung [the emperor] was so taken aback by this news that he forgave Hai for his impertinence.[2]

Hongwu was born to a family of poor peasants who had lost their land. So he looked with favor on agriculture and was sympathetic to the plight of the small farmer, not the landlord. All fields were surveyed and recorded in "yellow registers" or "fish-scale registers." Land tax revenues were twice as great as they had been under the Mongols, providing the government with adequate funding well into the sixteenth century. Hongwu despised commerce, subjecting it to harsh laws, abolished government monopolies, and banned foreign trade. Only later in the dynasty, as these stringent measures were relaxed, did the Ming–Qing commercial revolution begin.

Another emperor of special note was Yongle (r. 1402–1424), whose name means "Eternal Happiness." (He usurped the throne from the second emperor, his nephew, who ruled for only four years.) Yongle's base of power was in the north and he eventually moved the capital to Beijing. One achievement of his reign was the compilation of a great encyclopedia, which contained the entire body of learning of his age and included most texts extant in China. Scholars, for whom the enterprise provided thousands of jobs, rejoiced. Today, only portions of the work survive.

His second achievement was the rebuilding of the Forbidden Palace in Beijing, an icon of the emperor's majesty. Unlike the Kremlin, which consists of a miscellaneous assortment of buildings inside a wall, the entire palace complex in Beijing focused on the single figure of the ruler. Designed geometrically, its massive outer and inner walls, vast courtyards, and halls progress level by level to the raised area of the audience hall. During the Tang, emperors sat together with their grand councillors while discussing affairs of state. In the Song, officials stood in the emperor's presence. By the Ming, the emperor sat on an elevated dais above the officials, who knelt before him. Behind the audience hall was the emperor's private chambers and his harem. In 1425, the palace had 6,300 cooks serving 10,000 persons daily. These numbers later increased. At the start of the seventeenth century, there were

[2]C. O. Hucker, *China's Imperial Past* (Stanford, CA: Stanford University Press, 1975), p. 206.

9,000 palace ladies and, by one estimate, 70,000 eunuchs. The effulgent supereminence of the emperor extended even to his family, whose members were awarded vast estates in north China.

Then, during the sixteenth and early seventeenth centuries, a series of emperors appeared with little interest in government. One spent his days on wine, women, and sports; another filled his hours with Daoist rites; still another, who never learned to write, passed his days making furniture. During these centuries, the emperor's authority was exercised either by grand secretaries or by eunuchs.

Officials

A second component of Ming rule was those who held offices. The formal organization of offices was little different from that in the Tang or the Song. At the top were the military, the censorate, and the executive. At times, each was a check on the others. Beneath the executive were the six ministries and the hierarchy of provincial, prefectural, and district offices. Most Chinese, if they had contact with officials at all, knew only the district magistrate. Given high tax revenues, another reason for good Ming finances was that the apparatus of government grew only slowly while the productivity of China steadily increased. (In modern parliamentary states, the temptation to increase spending faster than economic growth is almost irresistible.) Government finances had ups and downs, but as late as the 1580s, huge surpluses accumulated at both the central and the provincial levels, arresting the pace of dynastic decline. Only during the last fifty years of the Ming did soaring military expenses exhaust government coffers.

The dilapidated remains of the examination stalls at Nanjing. Doors to individual cubicles can be seen to the right and left of the three-story gate. Thousands of such cubicles made up the old examination stalls. Those who passed the exams governed China.
[CORBIS-NY]

THE SEVEN TRANSFORMATIONS OF AN EXAMINATION CANDIDATE

The Chinese civil service examination was a grueling ordeal. Like a chess tournament, it required physical strength. Chinese critics said, "To pass the provincial examination a man needed the spiritual strength of a dragon-horse, the physique of a donkey, the insensitivity of a wood louse, and the endurance of a camel." The following selection is by a seventeenth-century writer who never succeeded in passing.

Is the style of this passage overdone or effective? What is distinctively Chinese about it?

When he first enters the examination compound and walks along, panting under his heavy load of luggage, he is just like a beggar. Next, while undergoing the personal body search and being scolded by the clerks and shouted at by the soldiers, he is just like a prisoner. When he finally enters his cell and, along with the other candidates, stretches his neck to peer out, he is just like the larva of a bee. When the examination is finished at last and he leaves, his mind in a haze and his legs tottering, he is just like a sick bird that has been released from a cage. While he is wondering when the results will be announced and waiting to learn whether he passed or failed, so nervous that he is startled even by the rustling of the trees and the grass and is unable to sit or stand still, his restlessness is like that of a monkey on a leash. When at last the results are announced and he has definitely failed, he loses his vitality like one dead, rolls over on his side, and lies there without moving, like a poisoned fly. Then, when he pulls himself together and stands up, he is provoked by every sight and sound, gradually flings away everything within his reach, and complains of the illiteracy of the examiners. When he calms down at last, he finds everything in the room broken. At this time he is like a pigeon smashing its own precious eggs. These are the seven transformations of a candidate.

From I. Miyazaki, *China's Examination Hell*, trans. by C. Schirokauer. Copyright © 1976, New York, Weatherhill, pp. 57–58.

If the Ming–Qing system can be spoken of as perfected, the good government it brought to China was largely a product of the ethical commitment and exceptional ability of its officials. No officials in the world today approach those of the Ming or Qing in power and prestige. When the Portuguese arrived early in the sixteenth century, they called these officials "mandarins." "Mandarin" began as a Sanskrit word for "counselor" that became Hindi, entered Malay, and was then picked up by the Portuguese and adopted by other Europeans. As in the Song, the rewards of an official career were so great that the competition to enter it was intense. As population grew and schools increased, entrance became evermore competitive.

A candidate, after being screened at the district office, first took the county examination. If he passed, he became a member of the gentry. He gained the cap and sash of the scholar and exemption from state labor service. Even this examination required years of arduous study. About half a million passed each year. The second hurdle was the provincial examination held every third year. Only one in one hundred or more was successful. The final hurdle was the metropolitan examination, also held triennially. During the Ming, fewer than ninety passed each year. As in earlier dynasties, regional quotas were set to prevent the Yangzi region from dominating the officialdom.

Eunuchs

To become a high official required years of study and great natural ability: Only the brightest and most determined succeeded. To become a palace eunuch required only that a boy with the necessary connections at the court be castrated. As keepers of the inner court, eunuchs were the playmates of future emperors and enjoyed great influence on the wives and consorts of emperors. Hongwu, fearing their influence, decreed that eunuchs not be educated but his decree was later ignored. Within the court government, eunuchs were a counterweight to officials. They were an alternate source of policies—like a "kitchen cabinet"—that emperors could play off against the authority of high officials. At moments, when emperors were weak, eunuchs determined policy and purged enemy officials; at other moments, officials gained the upper hand and purged once-powerful eunuchs. Eunuchs have been little studied.

Gentry

A final component in the Ming–Qing system—if not new, vastly more important than in earlier dynasties—was the local elite known as the gentry or literati. They formed an intermediate layer between the elite bureaucracy above—of which the lowest tier was the district magistrate—and villages below. Though the Ming and Qing population increased sixfold, the number of district magistrates increased only from 1,171 to 1,470. Consequently, the average district, which had a population of 50,000 in the early Ming and 100,000 in the late Ming, had two or three times that number by the early nineteenth century. The district magistrate came to his district as an outsider. The "law of avoidance," designed to prevent conflicts of interest, prevented him from serving in his home province. His office compound had a large staff of secretaries, advisers, specialists, clerks, and runners; but even then, he could not govern such a large population directly. To govern effectively, the magistrate had to obtain the cooperation of the local literati or gentry.

The Chinese literati were not a rural elite like English squires. They were largely urban, living in market towns or district seats. Socially and educationally, they were of the same class as district magistrates—a world apart from the less educated clerks, runners, and village headmen. They sent their children to private academies. They usually owned land they did not work and were exploitative toward the sharecroppers who tilled their soil. Rebels at the end of the Ming attacked landlords as they did government offices. But gentry were also local leaders. They represented community interests, which they interpreted conservatively, vis-à-vis the bureaucracy. They performed quasi-official functions on behalf of their communities: maintaining schools and Confucian temples; repairing roads, bridges, canals, and dikes; and writing local histories.

The gentry class was the matrix from which officials arose; it was the local upholder of Confucian values. During the mid-nineteenth century, at a time of crisis, it would come to the rescue of the dynasty.

MING FOREIGN RELATIONS

In the past, scholars often contended that in Ming (and Qing) times, Chinese character was neither aggressive nor warlike. They cited the Chinese inability to resist foreign conquest; the civility, self-restraint, and gentlemanliness of officials; and the Song adage that good men should not be used to make soldiers just as good iron is not used to make nails. The actions of early Ming emperors convincingly disprove this contention. Hongwu inherited large numbers of troops that had formerly served the Mongols. He oversaw the vigorous expansion of China's borders. At his death, China controlled the northern steppe from Hami at the gateway of Central Asia to the Sungari River in Manchuria and had regained control of the southern tier of Chinese provinces as well. Yongle continued the policies of the Ming founder: He personally led five expeditions into the Gobi Desert against the Mongols. He also ordered the invasion of Vietnam and for twenty years attempted to make that country a part of China. (Vietnam, we recall, had been a part of China for the millennium from 111 B.C. to 939 A.D.)

A second enterprise of Yongle was to send maritime armadas to Southeast Asia, India, the Arabian gulf, and east Africa between 1405 and 1433 (see Map 4–2). Their commander was Zheng He, a eunuch and a Muslim from Yunnan. The first armadas had sixty-two major ships and hundreds of smaller vessels and carried 28,000 sailors,

Map 4–2   Ming empire and the voyages of Zheng He.   The ships of Zheng He, venturing beyond Southeast Asia and India, reached the coast of east Africa.

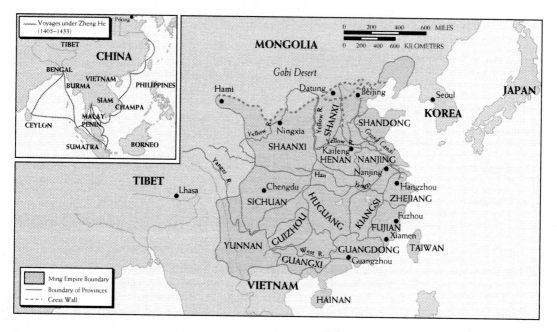

soldiers, and merchants. Navigating by compass and star maps, the expeditions followed the sea routes of Arab traders. Trade was not the primary purpose of the expeditions, although some eunuchs used the opportunity to make fortunes, and records show that giraffes, zebras, and other exotic items were presented to the emperor. Their purpose, rather, was to make China's glory known to distant kingdoms and to enroll them in the tribute system. Zheng He's soldiers installed a new king in Java, captured and brought back to China hostile kings from Borneo and Ceylon, and signed up nineteen other states as Chinese tributaries. The expeditions ended as abruptly as they had begun. They were costly and offered little return at a time when the dynasty was fighting in Mongolia and building the new capital at Beijing. What is remarkable is not that these expeditions came a half-century earlier than the Portuguese voyages of discovery, but that China possessed the maritime technology needed to explore the globe and decided not to use it. China lacked the combination of restlessness, greed, faith, and curiosity that would motivate the Portuguese.

After Yongle, the Chinese court was primarily concerned to secure its expanded frontiers. One means was "to use the barbarian to control the barbarian." Even after the collapse of the Yuan dynasty, the chief threat to China came from the Mongols,

Giraffe with attendant. Some emperors had private zoos and gladly received exotic animals as gifts from tribute states. A painting by Shen Du (1357–1438).
[1977-42-1. Tu, Shen. "The Tribute Giraffe with Attendant". Philadelphia Museum of Art: Gift of John T. Dorrance, 1977]

who had broken into eastern, western, and southern divisions. The Chinese made allies of the southern Mongols (those settled just north of the Great Wall) against the more fearsome grassland Mongols. This policy worked most of the time, but twice the Mongols formed confederations—pale imitations of the war machine of Genghis—strong enough to defeat Chinese armies. In the 1430s, they captured the emperor, and in 1550, they overran Beijing. The Mongol forces involved in the latter attack were defeated by a Chinese army in the 1560s and signed a peace treaty in 1571.

The second means of handling potentially hostile forces beyond China's borders was the "tribute system." In this system, the ambassadors of foreign vassal kings ceremonially acted out their political subordination to the universal ruler of the celestial kingdom. An ambassador approached the emperor respectfully, performed the kowtow (kneeling three times and bowing his head to the floor nine times), and presented his gifts. In return, the kings they represented were sent seals confirming their status, given permission to use the Chinese calendar and year-period names, and appointed to the Ming nobility.

Few countries (Korea is a possible exception) on China's borders accepted the system at face value. They participated to obtain its benefits and to placate their powerful neighbor. While in Beijing, the ambassadors were housed and fed in a style appropriate to their status. The gifts they received were often more valuable than those they gave. (A study of Korean embassies, however, demonstrates that at times they gave more than they got.) In addition, they were permitted to trade private goods in the markets of the city. So attractive were these perquisites that some Central Asian merchants invented imaginary kingdoms of which they appointed themselves the emissaries. Eventually, China set limits on the size, frequency, and cargos of these missions.

THE PATTERN OF QING RULE

The late Ming was weakened by wars with the Mongols, by the Sino-Japanese pirate state of Koxinga in Taiwan, by war with the Japanese on the Korean peninsula, and by internal revolts. The final foreign threat was the Manchus—the mouse that swallowed the elephant.

In the late sixteenth century, an extremely able leader had unified the Manchurian tribes and proclaimed a Manchu dynasty. While still based in Mukden (more recently, Shenyang), the dynasty established a Confucian type of government with six ministries, a censorate, and other Chinese institutions. When rebel forces arose and the Ming was failing, the Manchus were invited into China to support the Ming, but they stayed to rule. They presented themselves as the conservative upholders of the Confucian order. Chinese gentry preferred Manchu to Chinese rebel leaders, whom they regarded as little more than bandits. A few Chinese scholars and officials became famous as Ming loyalists, but most quietly shifted their loyalty to the new dynasty. The Qing as a Chinese dynasty dates from 1644, when the capital was moved from Mukden to Beijing.

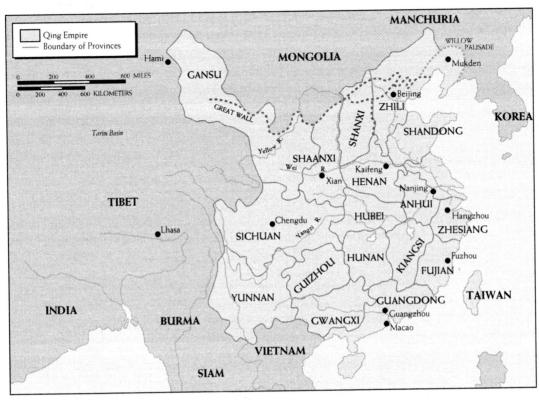

Map 4–3 The Qing empire at its peak.   The willow palisade was the line of demarcation between the Manchurian homeland of the Qing rulers and China. Chinese were excluded from Manchuria.

The early decades of Manchu rule were taken up with consolidation. South China was taken in 1659, with the aid of Ming generals who switched their allegiance to the new regime. The last Ming prince was pursued into Burma and killed in 1662. In 1673, three Chinese generals who controlled the south rebelled, but most Chinese troops in Manchu banners remained loyal, and the revolts were suppressed by 1681. In 1683, troops took Taiwan, which became a part of China for the first time (see Map 4–3).

Politically, the collapse of the Ming dynasty and the establishment of Manchu rule was less of a break than might be imagined. For not only was the transition short, but, unlike the Mongols, the Manchus were already partially Sinicized at the time of the conquest. They had been vassals of the Chinese state during the Ming, organized by tribal units into commanderies. Even before entering China, they were experienced in governing the Chinese who had settled in Manchuria to the north of the Great Wall.

Two features of Qing rule are noteworthy: First was the rule of two exceptionally able and long-lived emperors, which lasted almost until the nineteenth century. Second was new institutions that enabled the Manchu minority to maintain its grip on power; these new institutions were added to the governmental institutions discussed earlier—the emperor, officials, eunuchs, and gentry.

Kangxi and Qianlong

The first outstanding Qing emperor was Kangxi (1661–1722). He was born in 1654, ten years after the start of the dynasty. He ascended the throne at the age of seven, began to rule at thirteen, and held sway until his death in 1722. A man of great vigor, he rose at dawn to read memorials (official documents) before beginning his daily routine of audiences with officials. He presided over palace examinations. Well versed in the Confucian classics, he won the support of scholars by his patronage of the *Ming History*, a new dictionary, and a 5,000-volume encyclopedia. He opened four ports to foreign trade and carried out public works, improving the dikes on the Huai and Yellow rivers and dredging the Grand Canal. During his reign he made six tours of China's southern provinces. Kangxi also displayed an interest in European science, which he studied with Jesuit court astronomers whom the Qing had inherited from the Ming. And he sired thirty-six sons and twenty daughters by thirty consorts—though most died in infancy. Kangxi, in short, was a model emperor. But he was also responsible for the various policies that sought to preserve a separate Manchu identity. Like Kublai Khan before him, he built a summer palace on the southern fringe of the Mongolian steppe, where he hunted, hawked, and rode horseback with the freedom of a steppe lord.

The second great emperor was Qianlong, who began his reign in 1736, fourteen years after the death of his grandfather Kangxi, and ruled until 1795. During his reign, the Qing dynasty attained its highest level of prosperity and power. Like Kangxi, he was strong, wise, conscientious, careful, and hard working. He visited south China on inspection tours. He patronized scholars on a grand scale: His *Four Treasures* of the classics, works on history, letters, and philosophy, put 15,000 copyists to work for almost fifteen years. (He was also responsible for a literary inquisition against works critical of Manchu rule.) Only in his last years did Qianlong lose his grip and permit a court favorite to practice corruption on an almost unprecedented scale. In 1796, the White Lotus Rebellion broke out. Qianlong's successor put down the rebellion and permitted the corrupt court favorite to take his own life. After this time, the ample financial reserves that had existed throughout the eighteenth century were never reestablished. China nevertheless entered the nineteenth century with its government intact and with a peaceful and stable society. There were few visible signs of what was soon to come.

New Institutions

The ultimate support of any government is its military, and this is especially critical when a minority rules. The basic unit of the Qing military was the banner—the unit took the name of its flag. There were eight Manchu banners, eight Mongol, and eight

Chinese. There were more companies (of three hundred men each) in the Manchu banners than in either of the other two; together with their steppe allies, the Mongols, the Manchu troops outnumbered the Chinese by more than two to one. Furthermore, the Chinese banners mainly consisted of Manchurian Chinese, who had been a part of the regime from its inception. Manchu garrison forces were segregated and not under the jurisdiction of Chinese officials. They were given stipends and lands to cultivate. They were not permitted to marry Chinese, their children had to study Manchu, and they were not permitted to bind the feet of their daughters. In 1668, the Manchu court cordoned off northern and central Manchuria by a willow palisade as a strategic tribal territory closed to Chinese immigrants.

In addition to the banners, there were also Chinese constabulary forces known as "armies of the green standard." At first, the distinction between the banners and the Chinese military was critical. Later, as the functioning of the dynasty became routinized, the ethnic basis of its military strength became less important.

The second feature of Manchu government was what has been termed "dyarchy," the appointment of two persons, one Chinese and one Manchu, to each key post in the central government. Early in the dynasty, the Chinese appointed were often bannermen or bond servants personally loyal to the Manchus. At the provincial level, Manchu governor-generals superintended Chinese governors. Beneath the governors, most officials and virtually all district magistrates were Chinese.

The third feature of Qing government was the role of the Manchu language, an Altaic tongue totally unlike Chinese. For centuries Manchu had evolved as an oral tongue, but from 1599, it borrowed the Mongolian script and became a written language. Tracing the writing system back, Mongolian came from Uighur (written vertically), which came from Sogdian (written horizontally), which came, ultimately, from Aramaic. Aramaic, we recall, was also the point of origin for the alphabets of Greek, Latin, and the modern European languages. Many imperial edicts were written in Manchu as well as in Chinese, and Manchu officials were expected to conduct their correspondence with the emperor in Manchu. Mark Elliott notes that in writing to the emperor, Han Chinese signed off as "your official," whereas Manchu officials used the more intimate "your servant/slave." Within Qing government, those of Manchu birth constituted an inner "clan" of sorts.

QING FOREIGN RELATIONS

As always, the principal foreign threats to China during Qing rule came from the north and northwest. Russia had expanded east across Siberia and south against the remnants of the Golden Horde during the reign of Ivan the Terrible (1533–1584). By the 1660s, Russian traders, trappers, and adventurers had reached the Amur River in northern Manchuria where they built forts and traded with the eastern Mongols. (We are reminded of the French penetration of Canada during the same decades.) To prevent a rapprochement between the Russians and Mongols, Kangxi set up military colonies in Manchuria during the 1680s and drove the Russians from the lower Amur. This victory during the early years of Peter the Great (1682–1725) led to the 1689 Treaty of Nerchinsk. Negotiated with the assistance of Jesuit translators, the treaty excluded Russia from northern Manchuria while permitting Russian caravans to visit Beijing.

In the west was a complex, three-corner relationship between Russia, the western Mongols, and Tibet. Kangxi, and then Qianlong, campaigned against the Mongols, invaded Tibet, and in 1727, signed a new treaty with Russia. During the campaigns, the Qing temporarily gained control of millions of square miles of new territories. These areas became protectorates under a "barbarian management office," separate from the provincial administration of China proper. It is a telling comment on the Chinese concept of empire that ever since that time, even after China's borders contracted during the nineteenth century, the Chinese have continued to insist that the Manchu conquests of non-Chinese peoples define their legitimate borders.

Contacts with the West

Europeans had made their way to China in the Tang and Yuan dynasties, but only with Europe's oceanic expansion during the sixteenth century did they arrive in considerable numbers. Some came as missionaries, of whom the most educated, calculating, disciplined, enterprising, and successful were the Jesuits. On first arriving in Ming China, they donned the robes of the Buddhist monk, but on learning something of the culture, they switched to the gowns of the Confucian scholar. They studied Chinese and the Confucian classics and engaged in conversation with scholars. They used their knowledge of astronomy, geography, engraving, and firearms to win entry to the court at Beijing and appointments in the bureau of astronomy.

When the Manchus came to power in 1644, after a brief struggle, the Jesuits kept their position. They appealed to the curiosity of the court with telescopes, clocks, and clavichords. They tried to propagate Christianity. They attacked Daoism and Buddhism as superstitions but argued that Confucianism as a rational philosophy complemented Christianity, just as Aristotle's teaching complemented Christian theology in Europe. They interpreted the Confucian rites of ancestor worship as secular and non-antagonistic to Christianity. A few high court officials were converted. Kangxi was sympathetic to the scholarly personalities of the Jesuits and appreciated the cannon they cast but was unsympathetic to their religion: "I had asked [the Jesuit] Verbiest why God had not forgiven his son without making him die, but though he had tried to answer I had not understood him."[3]

Meanwhile, Franciscan and Dominican rivals had reported to Rome that the Jesuits condoned the Confucian rites. The ensuing debate was long and complex, but

---

[3] J. D. Spence, *Emperor of China: A Self-Portrait of K'ang Hsi* (New York: Alfred A. Knopf, 1974), p. 84.

in the end, papal bulls issued in 1715 and 1742 decided against the Jesuits and forbade Chinese Christians to participate in the family rites of ancestor worship. Thereupon, though a few Jesuits remained in service at the court, Christianity was banned, churches were seized, missionaries were forced to flee, and congregations declined.

Other Europeans came to China to trade. The Portuguese came first in the early sixteenth century but behaved badly and were expelled. They returned in midcentury and were permitted to trade, but only on a tiny peninsula at Macao that was walled off from China. They were followed by Dutch from the East Indies (Indonesia), by the British East India Company in 1699, and by Americans in 1784. At first, the Westerners mingled with merchants from Southeast Asia in a fairly open multiport pattern of trade. Then, during the early eighteenth century, the more restrictive "Canton system" evolved. Westerners were permitted to trade only at Guangzhou—which they called "Canton." They were barred from entering the city proper but were assigned land outside its walls along the river. They could not bring their wives to China. They were subject to the dispositions of Chinese law. They were under the control of official merchant guilds. Nevertheless, both they and their Chinese counterparts prospered.

QIANLONG'S EDICT TO KING GEORGE III OF ENGLAND

The Chinese emperor rejected the requests of the 1793 Macartney mission for change in the restrictive Canton system. His edict reflects the Chinese sense of their superiority to other peoples and their belief that China was the "central kingdom" of the world.

What philosophical principles underlie the emperor's sense of superiority?

You, O King, are so inclined toward our civilization that you have sent a special envoy across the seas to bring to our Court your memorial of congratulations on the occasion of my birthday and to present your native products as an expression of your thoughtfulness. On perusing your memorial, so simply worded and sincerely conceived, I am impressed by your genuine respectfulness and friendliness and greatly pleased.

The Celestial Court has pacified and possessed the territory within the four seas. Its sole aim is to do its utmost to achieve good government and to manage political affairs, attaching no value to strange jewels and precious objects. The various articles presented by you, O King, this time are accepted by my special order to the office in charge of such functions in consideration of the offerings having come from a long distance with sincere good wishes. As a matter of fact, the virtue and prestige of the Celestial Dynasty having spread far and wide, the kings of the myriad nations come by land and sea with all sorts of precious things. Consequently there is nothing we lack, as your principal envoy and others have themselves observed. We have never set much store on strange or ingenious objects, nor do we need any more of your country's manufactures.

From *China's Response to the West* by S. Y. Teng and J. K. Fairbank (Cambridge, MA: Harvard University Press). Copyright © 1954, 1979 by the President and Fellows of Harvard College. Reprinted by permission of Harvard University Press.

The British East India Company developed a triangular commerce between China, India, and Britain that enabled the English to drink tea and wear silk. Private fortunes were built. Specie flowed into China and the Chinese officials in charge grew immensely wealthy. Chafing under various restrictions, the British government in 1793 sent the Macartney mission to China to negotiate the opening of other ports, fixed tariffs, representation at Beijing, and so on. The emperor Qianlong permitted Macartney to present his gifts—which the Chinese described as tribute, even though Macartney refused to perform the kowtow—but turned down Macartney's requests. Western trade remained encapsulated at Guangzhou, distant from Beijing and little noted elsewhere in China.

MING–QING CULTURE

One thing that can be said of Ming–Qing culture, like population or agricultural crops, is that there was more of it. Whether we speak of gentry, scholar officials, or a professionalized class of literati, their numbers and works were far greater than in previous dynasties. Even local literary figures and philosophers were likely to publish their collected works or have them published by admiring disciples. Bookstores came of age in the Ming: They sold the Confucian classics and commentaries on them; collections of Tang and Song poetry; as well as colored prints, novels, erotica, and collections of model answers for the civil service examinations.

Chinese culture had begun to turn inward during the Song in reaction to Buddhism. This tendency was accelerated by the Chinese antipathy to Mongol rule and continued into the Ming and Qing, when Chinese culture became largely impervious to outside influences. Manchu rule seems to have affected this only marginally. Even works on mathematics and science translated into Chinese by the Jesuits left few traces in Chinese scholarship. Chinese cultural self-sufficiency, of course, reflected a tradition and a social order that had stood the test of time, but it also constituted a closed system of ideas with weaknesses that would become apparent in the nineteenth century. Orthodox thought during these five centuries was Zhu Xi Neo-Confucianism. From the mid- to the late Ming, some perturbations were caused by the Chan-like teachings of the philosopher Wang Yangming (1472–1529), whose activism caused him to be jailed, beaten, and at one point exiled during an otherwise illustrious official career.

Several other original thinkers' refusal to accept bureaucratic posts under the Qing won them plaudits during the anti-Manchu nationalism of the early twentieth century, but they had only a limited influence on their own times. The most innovative was Gu Yanwu, who wrote on both philology and statecraft. He used philology and historical phonetics to plumb the original meanings of the classics and contrasted their practical ethics with the "empty words" of Wang Yangming. Gu's successors extended his philological studies, developing empirical methods for textual studies, but lost sight of their implications for politics. The Manchus clamped down on unorthodox

Late Imperial China

Ming Dynasty 1368–1644

1368–1398	Reign of first Ming emperor; Chinese armies invade Manchuria, Mongolia, and eastern Central Asia
1402–1424	Reign of third Ming emperor; Chinese armies invade Vietnam and Mongolia
1405–1433	Voyage of Zheng He to India and Africa
1415	Grand Canal reopened
1472–1529	Wang Yangming, philosopher
1592–1598	Chinese army battles Japanese army in Korea

Qing (Manchu) Dynasty 1644–1912

1668	Manchuria closed to Chinese immigrants (by willow palisade)
1661–1722	Reign of Kangxi
1681	Suppression of revolts by Chinese generals
1683	Taiwan captured
1689	China and Russia sign Treaty of Nerchinsk
1736–1795	Reign of Qianlong
1793	Macartney mission

thought, and the seventeenth-century burst of creativity guttered out into a narrow, bookish, conservative scholasticism. Not until the end of the nineteenth century did thinkers draw from these studies the kind of radical inferences that philological studies of the Bible had produced in Europe.

Ming and Qing Chinese esteemed most highly, and not without reason, the traditional categories of high culture: painting, calligraphy, poetry, and philosophy. Porcelains of great beauty were also produced. In the early Ming, blue-on-white glazes predominated. During the later Ming and Qing, more decorative wares with enamel painted over the glaze became widespread. The pottery industry of Europe was begun during the sixteenth century in an attempt to imitate these wares, and Chinese and Japanese influences have dominated Western ceramics down to the present. Chinese today, however, look back and view the novel as the most remarkable cultural achievement of the Ming and Qing.

The novel in premodern China grew out of plot-books used by earlier storytellers. Like the stories, Chinese novels consisted of episodes strung together, and chapters in early novels often ended with an admonition to the reader not to miss the next exciting development. Scholars who had failed the examinations were usually the authors of Ming and Qing novels, which may account for their caustic comments on officials. As most novels were written in colloquial Chinese, which was not quite respectable in scholarly circles, their authors wrote under pseudonyms. Two collections of lively short stories are available in English: *Stories from a Ming Collection* and *The Courtesan's Jewel Box*. Many stories (although not those in these two collections) were pornographic. In fact, the Ming may have invented the humorous pornographic novel. Examples now available in English are *The Carnal Prayer Mat* and *The Golden Lotus*. This genre was suppressed in China during the straitlaced Qing rule and rediscovered in Japanese collections during the twentieth century.

Short descriptions of several major novels may convey something of their flavor:

1. *The Romance of the Three Kingdoms*, published in 1522, tells of the political and military struggles in China in the aftermath of the Han dynasty. Like Shakespeare, the author, whose identity is uncertain, used a historical setting to create a dramatic world in which human character determines the outcome of events. More than twenty editions had appeared by the end of the Ming, and it was also extremely popular in Japan and Korea.

2. *All Men Are Brothers* (also translated as *The Water Margin*) tells of 108 bandit heroes who flee government repression during the late northern Song, establish a hideout on a mountain amid marshes, and like Robin Hood, avenge the wrongs perpetrated by corrupt officials. Separate episodes tell why each hero had to leave society and of their many daring and amusing adventures. Of all Chinese novels, this was the most popular. Though officially banned as subversive during the Qing, it was widely read nonetheless.

3. *The Golden Lotus* is a pornographic novel about the sexual adventures of an urban merchant. It gives vivid descriptions of individual women and satirical descriptions of venal officials and greedy monks. In the end, the hero dies of his excesses and his family—all six wives and their children—disintegrates. The early English translation of this novel had long passages in Latin to protect those whose minds were not disciplined by the study of that language. (Despite its literary merits, the book, like others of its genre, was proscribed during the era of Mao Zedong. In recent decades, it has again become available.)

4. *The Dream of the Red Chamber* (also translated as *The Story of the Stone*) is generally considered China's greatest novel. It tells the story of a youth growing up in a wealthy but declining family during the early Qing. Critics praise its subtlety and psychological insight. Anthropologists mine the novel for information on the Chinese extended family and for its depiction of social relations. Like other Ming and Qing novels, it was recognized as a respectable work of art only during the twentieth century, after Western novels entered China.

5. *The Scholars* is an early Qing satire that pokes fun at scholars and officials.

A STAR IN HEAVEN

Among the officials whose stories are told in *The Scholars* is Fan Jin, thin and sallow with a grizzled beard and threadbare linen gown, who finally passes the county examination at the age of fifty-four. On his return home, he is given a feast and advice by his domineering father-in-law, Butcher Hu. But when Fan asks Hu for money to travel to the provincial examination, he gets the following reaction.

Why did a satire such as The Scholars *not undermine the premises on which Qing society rested?*

Butcher Hu spat in his face and let loose a stream of abuse. "Don't forget who you are!" he bellowed. "Just passing one examination and you become like a toad thinking to dine on the flesh of a swan. I hear you passed the examination not because of your essay, but because the examiner took pity on your old age. Now, like a fool, you aspire to be an official. Don't you know that those who have passed the higher examination are all stars in heaven! Haven't you seen the Changs in the city? Those officials all have tons of money and generously proportioned faces and ears. Now look at you with your protruding mouth and monkey chin. Piss on the ground and take a good look at yourself in the puddle! A miserable creature like you can't even hope to swallow a swan's fart! Forget it!"

[Fan takes the examination anyway. When he returns home, he discovers that his family has been hungry for two days. Fan goes to the market to sell a chicken. In the meantime, heralds on horseback arrive to proclaim he has passed the provincial examination. Returning home, Fan sees the posted announcement and falls into a dead faint. When revived, he begins ranting incoherently. A herald suggests that Butcher Hu, whom Fan fears, bring him to his senses with a slap. Butcher Hu demurs.]

"He may be my son-in-law," he said, "but now he has become a member of the gentry, a star in heaven. How can I hit a star in heaven? I've heard from Buddhist priests that whoever strikes a star in heaven will be carried away by the King of Hell, struck one hundred times with an iron rod, consigned to the eighteenth hell, and never return to human form again. I wouldn't dare do it."

[Eventually Butcher Hu slaps him, and Fan recovers in time to receive a visit from a member of the local gentry, who is wearing "an official's gauze cap, sunflower-coloured gown, gilt belt and black shoes." "Sir," he says to Fan, "although we live in the same district, I regret that we have never become acquainted." After paying his respects, the visitor presents Fan with fifty taels of silver and a more appropriate house. Soon others give him land, goods, money, rice, and servants. The chapter ends with the maids cleaning up under the supervision of Fan's wife after several days of feasting. Fan's mother enters the courtyard.]

"You must be very careful," the old lady warned her daughter-in-law and the maids. "These things all belong to someone else, so don't break them."

The maids replied: "How can you say they belong to others, madam? They all belong to you."

"Oh no! How could our house have such things?" she said with a smile. "How can you talk of their belonging to others?" the maids replied in unison. "And not only these things, but all of us and the house, too, belong to you."

When the old lady heard this, she picked up the bowls and dishes of fine porcelain and the cups and chopsticks inlaid with silver and examined them one by one. She burbled: "These things are all mine." Laughing wildly, she fell over backward, choked on phlegm, and lost consciousness.

If you want to know what became of the old lady, please read the next chapter.

Translation by Shang Wei.

LATE IMPERIAL CHINA IN HISTORICAL PERSPECTIVE

Why did Europe, and not China or anywhere else, open the door to modernity? Why did an industrial revolution not occur within the sophisticated commercial economy of China (or, for that matter, that of Japan)? Until about 1500, by most objective measures, China was ahead of Europe. The answer, obviously, must be found within European history. Still, a few comparisons may illuminate.

1. The sociologist Max Weber saw European capitalism as inspired by the Protestant ethic—which he found absent in China, India, and Catholic Europe. But is the Chinese family-centered ethic of frugality, saving, and hard work not a "Protestant" ethic of sorts? Or, if a deeper Calvinist anxiety about salvation is required for industrial development, as Weber argued, why have Japan, China, and the rest of East Asia been able to achieve such explosive growth since World War II?

2. Was it science that made the difference? Mathematics and Greek and Arab sciences were taught in European Renaissance universities, and these, eventually, led to Copernicus and Newton. Was it the absence of such subjects in the Chinese course of studies that prevented a breakthrough in China? Some historians would question this premise, contending that the industrial revolution in the West was well under way before science made a substantial contribution.

3. The self-educated technicians of England who invented the water loom and steam engine reaped enormous honors and rewards. In China, no patents protected inventors and no economists wrote of inventors as the benefactors of society. Wealth and honors were reserved for officials and gentry, who were political and literary in orientation and despised those who worked with their hands. (Of course, in earlier dynasties, Chinese had been brilliantly inventive without patent protection.) All agree, however, that Ming and Qing commercial growth did not lead to a breakthrough in machine industry.

4. Another factor was capital. In Europe, as merchants and commercial banks invested in machines, commercial capital was transformed into industrial capital. In China, Ming and Qing merchants were more apt to invest in land, which was honorable and secure from rapacious officials, or to expand their commercial activities. Cheap labor, also, may have made it unprofitable to reach out for Western machinery even during the nineteenth century.

5. Bureaucracy is a key component of modernity. It does for administration what the assembly line does for manufacturing, breaking complex tasks into simple ones to achieve huge gains in efficiency. In the West, bureaucracies appeared only in recent centuries. They were recruited from the new middle class to strengthen monarchies and then nation-states against landed aristocrats;

they represented the triumph of ability over hereditary privilege. Chinese bureaucrats shared many of the same virtues. They made government efficient. They were an elite of talent, educated in the Chinese classics, just as British officials were educated in those of Greece and Rome. Yet Chinese officials were somehow different. Instead of opposing an older establishment, they were the establishment. They had wielded power for at least a millennium and were a segment of a landed gentry from which hereditary aristocrats had long since disappeared. Despite their talent, in the nineteenth century, Chinese officials would constitute a major obstacle to modernity.

6. A final point that bears repetition was the Chinese disinterest in other civilizations and peoples, which they dismissed as barbarian. When the Jesuits tried to introduce science—a subject, to be sure, for which the Jesuits had limited enthusiasm, the Chinese response was occasional curiosity and massive indifference. A few Jesuits were appointed as interpreters and court astronomers, or were used to cast cannon. The Chinese lack of interest in others may be explained by their deep appreciation for the richness of their own civilization and by the coherence of the core institutions of their government—the emperor, bureaucracy, the examination system, the gentry, and Confucian schools—that had been in place for centuries. Having proved their worth, their institutions were so deeply rooted and their beliefs so internalized as to approximate a closed system.

REVIEW QUESTIONS

1. Why did the economy grow in late traditional China?
2. How did the Ming and Qing govern as well as they did for as long as they did?
3. Was Manchu rule more like that of the Mongols or more like that of the Ming? In what regards were Kangxi and Qianlong indistinguishable from Chinese emperors?
4. Ming–Qing foreign relations set the stage for China's nineteenth-century encounter with the West. How would you describe the setting?

SUGGESTED READINGS

BODDE, D., AND MORRIS, C. *Law in Imperial China* (1967). Focuses on the Qing Dynasty (1644–1911).

BROOK, T. *The Confusions of Pleasure: Commerce and Culture in Ming China* (1988).

CHANG, C. S., AND S. L. H. *Crisis and Transformation in Seventeenth Century China: Society, Culture, and Modernity* (1992).

CROSSLEY, P. *Translucent Mirror: History and Identity in Qing Imperial Ideology* (1999).

DE BARY, W. T. *Learning for One's Self: Essays on the Individual in Neo-Confucian Thought* (1991). A useful corrective to the view that Confucianism is simply a social ideology.

ELLIOTT, M. C. *Emperor Qianlong: Son of Heaven, Man of the World* (2009).

ELLIOTT, M. C. *The Manchu Way: The Eight Banners and Ethnic Identity in Late Imperial China* (2001). The best work on the subject. Compare to Crossley above.

ELMAN, B. *On Their Own Terms: Science in China, 1550–1900* (2005).

ELMAN, B. *A Cultural History of Civil Examinations in Late Imperial China* (2000).

ELVIN, M. *The Pattern of the Chinese Past: A Social and Economic Interpretation* (1973). A controversial but stimulating interpretation of Chinese economic history in terms of technology. It brings in earlier periods as well as the Ming, Qing, and modern China.

FAIRBANK, J. K., ED. *The Chinese World Order: Traditional China's Foreign Relations* (1968). An examination of the Chinese tribute system and its varying applications.

FAIRBANK, J. K., AND TWITCHETT, D., EDS. *The Cambridge History of China.* Volumes 7 and 8 (1988, 1998) treat the Ming Dynasty, 1368–1644; Volume 9 (2002) treats the Qing Dynasty to 1800.

HUANG, R. *1587, A Year of No Significance: The Ming Dynasty in Decline* (1981).

KAHN, H. L. *Monarchy in the Emperor's Eyes: Image and Reality in the Ch'ien-lung Reign* (1971). A study of the Chinese court during the mid-Qing period.

KUHN, P. *Chinese among Others: Emigration in Modern Times* (2008)

KUHN, P. *Soulstealers: The Chinese Sorcery Scare of 1768* (1990).

LI YU. *The Carnal Prayer Mat,* trans. by P. HANAN (1990).

NAQUIN, S. *Peking Temples and City Life, 1400–1900* (2000).

NAQUIN, S., AND RAWSKI, E. S., *Chinese Society in the Eighteenth Century* (1987).

PARSONS, J. B. *The Peasant Rebellions of the Late Ming Dynasty* (1970).

PERDUE, P. C. *China Marches West: The Qing Conquest of Central Asia* (2005).

PERDUE, P. C. *Exhausting the Earth: State and Peasant in Hunan, 1500–1850* (1987).

PERKINS, D. H. *Agricultural Development in China, 1368–1968* (1969).

RAWSKI, E. *The Last Emperors: A Social History of Qing Imperial Institutions* (1998).

RICCI, M. *China in the Sixteenth Century: The Journals of Matthew Ricci, 1583–1610* (1953).

ROWE, W. *Hankow* (1984). A study of a city in late imperial China.

SKINNER, G. W. *The City in Late Imperial China* (1977).

SPENCE, J. D. *Ts'ao Yin and the K'ang-hsi Emperor: Bondservant and Master* (1966). An excellent study of the early Qing court.

SPENCE, J. D. *Emperor of China: A Self-Portrait of K'ang-hsi* (1974). The title of this very readable book does not adequately convey the extent of the author's contribution to the study of the early Qing emperor.

SPENCE, J. D. *Treason by the Book* (2001). An account of the legal workings of the authoritarian Qing state that reads like a detective story.

STRUVE, L. A., TRANS. and ED. *Voices from the Ming–Ch'ing Cataclysm* (1993). Readings from Chinese sources that describe the suffering and turmoil of a dynastic transition.

WAKEMAN, F. *The Great Enterprise* (1985). On the founding of the Manchu dynasty.

CHAPTER FIVE

Modern China (1839–1949)

Sun Zhongshan (1866–1925), father of China's 1911 republican revolution.
[United Press International]

CHAPTER OUTLINE

The Close of Manchu Rule
From Dynasty to Warlordism (1895–1926)
Cultural and Ideological Ferment: The May Fourth Movement (1914–1920s)
Nationalist China
Modern China in Historical Perspective

From the mid-nineteenth century, the West was the expanding, aggressive, imperialistic force in world history. Its industrial goods and gunboats reached every part of the globe. It believed in free trade and had the military might to impose it on others. It was the trigger for change throughout the world. But the response to the Western impact varied immensely according to the internal array of forces in each country. In fact, the "response to the West" was only one small, though vital, part of the history of each country. In nineteenth-century China, hundreds of millions of people passed their entire lives without "responding" at all.

Casting China's modern history in a positive light, we can say it was fairly successful in its response, for although it became subject to the so-called unequal treaties, it escaped the colonial fate of Asian countries such as India, Burma, Vietnam, Malaya, Indonesia, and Korea. Also, looking back from the perspective of the present, we note that Confucianism proved less of a barrier to science and modern ideas than did more otherworldly religions elsewhere. Unlike Islam, Hinduism, or Christianity, Confucianism was just secular enough to crumble in the face of the more powerful secularism of nineteenth-century science and its associated doctrines. Of course, many Confucian values, deeply embedded in the society, survived the philosophy of which they had once been a part. In fact, one of the "breakdown products" of the Confucian sociopolitical identity was a new and powerful nationalism.

But the picture of this century of Chinese history may also be colored in darker hues. We call it modern China, but it was not the century in which China became modern as much as the century in which it encountered the modern West. The first phase, from the Opium War (1839–1842) to the fall of the Qing dynasty (1912), was, certain particulars apart, remarkably little affected by Western impact. Even after the Opium War, an event of much greater magnitude than Commodore Perry's visits to Japan in 1853 and 1854, it took seventy years for the dynasty to collapse. The ruling elite of Manchus and scholar-officials demonstrated a remarkable staying power. This was partly due to deeply internalized Confucian teachings, partly to a system of coherent institutions—central and local government offices, the examination system, schools, and family and clan organizations—and partly to a lack of viable alternatives. The dynastic system was also reinvigorated in the mid-nineteenth century by the effectiveness of local leaders in rebuilding after the devastation of the Taiping Rebellion. Only in China's relations with the Western powers did traditional methods not work: Being confronted on its seaboard by nations more powerful than itself was a new experience for China. During the seventy years before 1912, the West grew stronger and China grew only more populous.

The second phase of China's modern history, from 1912 to the establishment of a Communist state in 1949, was an era of turmoil and suffering. The warlords that appeared after the fall of the Qing may be viewed as a normal interdynastic phenomenon, which, other things being equal, might have led in time to a new dynasty. But other things were not. The radical critique of tradition by the May Fourth Movement spelled the end of the Confucian state. The era of warlords was followed by a partial military unification and continual military campaigns, by war with Japan, and then, while most countries were returning to peace, by four bitter years of civil war. The darker view that China had in some sense "failed" during this modern century is not a Western view imposed on China; it is the view held by the Chinese themselves.

THE CLOSE OF MANCHU RULE

Opium War and Its Aftermath (1839–1860)

The eighteenth-century three-country trade—British goods to India, Indian cotton to China, and Chinese tea to Britain—favored China. Silver flowing into China spurred the further monetization of Chinese markets. Then the British replaced cotton with Indian opium. By the 1820s, the balance of trade was reversed, and silver began to flow out of China.

A crisis emerged in the 1830s, when the British East India Company lost its monopoly on British trade with China. The opium trade opened wide. To check the evil of opium and the outflow of specie, the Chinese government in 1836 began to enforce an earlier ban on opium, closing dens where it was smoked and executing Chinese dealers. In 1839, the government sent Imperial Commissioner Lin Zexu to Guangzhou (Canton) to superintend the ban. He continued the crackdown on Chinese dealers and destroyed over 20,000 chests—a six-month supply—of opium belonging to foreign merchants. This action led to a confrontation between the Chinese and British.

War broke out in November 1839 when Chinese war junks clashed with a British merchantman. The following June, sixteen British warships arrived at Hong Kong, and for the next two years, the British bombarded forts, fought battles, seized cities, and attempted negotiations. Chinese troops, with their antiquated weapons and old-style cannon, were ineffective. The war finally ended in August 1842, with the Treaty of Nanjing, the first of the unequal treaties.

The treaty not only ended the "Canton System," which restricted Western trade to the city of Guangzhou, but also provided Britain with a superb deepwater port at Hong Kong, a huge indemnity, and the opening of five additional ports: Hong Kong, Shanghai, Xiamen (Amoy), Ningbo, and Fuzhou. British merchants and their families were permitted to reside in the ports and to engage in trade; Britain could appoint a consul for each city; and British residents gained extraterritoriality, under which they were subject to British law, not that of China. The treaty also contained a "most-favored-nation" clause, which provided that any further rights gained by any other nation would automatically accrue to Britain. The treaty with Britain was followed in 1844 by similar treaties with the United States and France. The American treaty permitted churches in treaty ports, and the French treaty permitted the propagation of Catholicism.

COMMISSIONER LIN URGES MORALITY ON QUEEN VICTORIA

In 1839, the British in China argued for free trade and protection for the legal right of their citizens. The Chinese position was that behind such lofty arguments, the British were pushing opium.

What does this document suggest about the Qing dynasty's view of China's place in the world in 1839? Does it still view China as a universal empire?

A communication: magnificently our great Emperor soothes and pacifies China and the foreign countries, regarding all with the same kindness. If there is profit, then he shares it with the peoples of the world; if there is harm, then he removes it on behalf of the world. This is because he takes the mind of heaven and earth as his mind.

The kings of your honorable country by a tradition handed down from generation to generation have always been noted for their politeness and submissiveness. We have read your successive tributary memorials saying, "In general our countrymen who go to trade in China have always received His Majesty the Emperor's gracious treatment and equal justice," and so on. Privately we are delighted with the way in which the honorable rulers of your country deeply understand the grand principles and are grateful for the Celestial grace. For this reason the Celestial Court in soothing those from afar has redoubled its polite and kind treatment. The profit from trade has been enjoyed by them continuously for two hundred years. This is the source from which your country has become known for its wealth. But after a long period of commercial intercourse, there appear among the crowd of barbarians both good persons and bad, unevenly. Consequently there are those who smuggle opium to seduce the Chinese people and so cause the spread of the poison to all provinces. Such persons who only care to profit themselves, and disregard their harm to others, are not tolerated by

the laws of heaven and are unanimously hated by human beings. His Majesty the Emperor, upon hearing of this, is in a towering rage. . . .

We find that your country is sixty or seventy thousand *li* [three *li* make one mile, ordinarily] from China. Yet there are barbarian ships that strive to come here for trade for the purpose of making a great profit. The wealth of China is used to profit the barbarians. That is to say, the great profit made by barbarians is all taken from the rightful share of China. By what right do they then in return use the poisonous drug to injure the Chinese people? Even though the barbarians may not necessarily intend to do us harm, yet in coveting profit to an extreme, they have no regard for injuring others. Let us ask, where is your conscience? I have heard that the smoking of opium is very strictly forbidden by your country; that is because the harm caused by opium is clearly understood. Since it is not permitted to do harm to your own country, then even less should you let it be passed on to the harm of other countries — how much less to China!

Suppose there were people from another country who carried opium for sale to England and seduced your people into buying and smoking it; certainly your honorable ruler would deeply hate it and be bitterly aroused. We have heard heretofore that your honorable ruler is kind and benevolent. Naturally you would not wish to give unto others what you yourself do not want.

Now we have set up regulations governing the Chinese people. He who sells opium shall receive the death penalty and he who smokes it also the death penalty. Now consider this: if the barbarians do not bring opium, then how can the Chinese people resell it, and how can they smoke it? The fact is that the wicked barbarians beguile the Chinese people into a death trap. How then can we grant life only to those barbarians? He who takes the life of even one person still has to atone for it with his own life; yet is the harm done by opium limited to the taking of one life only? Therefore in the new regulations, in

(continued)

regard to those barbarians who bring opium to China, the penalty is fixed at decapitation or strangulation. This is what is called getting rid of a harmful thing on behalf of mankind.

[However] All those who within the period of the coming one year (from England) or six months (from India) bring opium to China by mistake, but who voluntarily confess and completely surrender their opium, shall be exempt from their punishment. This may be called the height of kindness and the perfection of justice.

After the signing of the treaties, Chinese imports of opium rose from 30,000 chests to a peak of 87,000 in 1879. Thereafter, imports declined to 50,000 chests in 1906, and ended during World War I. But other kinds of trade did not grow as much as had been hoped, and Western merchants blamed the lack of growth on artificial restraints imposed by Chinese officials. They also complained that, despite the treaties, Guangzhou remained closed to trade. The Chinese authorities, for their part, were incensed by the export of coolies to work under harsh conditions on plantations in Cuba and Peru. A second war broke out in 1856, which continued sporadically until Lord Elgin, the British commander, together with a French contingent, captured Beijing in 1860. A new set of conventions and treaties provided for indemnities, the opening of eleven new ports, the stationing of foreign diplomats in Beijing, the propagation of Christianity anywhere in China, and the legalization of the opium trade.

While the British fought China for trading rights, the Russians were encroaching on China's northern frontier. During the 1850s, Russia established settlements along the Amur River. In 1858, China signed a treaty ceding the north bank of the Amur to Russia, and in 1860, China signed another treaty, giving Russia the Maritime Province between the Ussuri River and the Pacific.

Rebellions Against the Dynasty (1850–1873)

Far more immediate a threat to Manchu rule than foreign gunboats and unequal treaties were the Taiping, Nian, and Muslim rebellions that convulsed China between 1850 and 1873 (see Map 5–1). The torment and suffering they caused were unparalleled in world history. Estimates of those killed during the twenty years of the Taiping Rebellion range from twenty to thirty million. Adding in losses due to other rebellions, droughts, and floods, China's population dropped by sixty million and did not recover to pre-rebellion levels until the end of the dynasty in 1912.

The Taipings were begun by Hong Xiuquan (1814–1864), a schoolteacher from a poor family in a minority Hakka group in the southern province of Guangdong. Hong had four times failed to pass the civil service examinations. He became ill and saw visions. Influenced by Protestant tracts that he had picked up in Guangzhou, Hong announced that he was the younger brother of Jesus and that God had told him to rid China of evil demons—including Manchus, Confucians, Daoists, and Buddhists.

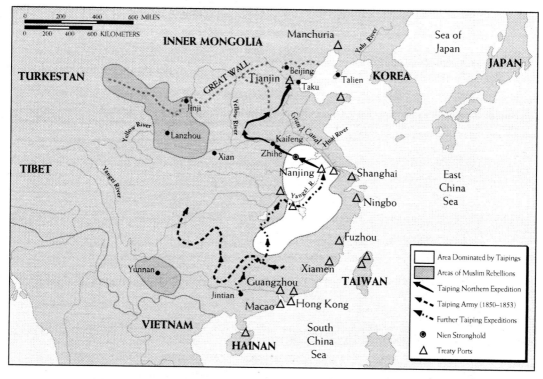

Map 5–1 The Taiping, Nian, and Muslim rebellions. Between 1850 and 1873, China was wracked by rebellions that almost ended the Manchu dynasty. The dynasty was saved by Chinese "gentry armies."

He formed the Association of God Worshipers. His followers cut off their queues as a sign of resistance to the Manchus, who called them "long-haired rebels." The Taipings began by attacking local Confucian temples, arousing the opposition of the gentry. The Taipings were soon joined by peasants, coal miners, charcoal workers, and unemployed transport workers. Hong proclaimed the Heavenly Kingdom of Great Peace in 1851 and two years later took Nanjing and made it his capital. The fighting spread until the Taipings controlled most of the Yangzi basin; their expeditions eventually entered sixteen of the eighteen Chinese provinces. By that time, their army numbered almost a million.

The Taiping doctrine joined Old Testament Christianity with an ancient text often used by reformers, the *Zhou Rites*. The puritanical ethics of the Taipings came from the former, and the notion of sharing property equally came from the latter. The Taipings prohibited opium, tobacco, alcohol, gambling, adultery, prostitution, and footbinding. They upheld filial piety. They maintained that women were men's equals and appointed them to administrative and military posts. In short, like earlier rebels, the Taipings combined moral reform, religious fervor, and a vision of a transformed egalitarian society.

The movement had several weaknesses. Most Taiping leaders were too poorly educated to govern effectively, and the Taipings could not draw on the gentry. When the Taiping area was divided into kingdoms, dissension broke out. The Taipings failed to cultivate the secret societies, which were also anti-Manchu. They also failed to cultivate Westerners, who had been neutral before the 1860 treaty settlements and aided the Manchu court thereafter. In addition, many Taiping ideals remained unfulfilled; for example, land was not redistributed, and, although Taiping teachings emphasized frugality and the sanctity of monogamous marriage, Hong lived with many concubines in the midst of luxury.

The other rebellions were of lesser note but longer duration. The Nian were located to the north of the Taipings along the Huai River. They began as bandits who lived in walled villages, were organized in secret societies, and lived by raiding the surrounding countryside. Eventually they built an army, collected taxes, and ruled 100,000 square miles. The Qing court feared that the Nian would join forces with the Taipings. An even longer revolt was of Muslims against Qing rule in the southwest and the northwest. One rebel set up an Islamic kingdom with himself as sultan. Like the Taiping Rebellion, these several rebellions took advantage of the weakened state of the dynasty and occurred in areas that had few Qing officials or troops.

Against these rebellions, the Manchu Banners and the Chinese Army of the Green Standard proved helpless: The former was useful only for defense, the latter only against unarmed peasants. The first effective step was taken in 1852, when the court sent Zeng Guofan (1811–1872) to Hunan Province in south-central China to organize a local army. Zeng was a product of the Confucian examination system and had served in Beijing. He saw the Manchu government, of which he was an elite member, as the upholder of morality and the social order, and Chinese rebels as would-be destroyers of that order. Arriving in Hunan, he recruited members of the gentry as officers. They were of the class that, since the Ming, had been growing in importance and performing many local government functions and, in some cases, organizing local militia. They were not only Confucian, but as landlords, they had the most to lose from rebel rule. They recruited soldiers from their local areas. Zeng's "Hunan Braves" stopped the Taipings' advance.

Until 1860, Manchu conservatives dominated the Qing court; they limited Zeng's role and dragged their feet in upholding the treaties. In 1860, the conservatives lost their footing when the British and the French occupied Beijing. A reform government replaced the conservatives, began internal changes, adopted a policy of cooperation with the Western powers, and put Zeng in charge of suppressing the rebellions. Zeng appointed able officials to raise other regional armies. Li Hongzhang (1823–1901), with his Anhui Army, was especially effective. Foreigners and Shanghai merchants gave their support. Revenues from the customs service and foreign ships and weapons were essential to Zeng's armies. The Taipings collapsed when Nanjing was captured in 1864 after protracted fighting. Zeng and Li suppressed the Nian by 1868, and Muslim rebellions were put down five years later. Scholar-officials, relying on local gentry, had saved the dynasty.

Self-Strengthening and Decline (1874–1895)

The two decades that followed the suppression of the mid-century rebellions illustrate the dictum that there is no single "correct" view of history. In comparison, for example, with the last years of the Song or Ming, the last decades of the nineteenth century look good. The dynasty's resiliency and capacity to rebuild were impressive—after unprecedented destruction and in view of the dynasty's advanced stage of administrative decentralization. Even on its borders, the Manchu state regained some territories while losing others. But if we ask instead how effective China's response was to the West, or if we compare China's progress with that of Japan, then China during the same decades looks almost moribund. Historians often call these years the period of "self-strengthening" after a catchphrase in vogue at the time. The term is not inappropriate, as the list of new initiatives taken during the period is long. Yet, since the firepower of Western naval forces doubled each decade, the forces that China faced at the end of the century were vastly more formidable than those of the Opium War. Despite self-strengthening, China was relatively weaker at the end of the period than at the start.

In 1895, Li Hongzhang met with Itō Hirobumi of Japan to negotiate a peace treaty after China's defeat in the Sino-Japanese War. Itō asked with uncharacteristic bluntness: "Ten years ago when I was at Tianjin, I talked about reform with the Grand Secretary (Li). Why is it that up to now not a single thing has been changed or reformed?" Li replied: "Affairs in my country have been so confined by tradition that I could not accomplish what I desired. . . . Now in the twinkling of an eye ten years have gone by, and everything is still the same. I am even more regretful. I am ashamed of having excessive wishes and lacking the power to fulfill them . . ." Itō responded blandly: "The providence of heaven has no affection, except for the virtuous."[1] Considering that Li was the single most powerful figure in China during these decades, Itō's puzzlement was not surprising.

The Court at Beijing The situation at the court partly explains China's inability to act effectively. Prince Gong (1833–1898) and the Empress Dowager Cixi (1835–1908) were coregents for the young emperor. For a Manchu noble, Prince Gong was a man of ideas. After signing the treaties of 1860, in 1861 he established a new office directly under the Grand Council to handle the court's relations with foreign diplomats in Beijing. The following year, he established a school to train Chinese in foreign languages. His position at the court, however, gradually grew weaker, and, outmaneuvered by the empress dowager, he was ousted in 1884.

[1]S. Y. Teng and J. K. Fairbank, *China's Response to the West* (Cambridge, MA: Harvard University, Press, 1954), p. 126.

IMPERIALISM, A CHINESE VIEW

Chinese scholars during the 1870s and 1880s talked of "self-strengthening," of building railroads, steamships, telegraphs, and modern arms to resist Westerners, who "stand like birds of prey, as covetous as wolves, with watering mouths and eyes, staring at Asia." But the Chinese diplomat Guo Songdao, who had dealt with foreigners, arrived at a different judgment of China's situation. He criticized scholar-officials at the Beijing court as "confused and stupid," and while negotiating with the "French barbarians" in 1884, he argued for prudence: "Give them trade and they will be satisfied."

Lenin argued that the imbalance between production and consumption in capitalist economies necessitated the export of capital, which led in turn to the capture of foreign markets and to their acquisition as colonies. Lenin's explanation apart, in fact, much of the world was taken as colonies. Is Guo arguing that Western powers will forego colonies if permitted to trade?

The European countries have concentrated on trade relations. . . . The areas they have occupied are as far away as several tens of thousands of *li*, all occupied on the pretext of commerce. At first they had no intention of resorting to war, but after [the local people] had repeatedly gone back on their promises, the foreigners inevitably took offense and so used military force. Nor had they any preconceived idea of fighting for territory; but the more they fought, the further they advanced and thereupon they took the opportunity to usurp territory. The various islands in Southeast Asia are almost completely invaded and occupied, and all by this process. Therefore, in negotiating with the European nations on commercial affairs, we can use reason to overcome them but should absolutely not resort to force in a dispute; we can inspire their confidence by sincerity and good faith, but should by no means gloss things over; we can make use of their power to plan to make ourselves strong, but we must not on any account be envious of their strength and so seek to challenge them.

Your minister once held that, of the requests the Europeans have made . . . there is none that cannot be settled by compromise according to reason; whereas, if war is resorted to, then they will not be easy to settle. This is because . . . their purpose is no more than to trade with us for profit; they cherish no hatred or grudge in their hearts. We have noticed that they do not speak lightly of war but argue with us back and forth, leaving themselves ample leeway to seek in each instance some advantage. If, on account of the fact that they do not speak of warfare easily, we goad them into acting with outrageous violence, then there will be a great deal of harm. Once warfare has been resorted to, the military expense they incur will eventually be sought from us as an indemnity.

The empress dowager was the daughter of a Manchu official. She had become an imperial concubine and had produced the only male child of the former emperor. She was educated, clever, petty, strong-willed, and narrow-minded. She did not oppose change, except by circumstance, nor did she favor it. She had no conception of how to reform China. Her single goal was to gather political power into her own hands. She did this by forging a political machine of conservative bureaucrats, military commanders, and eunuchs, and by maintaining a balance between the court and the regional strength of the powerful governor-generals. The result was a court barely able to survive, too weak to govern effectively, and not inclined to do more than approve of initiatives taken at the provincial level.

Regional Governments   The most vital figures during these decades were a handful of governors-general whose names are legend: Zeng Guofan, Li Hongzhang, Zuo Zongtang (1812–1885), and Zhang Zhidong (1837–1909). Each had a staff of two hundred or three hundred and an army, and was in charge of two or three provinces. They were loyal to the dynasty that they had restored in the face of almost certain collapse, and in return for their allegiance, they were allowed great autonomy.

Their first task was reconstruction. The rebellions in central China had destroyed the mulberry trees on which the silkworms fed, and those in the northwest, the irrigation systems. Millions were hungry or homeless. The leaders' response to these ills was massive and effective. Just as they had mobilized the gentry to suppress the rebellions, now they obtained their cooperation in rebuilding. They set up refugee centers and soup kitchens, reduced taxes in the devastated Yangzi valley, reclaimed lands gone to waste, began water-control projects, and built granaries. By the early 1890s, a measure of well-being had been restored to China's late dynastic society.

Their second task was self-strengthening—the adoption of Western arms and technology. The governors-general were keenly aware of China's weakness. To strengthen China, they built arsenals and shipyards during the 1860s and 1870s, and during the 1870s and 1880s, they began commercial ventures as well. The China Merchants Steam Navigation Company was established in 1872, the Kaiping Coal Mine in 1876, and then a telegraph company, short stretches of railways, and cotton mills. The formula applied in running these enterprises was "official supervision and merchant operation." Major decisions were made by scholar-officials like Zeng, but day-to-day operations were left to merchants.

This division of labor led to contradictions. The China Merchants Steam Navigation Company, for example, was funded partly by the government because private capital was inadequate.

Li Hongzhang awarded the company a monopoly on shipments of tax rice and official cargos to Tianjin and won tariff concessions for the company as well. For a time, these advantages enabled it to compete successfully with foreign lines. But Li also used company ships to transport his troops; he took company funds to reward his political followers; and he interfered in the company by hiring and firing managers. Under these conditions, both investors and managers took their profits quickly and did not reinvest in the line. Soon British lines once again dominated shipping in China's domestic waters.

Treaty Ports   Conditions in the treaty ports, of which there were fourteen by the 1860s, were different from the rest of China. The ports were little islands of privilege where foreigners lived in mansions staffed with servants, raced horses at the track, participated in amateur theatricals, drank (in Shanghai, at the longest bar in the world), and went to church on Sunday. But the ports were also islands of security, under the rule of foreign consuls, where capital was safe from confiscation, trade was free, and "squeeze" (extortion by officials) was the exception and not the rule. Foreign companies quite naturally located in the ports. The Hong Kong and Shanghai Bank, for example, was funded in 1865 by British interests to finance international trade and make loans to Chinese firms and banks. Chinese merchants were also attracted by these conditions and located their businesses on rented lands in the foreign concessions. Joint ventures, such as steamboats on the Yangzi, were begun by Chinese and foreign merchants. Well into the twentieth century, the foreign concessions (treaty port lands leased in perpetuity by foreigners) remained the vital sector of China's modern economy.

The effects of the treaty ports and of Western imperialism on China were largely negative. Under the low tariffs mandated by the treaties, Chinese industries had little protection from imports. Native cotton spinning was almost destroyed by imports of yarn—although the cloth woven from the yarn remained competitive with foreign cloth. Chinese tea lost ground to Indian tea and Chinese silk to Japanese silk, as these countries developed products of standard quality and China did not. China had few products to export: pig bristles, soybeans, and vegetable oils. The level of foreign trade stayed low, and China's interior markets were affected only slightly.

By the 1870s, the foreign powers had reached an accommodation with China. They counted on the court to uphold the treaties; in return, they became a prop for the dynasty during its final decades. By 1900, for example, the court's revenues from customs fees were larger than those from any other source, including the land tax. The fees were collected by the Maritime Customs Service, an efficient and honest treaty-port institution. It was headed by an Irishman, Robert Hart, who saw himself as serving the Chinese government. In 1895, the Maritime Customs Service had 700 Western and 3,500 Chinese employees.

The Borderlands

China's other foreign relations were with fringe lands inhabited by non-Chinese but which China claimed by right of past conquest or tribute relations. Often distant from the pressing concerns of Chinese government, the tributaries were nonetheless the mirrors in which China saw reflected its own self-image as a universal empire. During the late nineteenth century, this image was strengthened in the northwest but dealt a fatal blow in Vietnam and Korea.

The Northwest Along the sweep of its northern and western frontiers, China confronted imperial Russia. Both countries had been expanding onto the steppe since the seventeenth century. Both had firearms. Caught in a pincers between them, the once proud, powerful, and independent nomadic tribes were gradually rendered impotent. Conservatives at the Manchu court ordered Zuo Zongtang, who had suppressed Muslim rebels within China, to suppress a Muslim leader who had founded an independent state in Chinese Turkestan (the Tarim Basin, the area of the old Silk Road). Zuo led his army across 3,000 miles of deserts, and by 1878, he had reconquered the area, which was subsequently renamed Xinjiang, or "New Territories." A treaty signed with Russia in 1881 also restored most of the Ili region in western Mongolia to Chinese control. These victories strengthened court conservatives who wished to take a stronger stance toward the West.

Vietnam   To the south was Vietnam, which had wrested its independence from China in 939 and periodically had repelled Chinese invasions thereafter. It saw itself as an independent and separate state, but it used the Chinese writing system, modeled its laws and government on those of China, and traded with China within the framework of the tribute system. China, more simply, saw Vietnam as a tributary that could be aided or punished as necessary.

During the 1840s, the second emperor of the Nguyen dynasty, which had begun in 1802, moved to reduce French influence and suppress Christianity. Among the thousands killed were French and Vietnamese priests. The French responded by seizing Saigon and the three provinces of Cochin China in 1859, establishing a protectorate over Cambodia in 1864, and taking three more provinces in 1867 and Hanoi in 1882. China, flush with confidence after its victories in Central Asia, in 1883 sent in troops to aid its tributary. The result was a two-year war in which French warships ranged the coast of China, attacking shore batteries and sinking ships. In 1885, China was compelled to sign a treaty abandoning its claims to Vietnam. By 1893, France had brought together Vietnam, Cambodia, and Laos to form the Federation of Indochina. Newly founded Cantonese newspapers contributed to a rising Chinese nationalism with inflammatory articles attacking French aggression. Indochina remained under French control until 1940.

Korea   The third area of contention was Korea, strategically located between Russia, China, and Japan. An ancient and proud state with an independent identity, Korea was about the size of England, Scotland, and Wales combined. Even while drawing heavily on Chinese laws, philosophy, history, and institutions, Korea had developed a distinctive culture and way of life. Yet unlike Vietnam, Korea saw itself as a tributary of China. Even at his own court, the Korean ruler styled himself as a king and not an emperor. It was the only rim area of China that accepted the tribute system on Chinese terms.

During the last decades of the long Choson dynasty (1392–1910), the Korean state was weak. It hung on to power, in part, by enforcing a policy of seclusion almost as total as that of Tokugawa Japan, which won it the name of the *Hermit Kingdom*. Its only foreign ties were its tribute relations with China and its trade and occasional diplomatic missions to Japan. In 1876, Japan "opened" Korea to international relations, using much the same tactics that Perry had used twenty-two years earlier against Japan. Japan then contended with China for influence in Korea's internal politics. Conservatives and moderate reformers in Korea looked to China for support. Radical reformers, weaker and fewer in number, looked to Japan, arguing that only sweeping changes such as those that followed Japan's Meiji Restoration would enable Korea to survive. The radicals, however, were soon suppressed.

In 1893, a popular religious sect unleashed a rebellion against the weak and corrupt Seoul government. When the government requested Chinese help to suppress the rebellion, China sent troops, but Japan sent more, and in 1894, war broke out between China and Japan. China and the Western powers expected an easy Chinese victory, but they had not understood the changes occurring within Japan. Japan won handily. Neither Chinese fleet nor Chinese armies were a match for the discipline and the superior tactics of the Japanese units. It was after this war that Taiwan became Japan's first colony. The defeat by Japan convinced many in China that fundamental changes were inevitable.

FROM DYNASTY TO WARLORDISM (1895–1926)

The officials who ruled China were steeped in the Confucian classics and in Chinese history and literature. Their minds were resistant to change. Most officials, living in China's interior, viewed the foreign crises of the nineteenth century as "coastal phenomena" that, like bee stings, were painful for a time but then forgotten. Few officials realized the magnitude of the foreign threat.

China's defeat in 1895 by Japan, another Asian nation and one for which China had had little regard, came as a shock. The response within China was a new wave of reform proposals. The most influential thinker was Kang Youwei (1858–1927), who described China as "enfeebled" and "soundly asleep atop a pile of kindling." For this state of affairs, Kang blamed the "conservatives." They did not understand, he argued, that Confucius himself had been a reformer and not simply a transmitter of past wisdom. Confucius had invented the idea of a golden age in the past in order to persuade the rulers of his own age to adopt his ideas. All of history, Kang continued, was evolutionary—a march forward from absolute monarchy to constitutional monarchy to democracy. Actually, Kang was not well versed in Western ideas; he equated the somewhat mystical Confucian virtue of humanity (*ren*) with electricity and ether. Nonetheless, his reinterpretation of the essentials of Confucianism removed a major barrier to the entry of Western ideas into China.

In 1898, the emperor himself became sympathetic to Kang's ideas and, on June 11, launched "one hundred days of reform." He took as his models not past Chinese monarchs but Peter the Great (r. 1682–1725) of Russia and Emperor Meiji (r. 1867–1912) of Japan. Edicts were issued for sweeping reforms of China's schools,

LIANG QICHAO URGES THE CHINESE TO REFORM (1896)

Next to Kang Youwei, Liang Qichao (1873–1929) was the most influential reformist thinker in late Qing China.

What kind of reform program do you imagine Liang advocated?

On the *Harm of Not Reforming.* Now here is a big mansion which has lasted a thousand years. The tiles and bricks are decayed and the beams and rafters are broken. It is still a magnificently big thing, but when wind and rain suddenly come up, its fall is foredoomed. Yet the people in the house are still happily playing or soundly sleeping and as indifferent as if they have seen or heard nothing. Even some who have noted the danger know only how to weep bitterly, folding their arms and waiting for death without thinking of any remedy. Sometimes there are people a little better off who try to repair the cracks, seal up the leaks, and patch up the ant holes in order to be able to go on living there in peace, even temporarily, in the hope that something better may turn up. These three types of people use their minds differently, but when a hurricane comes they will die together. . . . A nation is also like this. . . .

India is one of the oldest countries on the great earth. She followed tradition without change; she has been rendered a colony of England. Turkey's territory occupied three continents and had an established state for a thousand years; yet, because of observing the old ways without change, she has been dominated by six large countries, which have divided her territory. . . . The Moslems in central Asia have usually been well known for their bravery and skill in warfare, and yet they observe the old ways without changing. The Russians are swallowing them like a whale and nibbling them as silkworms eat mulberry leaves, almost in their entirety.

The age of China as a country is equal to that of India and the fertility of her land is superior to that of Turkey, but her conformity to the defective ways which have accumulated and her incapacity to stand up and reform make her also like a brother of these two countries. . . . Whenever there is a flood or drought, communications are severed, there is no way to transport famine relief, the dead are abandoned to fill the ditches or are disregarded, and nine out of ten houses are emptied. . . . The members of secret societies are scattered over the whole country, waiting for the chance to move. Industry is not developed, commerce is not discussed, the native goods daily become less salable. . . . "Leakage" [i.e., squeeze] becomes more serious day by day and our financial sources are almost dried up. Schools are not well run and students, apart from the "eight-legged" essays, do not know how to do a thing. The good ones are working on small researches, flowery writing, and miscellaneous trifles. Tell them about the vast oceans, they open their eyes wide and disbelieve it.

railroads, police, laws, military services, bureaucracy, post offices, and examination system. But the orders were implemented in only one province; conservative resistance was nationwide. Even at the court, after the one hundred days, the empress dowager regained control and ended the reforms. Kang and most of his associates fled to Japan. They were later called "the six gentlemen of 1898." One reformer who remained behind was executed.

An American view of the "Open Door." The combination of high
self-esteem and anti-foreignism at the turn of the century was not
a Chinese monopoly.
[CORBIS-NY]

The response of the Western powers to China's 1895 defeat has been
described as "carving up the melon." Each nation tried to define a sphere of interest, which usually consisted of a leasehold, railway rights, and special commercial
privileges. Russia gained a leasehold at Port Arthur in the area that it had denied to
Japan in 1895; Germany acquired one in Shantung; and Britain got the New
Territories adjoining Jiulong (Kowloon) at Hong Kong. New ports and cities were
opened to foreign trade. The United States, busy acquiring the Philippines and
Guam, was in a weaker position in China. So it enunciated an "open-door" policy:
equal commercial opportunities for all powers and the preservation of the territorial
integrity of China.

There was in China at this time an antiforeign religious society known as the Boxers. The Chinese name translates more literally as the "Righteous and Harmonious Fists." The Boxers had rituals, spells, and amulets that they believed made them impervious to bullets. They rebelled first in Shantung in 1898, and, gaining court support, entered Beijing in 1900. The court declared war on the treaty powers, and there followed a two-month siege of the foreign legation quarter. Pent-up resentments against decades of foreign encroachments fueled support for the rebellion. Eventually an international force captured Beijing, won a huge indemnity, and obtained the right to maintain permanent military forces in the capital. In the aftermath of the Boxer Rebellion, the Russians occupied Manchuria.

The defeat of the Boxers convinced even conservative Chinese leaders of the futility of clinging to old ways. A more powerful reform movement began, with the empress dowager herself positioned in its vanguard. But as the movement gained momentum, the dynasty could not stay far enough in front and eventually was overrun.

Educational reforms began in 1901. Women, for the first time, were admitted to newly formed schools. In place of Confucianism, the instructors taught science, mathematics, geography, and an anti-imperialist version of Chinese history that fanned the flames of nationalism. Western doctrines such as classical economics, liberalism, socialism, anarchism, and social Darwinism were also introduced. Most entered via translations from Japanese, and in the process, the modern vocabulary coined by Japanese scholars was implanted in China. By 1906, there were 8,000 Chinese students in Japan, which had become a hotbed of Chinese reformist and revolutionary societies.

Military reforms were begun by Yuan Shikai (1859–1916), whose New Army drew on Japanese and Western models. Young men from gentry families, spurred by patriotism, broke with the traditional Chinese animus against military careers and joined the New Army as officers. Their loyalty was to their commanders and country, not to the ruling dynasty.

Political reforms began with a modification of the examination system to accommodate the learning at the new schools. Then, in 1905, the examination system was abolished altogether. Henceforth, officials were to be recruited from the graduates of the schools and those who had studied abroad. Provincial assemblies were formed in 1909, and a consultative assembly with some elected members was established in Beijing in 1910. These representative bodies were intended to rally the new gentry nationalism in support of the dynasty, but they turned into forums for the expression of ideas and interests at odds with those of the dynasty.

In sum, during the first decade of the twentieth century, the three vital components of the imperial system—Confucian education, bureaucracy, and gentry—had been discarded or modified in ways that even a few decades earlier would have been unimaginable. These changes sparked the 1911–1912 revolution. It began with an uprising in Sichuan province against a government plan to nationalize the main railways. The players were:

1. Gentry who stood to lose their investments in the railways.

2. Qing military commanders who broke with Beijing, declaring their provinces independent.

3. Sun Zhongshan (or Sun Yat-sen) (1866–1925), a republican revolutionary. Born a peasant, he had learned English and become a Christian in Hawaii; he then studied medicine in Guangzhou and Hong Kong. He organized the Revolutionary Alliance in Tokyo in 1905, and was associated with the Nationalist Party (*Guomindang*) formed in 1912.

4. Yuan Shikai, a Qing general who was called on by the court to preserve the dynasty. Instead, he arranged for the last child emperor to abdicate in February 1912, for Sun to step aside, and for himself to become president of the new Republic of China.

The Nationalists won the election called in 1913. Yuan thereupon had their leader assassinated, crushed the pro-Nationalist military-governors of the southern provinces who supported them, and forced Sun Zhongshan and other revolutionaries to flee again to Japan. Yuan emerged as the uncontested ruler of China. Mistaking the temper of the times, in December 1915, he proclaimed a new dynasty with himself as emperor. The idea of yet another dynasty met implacable opposition from all quarters, forcing Yuan to abandon the attempt. He died three months later in June 1916. After Yuan, a national government led a shadow existence in Beijing, but China fell into the hands of warlord armies. A few were concerned for local welfare but most were despots who cruelly exploited the populations they controlled. The years until the late 1920s were a time of agony, frustration, and travail for the Chinese people. But they also were a time of intense intellectual ferment.

CULTURAL AND IDEOLOGICAL FERMENT: THE MAY FOURTH MOVEMENT (1914–1920S)

In the century after the Opium War, China's leading thinkers responded to the challenge of the West in terms of four successive modes of thought:

1. Traditional Confucian teachings predominated during the 1840s, 1850s, and into the 1860s. The key event of these years was the Taiping Rebellion. The success of the court in putting down the rebellion and restoring the social order underlined the effectiveness, vitality, and validity of those teachings.

2. From the 1860s to the 1890s, the dominant intellectual modality was "*ti-yung* reformism." The essence (*ti*) was to remain Confucian, but useful contrivances (*yung*) could be borrowed from the West. This formula enabled a restabilized China to borrow and reform in small ways—building arsenals and railroads—while remaining Chinese at heart. It was the ideology of the "self-strengthening" movement.

3. Then, after China's defeat in the Sino-Japanese War of 1894–1895 and during the decade after the turn of the century, the *ti-yung* distinction came to be seen as inadequate. The Confucian essence (*ti*) itself had to be reinterpreted. The dominant view was that of Kang Youwei, who argued that Confucius had been a reformer and that Confucianism, properly understood, was a philosophy of change. Such thought was behind the rash of reforms of 1900–1911.

4. In the fourth stage, Chinese thinkers abandoned attempts to reform Confucianism and turned to embrace Western ideas. This began in 1914, two years after the overthrow of the Qing dynasty, and extended into the 1920s. It is called the *May Fourth Movement* after an incident in Beijing in 1919 in which thousands of students protested the settlement at Versailles that awarded former German possessions in Shandong to Japan. The national feelings that led the students to demonstrate in the streets were a part of this transformation. Instead of appealing to tradition, leading thinkers began to judge ideas in terms of their value in solving China's problems. It was not accidental that this era of intellectual openness and ferment corresponded almost exactly with the period of warlord rule—which afforded a breathing space between the ideological constraints of the old dynasty and those of the Nationalist and Communist eras that would follow.

Scholars who returned from abroad during the last years of Qing rule often located in the safety of the treaty ports. During the May Fourth Movement era, however, the center of advanced thought was Beijing. Cai Yuanpei (1868–1940), who had been minister of education under the republic, became the chancellor of Beijing University, and Chen Duxiu (1879–1942) became his dean of letters. Both men had had a classical education and had passed the traditional examinations. Cai joined the party of Sun Zhongshan and went to study in Germany, where he earned a Ph.D. After the fall of Yuan Shikai, he made Beijing University a haven for scholars who had returned from study in Japan or the West.

Chen Duxiu, a Francophile, had studied in Japan. In 1915, he launched *New Youth*, a magazine that played a role in the intellectual revolution of early twentieth-century China comparable to the *cahiers* in the French Revolution or the pamphlets of Thomas Paine in the American Revolution. In his magazine, Chen placed the blame for Chinese ills on the teachings of Confucius. He called for a generation of progressive, cosmopolitan, and scientific youth who would uphold the values of liberty, equality, and fraternity.

CHEN DUXIU'S "CALL TO YOUTH" IN 1915

Struggle, natural selection, and organic process are the images of Chen Duxiu. How different from those of Confucianism!

How does Chen's "Call to Youth" relate to the political conditions in China in 1915?

The Chinese compliment others by saying, "He acts like an old man although still young." Englishmen and Americans encourage one another by saying, "Keep young while growing old." Such is one respect in which the different ways of thought of the East and West are manifested. Youth is like early spring, like the rising sun, like trees and grass in bud, like a newly sharpened blade. It is the most valuable period of life. The function of youth in society is the same as that of a fresh and vital cell in a human body. In the processes of metabolism, the old and the rotten are incessantly eliminated to be replaced by the fresh and living. . . . According to this standard, then, is the society of our nation flourishing, or is it about to perish? I cannot bear to answer. As for those old and rotten elements, I shall leave them to the process of natural selection. . . .

I only, with tears, place my plea before the young and vital youth, in the hope that they will achieve self-awareness, and begin to struggle.

What is the struggle? It is to exert one's intellect, discard resolutely the old and the rotten, regard them as enemies and as the flood or savage beasts, keep away from their neighborhood and refuse to be contaminated by their poisonous germs. Alas! Do these words really fit the youth of our country? I have seen that, out of every ten youths who are young in age, five are old in physique; and out of every ten who are young in both age and physique, nine are old in mentality. Those with shining hair, smooth countenance, a straight back and a wide chest are indeed magnificent youths! Yet if you ask what thoughts and aims are entertained in their heads, then they all turn out to be the same as the old and rotten, like moles from the same hill. . . . It is the old and rotten air that fills society everywhere. One cannot even find a bit of fresh and vital air to comfort those of us who are suffocating in despair.

The greatest modern Chinese writer was Lu Xun (1881–1936). Like most other leading intellectuals of the period, he had been born in a scholar-official family. He went to Japan for eight years to study medicine but switched in midcourse to literature. His first work, *A Madman's Diary*, appeared in *New Youth* in 1918. Its protagonist is a pathetic figure, whose madness takes the form of a belief that people eat people. Lu Xun's message was that only the vision of a madman could truly comprehend an abnormal and inhumane society.

As the May Fourth Movement developed, ideas propounded in Beijing quickly spread to the rest of China, especially to its urban centers. Protest demonstrations against imperialist privilege broke out in Shanghai, Wuhan, and Guangzhou, as they had in the capital. Nationalism and anti-imperialist sentiment were stronger than liberalism, though most thinkers spoke out for democracy. Only members of an older generation of reformers, such as Kang Youwei or Liang Qichao, came full circle and,

LU XUN

Like Chen Duxiu and other writers of the May Fourth Movement, Lu Xun saw China's old society as rotten and corrupt. Only a radical reform, he felt, would enable the Chinese to realize their humanity.

Making an Argument

I dreamed I was in a primary school classroom preparing to write a composition, and I asked my teacher how to make an argument.

"That's hard." Looking at me sharply over the rim of his glasses, he said: "Let me give you an example."

"A son was born to a family and the entire household was overjoyed. When the boy was one month old, they brought him out and displayed him to guests—expecting, naturally, to hear predictions of good fortune.

One said, 'This child will become rich.' For his words he was thanked profusely.

One said, 'This child will become an official.' He received compliments in turn.

But another guest said, 'One day this child will die.' He was soundly beaten by the entire household.

That the child will die is inevitable, while to say he will become rich or attain high position is probably a lie. Those who lie are rewarded while those who speak the truth are beaten. You. . .

'But sir, I don't want to lie, and I don't want to be beaten, so how should I speak?'

In that case you can say: 'Aha! This child. Just look at him! Oh my. Hehe! He! Hehehehe!'"

Observations

Downstairs a man is dying,
Next door the family is listening to a victrola,
Across the lane they are playing with children.
Upstairs two persons are laughing with abandon, and there is the clack of mahjong tiles.
In a boat on the river a woman is wailing for her dead mother.
Human grief and joy do not extend to others;
I feel only that they are noisy.
It is in woman's nature to be a mother and to be a daughter—but not to be a wife.
A wifely nature is something forced—a mixture of her motherly and daughterly natures.
On seeing short sleeves,
they immediately think of bare arms,
they immediately think of the naked body,
they immediately think of the sexual organs,
they immediately think of copulation,
they immediately think of promiscuity,
they immediately think of illegitimate children.
Only at this level is the imagination of the Chinese capable of advancing by leaps and bounds.

Translation by A. Craig

---

appalled by the slaughter of World War I and the evils of Western materialism, advocated a return to traditional Chinese philosophies.

At the onset of China's intellectual revolution, Marxism had small appeal; Marx's critique of capitalist society did not fit Chinese conditions. More popular was the anarchism of Peter Kropotkin (1842–1921), who taught that mutual aid was as much a part of evolution as the struggle for survival. But after the Russian Revolution of 1917, Marxism–Leninism entered China. The Leninist definition of imperialism as the last crisis stage of capitalism had an immediate appeal, for it put the blame for China's ills on the West and offered "feudal" China the possibility of leapfrogging over capitalism to socialism. As early as 1919, an entire issue of *New Youth* was devoted to Marxism.

Marxist study groups formed in Beijing and other cities. In 1919, a student from Hunan, Mao Zedong, who had worked in the Beijing University library, returned to Changsha to form a study group. Chen Duxiu was converted to Marxism in 1920. Instructed in organizational techniques by a Comintern agent, Chen and others formed the Chinese Communist Party in Shanghai in 1921; Zhou Enlai (1898–1976) formed a similar group in Paris during the same year. The numbers involved were small but grew steadily.

NATIONALIST CHINA

Guomindang Unification of China and the Nanjing Decade (1927–1937)

Sun Zhongshan had fled to Japan during the 1913–1916 rule by Yuan Shikai. He returned to Guangzhou in 1916, but despite his immense personal attractiveness as a leader, he was a poor organizer, and his Guomindang (GMD), or Nationalist Party, made little headway. For a time, in 1922, he was driven out of Guangzhou by a local warlord. From 1923, Sun began to receive Soviet advice and support. With the help of Comintern agents like Michael Borodin, he reorganized his party on the Leninist model, with an executive committee on top of a national party congress, and, below this, provincial and county organizations and local party cells.

Since 1905 Sun had enunciated his "three principles of the people": nationalism, people's livelihood, and people's rights. Sun's earlier nationalism had been directed against Manchu rule; it was now redirected against Western imperialism. The principle of "people's livelihood" was defined in terms of equalizing landholdings and nationalizing major industries. By "people's rights," Sun meant democracy, although he argued that full democracy must be preceded by a preparatory period of tutelage under a single-party dictatorship. Sun sent his loyal lieutenant Jiang Jieshi (Chiang Kai-shek) (1887–1975) to the Soviet Union for study. Jiang returned after four months with a cadre of Russian advisers and established a military academy at Huangpu to the south of Guangzhou in 1924. The cadets of Huangpu were to form a "party army." Sun died in 1925. By 1926, the Huangpu Academy had graduated several thousand officers, and the GMD army numbered almost 100,000. The GMD had grown to become the major political force in China, with 200,000 members; its leadership was divided between a left and a right wing.

Changes occurring within Chinese society spurred the growth of the party. Industries arose in the cities. Labor unions were organized in tobacco and textile factories. New ventures were begun outside the treaty ports, and chambers of commerce were established even in medium-sized towns. Entrepreneurs, merchants, officials, journalists, and the employees of foreign firms formed a new and politically conscious middle class.

The quicksilver element in cities was the several million students at government, Catholic, and Protestant schools. In May 1925, students demonstrated against the treatment of workers in foreign-owned factories at Shanghai. Police in the international settlement fired on the demonstrators, killing thirteen and wounding fifty. This further inflamed national and anti-imperialist feelings, and strikes and boycotts of foreign goods were called throughout China. Those in Hong Kong lasted fifteen months.

Under these conditions, the Chinese Communist Party (CCP) also grew; in 1926, it had about 20,000 members. The party was influential in student organizations, labor unions, and even within the GMD. By an earlier agreement, Sun had permitted CCP members to join the GMD as individuals but had enjoined them from organizing CCP cells within the GMD. Moscow approved of this policy; it felt that the CCP was too small to accomplish anything on its own and that by working within the GMD, its members could join in the "bourgeois, national, democratic struggle" against "imperialists and feudal warlords." Zhou Enlai, for example, became deputy head of the Political Education Department of the Huangpu Academy.

By 1926, the GMD had established a base in the area around Guangzhou, and Jiang Jieshi felt ready to march north against the warlord domains. He was worried about the growing Communist strength, however, and before setting off, he ousted the Soviet advisers and CCP members from the GMD offices in Guangzhou. The march north began in July. By the spring of 1927, Jiang's army had reached the Yangzi, defeating, and often absorbing, warlord armies as it advanced (see Map 5–2).

After entering Shanghai in April 1927, Jiang carried out a sweeping purge of the CCP—against its members in the GMD, against its party organization, and against the labor unions that it had come to dominate. Hundreds were killed. The CCP responded by trying to gain control of the GMD left wing, which had established a government at Wuhan, and by armed uprisings. Both attempts failed. The surviving CCP members fled to the mountainous border region of Hunan and Jiangxi to the southwest and established the "Jiangxi Soviet." The left wing of the GMD, disenchanted with the Communists, rejoined the right wing at Nanjing, China's new capital. Jiang's army continued north, took Beijing, and gained the nominal submission of most northern Chinese warlords in 1928. By this time, most foreign powers had recognized the Nanjing regime as the government of China.

Jiang Jieshi was the key figure in the Nanjing government. By training and temperament he believed in military force. He was unimaginative, strict, feared more than loved, and, in the midst of considerable corruption, incorruptible. Jiang venerated Sun Zhongshan and his "three principles of the people." The grandeur of Sun's tomb in Nanjing surpassed that of the Ming emperors. But where Sun, as a revolutionary, had looked back to the zeal of the Taiping rebels, Jiang, trying to consolidate his rule over provincial warlords, looked back to Zeng Guofan, who had put down the rebels and

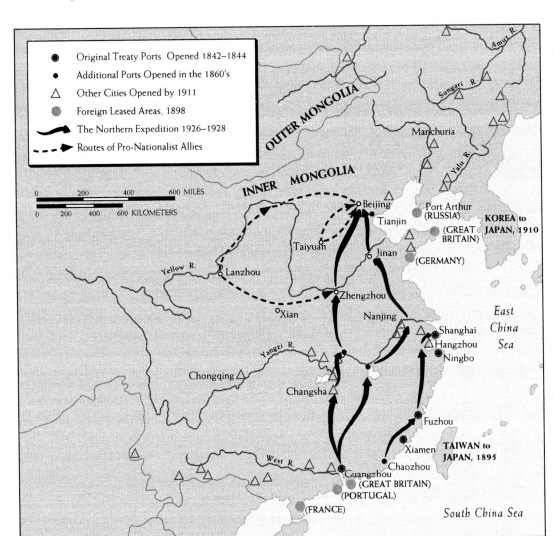

Map 5–2 The northern expeditions of the GMD. These expeditions, from 1926 to 1928, unified most of China under the Nationalist (GMD) government of Jiang Jieshi, inaugurating the Nanjing decade. Warlord armies continued to hold power on the periphery.

restabilized China. Like Zeng, Jiang was conservative and, though a Methodist, often appealed to Confucian values. The New Life Movement begun by Jiang in 1934 was an attempt to revitalize these values.

Jiang's power rested on the army, the party, and the government bureaucracy. The army was dominated by the Huangpu clique, which was personally loyal to Jiang, and by officers trained in Japan. After 1927, German military advisers replaced Soviet

Jiang Jieshi (1887–1975).
[CORBIS-NY]

advisers. They reorganized Jiang's army along German lines with a general staff system. The larger part of GMD revenues went to the military, which was expanded into a modernized force of 300,000. Huangpu graduates also controlled the secret military police and used it against Communists and any others who opposed the government. The GMD was a dictatorship under a central committee. Jiang became president of the party in 1938.

The densely populated central and lower Yangzi provinces were the area of GMD strength. The party, however, was unable to control outlying areas occupied by warlords, Communists, and Japanese. Some gains were made during the Nanjing decade: Jiang's armies defeated the northern warlords in 1930, put down a rebellion in the coastal province of Fujian in 1934, and extended their control over southern and southwestern China two years later. But warlords ruled other areas until 1949. In 1931, Jiang launched a series of campaigns against the Jiangxi Soviet. In 1934, the Communists were forced to abandon their mountain base and flee to the southwest and then to Shaanxi province in northwestern China. Of the 90,000 troops that set out on this epic "Long March" of 6,000 miles, only 20,000 survived. It was during this march that Mao Zedong wrested control of the CCP from the Moscow-trained, urban-oriented leaders and established his unorthodox view that a revolutionary Leninist party could base itself on the peasantry.

The Japanese had held special rights in Manchuria since the Russo-Japanese War of 1905. When Jiang's march north and the rise of Chinese nationalism threatened the Japanese position, field-grade officers of Japan's forces engineered a military coup in 1931, and in 1932 established a puppet state and proclaimed the independence of Manchuria. In the years that followed, Japanese army units moved south as far as the Great Wall. Chinese national sentiment demanded that Jiang resist, but Jiang, well aware of the disparity between his armies and those of Japan, decided that the internal unification of China must take precedence over war against a foreign power. On a visit to Xian in 1936, Jiang was captured by a northern warlord and held prisoner until he agreed to join with the CCP in a united front against Japan. The following year, however, a full-scale war with Japan broke out, and China's situation again changed.

War and Revolution (1937–1949)

In 1937, the GMD controlled most of China and was recognized nationally and internationally as its government, whereas the CCP survivors of the Long March had just begun to rebuild their strength in arid Shaanxi, an area too remote for Jiang's army to penetrate. But by 1949, CCP forces had conquered China, including border areas never under GMD rule, and Jiang and the GMD were forced to flee to Taiwan. What had happened?

The war with Japan was the key event. It began in July 1937 with an unplanned clash at Beijing and then spread. Battlefield victories soon convinced the Japanese military leaders to abandon negotiations for a truce in favor of a knockout blow. Beijing and Tianjin fell within a month, Shanghai was attacked in August, and Nanjing fell in December. During the following year, the Japanese took Guangzhou and Wuhan and set up puppet regimes in Beijing and Nanjing. In 1940, frustrated by trying to work with Jiang, a rival party leader and many of his associates joined the Japanese puppet government. Japan proclaimed its "New Order in East Asia," which was to replace the system of unequal treaties. It expected Jiang to recognize his situation as hopeless and submit. Instead, in 1938 Jiang relocated his capital in Chongqing, far to the west behind the gorges of the Yangzi. He was joined by thousands of Chinese, students and professors and factory managers and workers, who moved from occupied China to free China.

Modern China

Close of Manchu Rule

1839–1842	Opium War
	Close of Manchu rule
1850–1873	Taiping and other rebellions
1870s–1880s	Self-strengthening movement
1894–1895	Sino-Japanese War
1898	One hundred days of reform
1898–1900	Boxer Rebellion
1912–1912	Republican revolution overthrows Qing dynasty

Warlordism

1912–1916	Yuan Shikai, president of Republic of China
1916–1928	Warlord era
1919	May Fourth Movement

Nationalist China

1924	Founding of Huangpu Academy
1926–1928	March north and GMD reunification of China
1928–1937	Nanjing decade
1934–1935	Chinese Communists' Long March to Yan'an
1937–1945	War with Japan
1945–1949	Civil war followed by the establishment of the People's Republic of China

Jiang's stubborn resistance to the Japanese won admiration from all sides. But the area occupied by the Japanese included just those eastern cities, railways, and densely populated Yangzi valley territories that had constituted the GMD base. The withdrawal to Chongqing cut the GMD off from most of the Chinese population, programs for modernization ended, and the GMD's former tax revenues were lost. Inflation increased geometrically, reducing the real income of officials, teachers, and soldiers alike. By the end of World War II and during the early postwar years, salaries were paid in large packages of almost worthless money, which was immediately spent on food or goods possessing real value. Inflation led to demoralization and exacerbated the already widespread corruption.

The United States sent advisers and military equipment to strengthen Jiang's forces after the start of the war in the Pacific (see Map 5–3). The advisers, however, were frustrated by Jiang, who wanted not to fight the Japanese but to husband his forces for

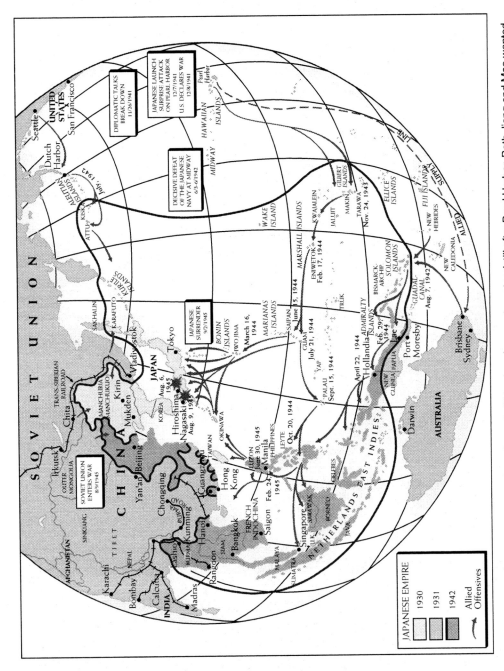

Map 5–3 **The war in the Pacific.** Japan's war in China largely came to a standstill after Pearl Harbor. Both Jiang and Mao wanted to save their troops for the civil war that they knew would follow the defeat of Japan. Large numbers of Japanese troops were required to maintain the occupied area of China. Most of the fighting in World War II, however, occurred in the Pacific campaigns.

the anticipated postwar confrontation with the Communists. Within his army, a gap divided officers and men. Conditions in camps were primitive, food poor, and medical supplies inadequate. The young saw conscription almost as a sentence of death. Jiang's unwillingness to commit his troops against the Japanese also meant that the surge of anti-Japanese patriotism was not converted to popular support for the GMD.

For the Communists, the Japanese occupation was an opportunity. Headquartered at Yan'an, they consolidated their base in Shaanxi province. They began campaigns to promote literacy and production drives to promote self-sufficiency. Soldiers farmed so as not to burden the peasants. The CCP abandoned its earlier policy of expropriating lands in favor of reductions in rents and interest. (This change led to the widespread American view that the CCP were not Communists but agrarian reformers, despite their protests to the contrary.) Party members took only those provincial and county offices needed to ensure their control and shared the rest with the GMD and other parties. They expanded village councils to include tenants and other previously excluded strata. But while compromising with other political and social groups, they strengthened their party internally.

Party membership expanded from 40,000 in 1937 to 1.2 million in 1945. Schools were established in Yan'an to train party cadres. Even as the party expanded, orthodoxy was maintained by a rectification campaign begun in 1942. Those tainted by liberalism, individualism, or other impure tendencies were criticized and made to confess their failings and repent at public meetings. Mao's thought was supreme. To the Chinese at large, Mao represented himself as the successor to Sun Zhongshan, but within the Communist Party, he presented himself as a theoretician in the line of Marx (1818–1883), Engels (1820–1895), Lenin (1870–1924), and Stalin (1879–1953).

Whereas the GMD ruled through officials and often in cooperation with local landlords, the Communists learned to operate at the grassroots level. They infiltrated Japanese-controlled areas and also penetrated some GMD organizations and military units. CCP armies were built up from 90,000 in 1937 to 900,000 in 1945. These armies were supplemented by a rural people's militia and by guerrilla forces in nineteen mountainous "base areas." By most accounts, the Yan'an leadership and its party, army, and mass organizations possessed a cohesion, determination, and high morale that were conspicuously lacking in Chongqing.

But the strength of the Chinese Communists as of 1945 should not be overstated. Most Chinese villagers were influenced by neither the CCP nor the GMD, and although intellectuals in free China had become disaffected with the GMD, most did not positively support the CCP. When the war in the Pacific ended in 1945, China's fate was unclear. The Soviet Union allowed CCP cadres to enter Manchuria, which it had seized during the last few days of the war, and blocked the entry of GMD troops until the following year. But even the Soviet Union recognized the GMD as the government of China and expected it to win the postwar struggle. The Allies directed Japanese armies to surrender to the GMD forces in 1945. The United States flew Jiang's troops from Chongqing to key eastern cities. His armies were by then three times the size of the Communists' and far better equipped.

MAO ON THE PEASANT MOVEMENT IN HUNAN

The following excerpts are from Mao Zedong's 1927 "Report on an Investigation of the Peasant Movement in Hunan." While the more orthodox, Moscow-trained leaders of the Chinese Communist Party still put their trust in the urban proletariat, Mao emphasized the revolutionary potential of the peasantry.

Does Mao's report seem overly optimistic or does it accurately foretell what would happen during the 1930s and 1940s? What does it say of Mao's belief in the Marxist theory of class struggle?

The present upsurge of the peasant movement is a colossal event. In a very short time, in China's central, southern and northern provinces, several hundred million peasants will rise like a mighty storm, like a hurricane, a force so swift and violent that no power, however great, will be able to hold it back. They will smash all the trammels that bind them and rush forward along the road to liberation. They will sweep all the imperialists, warlords, corrupt officials, local tyrants and evil gentry into their graves. Every revolutionary party and every revolutionary comrade will be put to the test, to be accepted or rejected as they decide. There are three alternatives. To march at their head and

lead them? To trail behind them, gesticulating and criticizing? Or to stand in their way and oppose them? Every Chinese is free to choose, but events will force you to make the choice quickly. . . .

The peasants are clear-sighted. Who is bad and who is not, who is the worst and who is not quite so vicious, who deserves severe punishment and who deserves to be left off lightly—the peasants keep clear accounts, and very seldom has the punishment exceeded the crime. . . . A revolution is not a dinner party, or writing an essay, or painting a picture, or doing embroidery; it cannot be so refined, so leisurely and gentle, so temperate, kind, courteous, restrained and magnanimous. A revolution is an insurrection, an act of violence by which one class overthrows another. A rural revolution is a revolution by which the peasantry overthrows the power of the feudal landlord class. Without using the greatest force, the peasants cannot possibly overthrow the deep-rooted authority of the landlords which has lasted for thousands of years. The rural areas need a mighty revolutionary upsurge, for it alone can rouse the people in their millions to become a powerful force. . . .

Selected Readings from the Works of Mao Tse-tung, Beijing: Foreign Languages Press, 1967, pp. 20–21, 25.

A civil war broke out early in 1946. Both sides recognized that the earlier united front had been a sham. Efforts by U.S. General George Marshall (1880–1959) to mediate were futile. Until the summer of 1947, GMD armies were victorious—even capturing the CCP stronghold of Yan'an. But the tide turned in July as CCP armies went on the offensive in north China. They captured American military equipment abandoned by the GMD forces, and by October 1948, the GMD forces had been driven from Manchuria. In January of 1949, Beijing and Tianjin fell. By late spring, CCP armies had crossed the Yangzi, taking Nanjing and Shanghai. A few months later, all of China was in Communist hands. Many Chinese fled with Jiang to Taiwan or escaped to Hong Kong; they included not only GMD officials and generals but entrepreneurs and academics as well. Not a few subsequently made their way to the United States.

In China, apprehension was mixed with anticipation. The disciplined, well-behaved soldiers of the "People's Liberation Army" were certainly a contrast to those of the GMD. As villages were liberated, lands were taken from landlords and given to the landless. In the cities, crowds gave every indication of welcoming the CCP troops as liberators. The feeling was widespread that the future of China was once again in the hands of the Chinese.

MODERN CHINA IN HISTORICAL PERSPECTIVE

From the late nineteenth century, most non-Western countries wanted to be modern. They coveted the military power and the material well-being that science and industry had produced in the West. They did not, however, wish to become Western, for that would have negated their own cultural identity. Still, they found it difficult to adopt Western technology without also borrowing a broad range of Western values and ideas. Nor was it easy to distinguish between what was truly modern and what was merely recent-Western.

The process of modernization may be thought of in terms of three stages: The first is the development of *preconditions*, of a base or platform within a country's late traditional culture from which it can reach out for the ideas and institutions of the West. The second is *Westernization*, the actual borrowing, and the third is *assimilation*, the fusion of what has been borrowed with indigenous values and institutions.

In terms of preconditions, Chinese "tradition" was quite advanced. Already in place was a high level of literacy, a stress on education as the means of getting ahead, an ethic emphasizing frugality and saving, a family system well adapted to small enterprises, a vigorous market economy, and many of the cultural ingredients for a modern nationalism. But China had liabilities as well. Chinese merchants did not participate in politics; they were not a bourgeoisie with representative bodies. Local Chinese society furnished no stable base for would be nation-builders—as evidenced by rebellions during the nineteenth century and local disorders thereafter. Sun Zhongshan compared it to "a sheet of loose sand." An examination elite ran the government and viewed foreigners as barbarians. The ingrained assumption of "middle kingdom" superiority is clearly reflected in Commissioner Lin's letter to Queen Victoria praising British kings for their "politeness and submissiveness." Consequently, when it came to Westernization, the government by Confucian literati that had long been China's outstanding asset became its chief liability. Until the end of the dynasty, the best that intellectuals could devise were limited reformulations of Confucianism. Large-scale Westernization and assimilation had to wait seventy years after the Opium War for the dynasty to collapse.

Then, in the maelstrom of the May Fourth Movement, intellectual changes occurred at a furious pace in China's main cities. But new doctrines alone could not provide a stable polity. Nationalism emerged as the common denominator of most Chinese thought. Sun Zhongshan appealed to it. The Nationalists (or GMD) drew on it at the Huangpu Academy, during the march north, and in founding the Nanjing government. But other groups could also appeal to it. The CCP won out in 1949.

Mao Zedong (1893–1976) at his cave headquarters in Shaanxi province during World War II. He wears a padded winter jacket and writes with a Chinese brush. On his desk are the *Collected Works* of Lu Hsun.
[Hulton Archive/Getty Images]

It is beguiling to view the CCP cadres as a new class of literati operating the machinery of a monolithic, centralized state, with the teachings of Marx and Lenin replacing those of Confucius, and local party cadres replacing the Confucian gentry. But this interpretation is too simple. Communism stressed science, materialism, class conflict, and the establishment of an ideal social order in the future. It broke with the Confucian emphasis on metaphysics, social harmony, and a golden age in the distant past.

Communism itself was modified as it was assimilated within China. Marx had predicted that socialist revolutions would break out in advanced economies where the contradictions of capitalism were sharpest. Lenin had shifted the emphasis from spontaneous revolutions by workers to the small but disciplined revolutionary party, the vanguard of the proletariat. He thereby changed Communism into what it has been ever since: a movement capable of seizing power only in backward nations. At the level of doctrine, Mao Zedong modified Lenin's ideas only slightly—by theorizing that "progressive" peasants were a part of the proletariat. But he went beyond this theory in practice, virtually ignoring city workers while relying on China's villages for recruits for his armies, who were then indoctrinated using Leninist techniques. Despite its low level of technology, the Peoples' Liberation Army, the Communist equivalent of a "citizen's army," was formidable in the field. It was also modern in the sense that it did not loot and despoil the areas it occupied.

But the organizational techniques that were so effective in creating a party and army would prove less so for economic development. It soon became clear that mass mobilization was no substitute for individual incentives.

REVIEW QUESTIONS

1. Which had the greater impact on China, the Opium War or the Taiping Rebellion? By what yardstick can this be measured?

2. How did the Qing (or Manchu) dynasty recover from the Taiping Rebellion? In what ways was the recovery inadequate to prevent the overthrow of the dynasty in 1912?

3. Did the May Fourth Movement prepare the way for the Nationalist revolution? For the Communist revolution? Or was it incidental to both?

4. In thinking about the rise of the Nationalists to power, how much weight do you give to ideas and how much to political and military organization? Was the balance different in the Communist rise to power?

SUGGESTED READINGS

COBLE, P. M. *Chinese Capitalists in Japan's New Order: The Occupied Lower Yangzi, 1937–1945* (2003).

COBLE, P. M. *The Shanghai Capitalists and the Nationalist Government, 1927–1937* (1986).

EASTMAN, L. E. *Seeds of Destruction: Nationalist China in War and Revolution, 1937–1949* (1984).

ELVIN, M. AND SKINNER, G. W. *The Chinese City Between Two Worlds* (1974). A study of the late Qing and the Republican eras.

ESHERICK, J. W. *The Cultural Revolution as History* (2006).

ESHERICK, J. W. *The Origins of the Boxer Rebellion* (1987).

ETO, S. *China's Republican Revolution* (1984).

FAIRBANK, J. K. AND GOLDMAN, M. *China: A New History* (1998). A survey of the entire sweep of Chinese history that is especially strong on the modern period. (Fairbank, the doyen of modern Chinese historical studies in the West, completed reading the page proofs the day before he died.)

FAIRBANK, J. K. AND TWITCHETT, D., EDS. *The Cambridge History of China.* Volumes 10 and 11 (1978, 1980) treat the late Qing dynasty, 1800–1911; volumes 12 and 13 (1983, 1986) treat Republican China, 1912–1949. Like the premodern volumes in the same series, the volumes on modern China represent a survey of what is known; each volume contains a comprehensive bibliography.

FITZGERALD, J. *Awakening China: Politics, Culture, and Class in the Nationalist Revolution* (1996)

HAO, C. *Chinese Intellectuals in Crisis: Search for Order and Meaning, 1890–1911* (1987).

KIRBY, W. *State and Economy in Republican China* (2001).

KUHN, P. A. *Origins of the Modern Chinese State* (2002).

KUHN, P. A., *Rebellion and Its Enemies in Late Imperial China; Militarization and Social Structure, 1796–1864* (1980). A study of how Confucian gentry saved the Manchu dynasty after the Taiping Rebellion.

LEVENSON, J. *Liang Ch'i-ch'ao and the Mind of Modern China* (1953). A classic study of a major Chinese reformer and thinker.

LU HSUN, *Selected Works* (1960). Novels, stories, and other writings by modern China's greatest writer.

LU HSUN, *Diary of a Madman and Other Stories* (1990).

MacFarquhar, R. *Mao's Last Revolution* (2006).

MacFarquhar, R. *The Politics of China: The Eras of Mao and Deng* (1997).

Schiffrin, H. Z. *Sun Yat-sen:, Reluctant Revolutionary* (1980). A biography.

Schoppa, R. K. *Revolution and its Past: Identities and Change in Modern Chinese History* (2006).

Schwartz, B. I. *In Search of Wealth and Power: Yen Fu and the West* (1964). An insightful study of a late-nineteenth-century thinker who introduced Western ideas into China.

Schwartz, B. I. *Chinese Communism and the Rise of Mao* (1951). A classic study of Mao, his thought, and the Chinese Communist Party before 1949.

Spence, J. D. *The Gate of Heavenly Peace: The Chinese and Their Revolution, 1895–1980* (1981). Historical reflections on twentieth-century China.

Szonyi, M. *Practicing Kinship: Lineage and Descent in Late Imperial China* (2002).

Teng, S. Y. and Fairbank, J. K. *China's Response to the West* (1954). Translations from Chinese thinkers and political figures, with commentaries.

White, T. H. and Jacoby, A. *Thunder Out of China* (1946). A view of China during World War II by two who were there.

China, the Recent Decades

Student activists construct a "Goddess of Democracy and Freedom," taking the Statue of Liberty as their model. The goddess was in place in Tiananmen Square shortly before tanks drove students from the Square in June 1989.
[Reuters/Ed Nachtrieb/Reuters Limited]

China's history since the rise to power of the Communist state in 1949 divides neatly into two periods: the China of Mao and China after Mao. During the later years of the first period, which lasted until 1976, China was wracked by successive political convulsions. Mao Zedong wanted "revolution" to continue, even under his own government. Millions died as a result. Moreover, in spite of gaining undisputed political authority over an area comparable to that of the Qing Empire—an area that included the non-Chinese peoples of Tibet, Central Asia, Inner Mongolia, and Manchuria—the government was unable to tap effectively the energies and talents of its people. To be sure, the problems faced by the government were immense but there were accomplishments. Still, the contrast between the low productivity of the Chinese in China and the remarkable productivity of the same people in Hong Kong and Taiwan was startling.

Map 6–1   China in contemporary Asia.

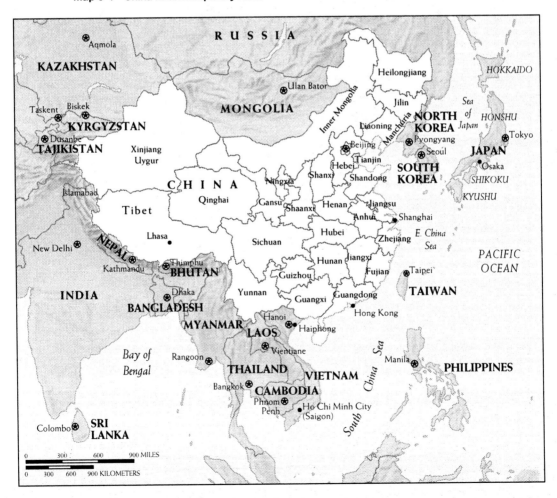

A marked reversal of earlier "socialist" policies occurred after Mao's death in 1976. This period might be called the China of Deng Xiaoping (1904–1997) and his successors. Deng maintained the dictatorship of the Communist Party, but also introduced many features of a market economy. The result was explosive growth and an export boom, first in southeastern coastal areas, where long-suppressed entrepreneurial abilities surfaced, and then throughout the country. Standards of living rose and the society became freer—though criticism of the government was not permitted and political dissidents were jailed. China was still a dictatorship, but under Deng and his successors it was no longer totalitarian.

MAO'S CHINA

Consolidation

Victory over the forces of Jiang Jieshi (Chiang Kai-shek) had come suddenly. The People's Republic of China was proclaimed in October 1949. Even after that, Chinese armies continued to push outward, conquering vast areas with non-Chinese populations. Tibet, for example, was seized in 1950. Once subdued, the areas inhabited by Tibetans, Uighur Turks, Mongols, and other minorities were designated "autonomous regions." Their governments were staffed mainly by members of the indigenous population but were tightly controlled by Chinese. Their lands were occupied by Chinese army units and over time were settled by a sufficient number of Chinese immigrants to change their ethnic complexion. Also in 1950, Chinese troops entered the Korean War to preserve Communist North Korea as a buffer state, and fought South Korean, American, and other UN troops to a standstill in mid-peninsula.

The Communists, who had gained power by war, found themselves the rulers of a country devastated and poor. The people were apprehensive. The Communist Party was small, with fewer than three million members in 1949. (By 1961, the figure would rise to seventeen million.) The new government proceeded cautiously. In central and south China, though some officials appointed by the Nationalist government were temporarily left in place, the Communist Party gripped all levers of power. Liberals and non-Marxist scholars continued for a time to teach in universities, though attacks during the 1957 anti-rightist campaign destroyed the effectiveness of many. Two-thirds of the large industries were already owned by the state, but for a time, the remaining one-third and small businesses were left in private hands. Under these relatively moderate policies, the economy began to recover. These early years were sometimes called the era of "New Democracy."

The Soviet Model

In 1950, the Sino-Soviet Alliance was formed. Thereafter, in a piecemeal fashion, the Soviet model was adopted for the government, army, economy, and schools. Mao was chairman of the Chinese Communist Party and the head of state. He ruled through the

Standing Committee of the Political Bureau (the Politburo) of the party's Central Committee. Below the Politburo were regional, provincial, and district committees, with party cells in every town, factory, school, and government office. Party members were ordered to energize and enforce the local implementation of party policies. The party also tightly controlled the military and public security forces. The driving ideology behind the adoption of this Soviet model was the Leninism-Stalinism of Mao and other party leaders.

China's first five-year plan was launched in 1953. The Soviet Union sent financial aid, engineers, and planners. Industries in Manchuria and the former treaty ports were integrated with those in the rest of China. Huge numbers of workers were mobilized to build new bridges, dams, roads, and railways. Better transport linked what had formerly been isolated regional economies. Private businesses were nationalized and brought under bureaucratic control.

Rural society underwent two fundamental changes: land redistribution and collectivization. In the early 1950s, teams of party cadres visited villages and held

Trial of a landlord. The judges, seated at tables with their hats beneath, are former tenants and Communist Party cadres. The accused, bound and guarded by soldiers, is a former landlord or village head. During the land reform of the early 1950s, the sentence was often death.

meetings at which landlords and rich peasants were denounced and made to confess their crimes. Some were rehabilitated, others were sent to labor camps, and hundreds of thousands—some scholars estimate several million—were executed. Their holdings were redistributed to the landless. Local responsibilities once borne by landlord gentry were shifted to peasant associations dominated by former tenant farmers, the most politically reliable of whom became local party cadres. Then, two years later, in 1955 and 1956, before the new landowners had time to put down roots and entrench themselves, all lands were collectivized. The timing was important: In the Soviet Union, collectivization had come six years after redistribution and was resisted by the *kulaks*, who had by then fully established their ownership of the land.

The Great Leap Forward

During the early 1950s, intellectuals and universities were singled out as a target for thought reform. The Chinese slang term was *brainwashing*. This involved study and indoctrination in Marxism, group pressure to produce an atmosphere of insecurity and fear, followed up by confession, repentance, and reacceptance by society. The thought reform was intended to strengthen party control. But beyond this was the optimistic belief that the inculcation of correct moral doctrines could mobilize human energies on behalf of the state—a belief that perhaps had Confucian roots. In 1956, Mao felt that intellectuals had been adequately indoctrinated, and concerned lest creativity be

---

MAO'S VIEW OF CHINA ON THE EVE OF THE GREAT LEAP FORWARD

The following passage is from "Introducing a Cooperative," which Mao wrote in 1958. It was written just as he broke with the Soviet model of five-year plans in favor of a "mass mobilization" of the energies of the Chinese people.

What was the basis of the optimism reflected in this passage? Why did the Great Leap Forward fail? Was Mao's view of the Chinese people as being "blank" at fault? How could the masses be both "inspired" and "blank"?

The political consciousness of the broad masses is rising rapidly. . . .

Judging from this, it will probably take less time than previously estimated for our industry and agriculture to catch up with that of the capitalist powers. In addition to the leadership of the Party, a decisive factor is our population of 600 million. More people mean a greater ferment of ideas, more enthusiasm and more energy. Never before have the masses of the people been so inspired, so militant and so daring as at present. . . .

Apart from their other characteristics, the outstanding thing about China's 600 million people is that they are "poor and blank." This may seem a bad thing, but in reality it is a good thing. Poverty gives rise to the desire for change, the desire for action and the desire for revolution. On a blank sheet of paper free from any mark, the freshest and most beautiful characters can be written, the freshest and most beautiful pictures can be painted. . . .

Selected Readings from the Works of Mao Tse-tung, Beijing: Foreign Languages Press, 1967, p. 403.

stifled, he said in a speech, "Let the hundred flowers bloom"—a reference to the lively discourse among the many schools of philosophy in ancient Zhou China. To his surprise, intellectuals responded with a torrent of criticism that did not spare the Communist Party. Mao thereupon reversed his position, mounted an anti-rightist campaign, and sent almost half a million writers and intellectuals to labor camps.

By the late 1950s, Mao had become disappointed with the results of collectivization and the first five-year-plan. In 1958 he abandoned a second plan (and the Soviet model) in favor of a mass mobilization to unleash the productive energies of the people. He called it the Great Leap Forward. One slogan was: "Hard work for a few years and happiness for a thousand." Campaigns were organized to accomplish vast projects, iron smelters were built in "backyards," instant industries were the order of the day. In the countryside, village-based collectives gave way to communes of 30,000 persons or more. The results were disastrous. Homemade iron was unusable, instant industries failed, and agricultural production plummeted. Scholars estimate that between 1958 and 1962 as many as twenty to thirty million Chinese starved to death. To reverse the damage, communes were broken into production brigades in 1959, and two years later these were further broken into production teams of dozens of households. Even these compromises could not overcome the ills of low incentives and collective responsibility; throughout the 1970s, agricultural production barely matched population growth.

It was also during the late 1950s that Sino-Soviet relations deteriorated. Disputes arose over borders. China was dissatisfied with the level of Soviet aid and embarrassed by the Soviet debunking of Stalin's cult of personality, since in China, Mao was still venerated as the "great helmsman." China felt that Soviet revisionism had betrayed the principles of Marx, Lenin, and Stalin. For its part, the Soviet Union condemned China's Great Leap Forward as "leftist fanaticism" and resented Mao's view of himself, after Stalin's death in 1953, as the foremost theoretician and exponent of world Communism. In 1960, the Soviet Union halted its economic aid and withdrew its engineers from China, and by 1963, the split was visible to the outside world. Each country deployed about a million troops along their common border. Had relations between the two Communist giants been amicable, these troops, deployed elsewhere, might have changed the history of Southeast Asia and Eastern Europe. The Sino-Soviet split was arguably the single most important development in postwar international politics.

The years between 1960 and 1965 saw conflicting trends. The utter failure of the Great Leap Forward led some Chinese leaders to turn away from Mao's reckless radicalism toward more moderate policies. Mao kept his position as the head of the party but was forced to give up his post as head of state to another veteran Communist official. Yet even as the government moved toward more realistic goals and stable bureaucratic management, General Lin Biao (1908–1971) reestablished within the army the party committees and procedures for ideological indoctrination that had lapsed after the failure of the Great Leap Forward. A new mass movement also began to transform education.

The Great Proletarian Cultural Revolution (1965–1976)

In 1965, Mao reemerged to dominate Chinese politics. Mao the revolutionary had never been able to make the transition to Mao the ruler of an established state. When he looked at the Chinese Communist Party and the government bureaucracy, he saw a new privileged elite; when he looked at younger Chinese, he saw a generation with no experience of revolution. Mao feared that the Chinese revolution—his revolution— would end up as a Soviet-style bureaucratic Communism run for the benefit of officials and not for the people; the beginnings of such a system had already appeared. He called for a new revolution to create a truly egalitarian culture.

Performance during Cultural Revolution. Members of the Xiangyang Commune in Jiangsu province take part in the campaign to "Criticize Lin Biao and Confucius," one of the last large "campaigns" dictated by members of Chinese government in charge of the Cultural Revolution. Here, the commune's amateur art troupe performs a ballad criticizing Confucius. The campaign began after the death of Lin Biao, who, though for a time was Mao Zedong's chosen successor, was accused of attempting to seize power.

Obtaining army support, Mao urged students and teenaged youth to form bands of Red Guards. In the early feverish phase of the Cultural Revolution, the guards invoked Mao's sayings, which were contained in the "Little Red Book," and revered almost as holy scripture. Mass rallies were held. Several were attended by a million or more, who then made "long marches" back to their home provinces to carry out Mao's program. Universities were shut down as student factions fought. Teachers were beaten, imprisoned, and subjected to such extremes of humiliation that many committed suicide. Books and artworks were destroyed in the campaign against the "four olds." Stone Buddhist sculptures that dated to the Song dynasty were smashed or defaced. Things foreign also came under attack. Homes were ransacked for foreign books, and Chinese who had studied abroad were persecuted. Even borrowing foreign technology was denigrated as "sniffing after foreigners' farts and calling them sweet." Red Guards attacked local party headquarters and government offices, and beat to death persons viewed as reactionaries, including some party cadres. High party officials were purged. Revolutionary committees replaced the crippled apparatus of Communist Party government. Chinese look back at these events as a species of mass hysteria and even today find them difficult to comprehend.

Mao eventually tired of the violence and near anarchy. In 1968 and 1969, he called in the army to take over the revolutionary committees. In 1969, a new Central Committee, composed largely of military men, was established, and General Lin Biao was named as Mao's successor. Violence came to an end as millions of students and intellectuals were sent to the countryside to work on farms. In 1970 and 1971, the revolutionary committees were reconstituted as party committees. Worsening relations with the Soviet Union also made China's leaders desire greater stability at home. In 1969, a pitched battle had broken out between Chinese and Russian troops over an island in the Ussuri River. After this incident, the Chinese built bomb shelters in their main cities. It was just at this time that President Nixon began to withdraw U.S. troops from Vietnam. When he proposed a renewal of ties, China quickly responded. Nixon visited Peking in 1972, opening a new era of diplomatic relations. Pundits debated: was America playing the "China card" or was China playing the "America card?"

The second phase of the Cultural Revolution, between 1969 and 1976, was moderate only in comparison with what had gone before. On farms and in factories, ideology continued to be seen as an adequate substitute for economic incentives. Universities reopened, but students were admitted by class background, not by examination. In 1971, Lin Biao, Mao's heir, was purged. According to the official account of his death, Lin tried to kill Mao and seize the government, but when the coup failed, he died in a plane crash while attempting to escape to the Soviet Union. After Lin's death, power was balanced between the so-called Gang of Four, which included Mao's wife and was abetted by the aging Mao, and other senior officials. Class struggle was revived, and an official campaign was launched attacking the rightist "political swindlers" Lin Biao and Confucius.

FROM DENG XIAOPING TO THE PRESENT

Political Developments

Mao's death in 1976 brought immediate change. Within four weeks, the Gang of Four and their radical supporters had been arrested. The role of the army was crucial. By the close of 1978, Deng Xiaoping (1904–1997) had emerged as the dominant figure in Chinese politics.

As a young man, Deng had been a student-worker for five years in France, where he became a member of the Chinese Communist Party; he was also a veteran of the Long March. Purged once during the 1930s and twice during the Cultural Revolution

DENG ON THE CULTURAL REVOLUTION

Deng Xiaoping recognized Mao's "immortal service" to the people of China; he wrote that Mao's "contributions are primary and his mistakes secondary." But he also wrote, "we cannot discuss the defects in our system of Party and state leadership without touching upon Comrade Mao Zedong's mistakes in his later years." Deng's approach was more practical than ideological; he once said that if a cat catches mice, what difference does it make whether it is black or white. His criticisms of the Cultural Revolution in "On the Reform of the System of Party and State Leadership" (1980) provided a basis for extensive changes in many spheres of life in China.

Do the problems of "bureaucracy" in China sound familiar? Or should we say that in China's highly centralized Communist state, these problems were magnified in a way that is difficult for us to comprehend? How do these passages relate to policy changes in China during the Deng era?

Bureaucracy remains a major and widespread problem in the political life of our Party and state. Its harmful manifestations include the following: standing high above the masses; abusing power; divorcing oneself from reality and the masses; spending a lot of time and effort to put up an impressive front; indulging in empty talk;

sticking to a rigid way of thinking; being hidebound by convention; overstaffing administrative organs; being dilatory, inefficient and irresponsible; failing to keep one's word; circulating documents endlessly without solving problems; shifting responsibility to others; and even assuming the airs of a mandarin, reprimanding other people at every turn, vindictively attacking others, suppressing democracy, deceiving superiors and subordinates, being arbitrary and despotic, practising favouritism, offering bribes, participating in corrupt practices in violation of the law, and so on. Such things have reached intolerable dimensions both in our domestic affairs and in our contacts with other countries.

During the "Cultural Revolution," when someone got to the top, even his dogs and chickens got there too; likewise, when someone got into trouble, even his distant relatives were dragged down with him. This situation became very serious. Even now, the abominable practice of appointing people through favouritism and factionalism continues unchecked in some regions, departments and units. There are quite a few instances where cadres abuse their power so as to enable their friends and relations to move to the cities or to obtain jobs or promotions. It is thus clear that the residual influences of clannishness must not be underestimated.

Selected Works of Deng Xiaoping, Beijing: Foreign Languages Press, 1984, pp. 317, 318.

for "rightist tendencies," he was once paraded around Beijing wearing a dunce cap, Deng was determined that such things not happen again, He ousted his enemies, rehabilitated those purged during the Cultural Revolution, and put his supporters in power. He advocated "socialism with Chinese characteristics," by which he meant a market economy and Chinese Communist Party rule. Fearing that elections would lead to a non-Communist government, he opposed "bourgeois liberalism," but nevertheless favored opening China to the world; for Deng, it was important to "seek truth from facts."

Portraits of Mao were removed from most public places in August 1980. After the lunacy of the Cultural Revolution, the establishment of a normal Communist Party dictatorship came as a welcome relief. The people began to enjoy a measure of security and the prospect of better lives. There persisted, however, a tension between the ruling party's determination to maintain its grip on power and its desire to obtain the benefits of a positive economic policy and a mild relaxation of restraints. This tension was most visible in China's intellectual life.

Deng's repudiation of the Cultural Revolution led to an outpouring of stories, plays, and reports. In Xu Hui's *Nightmare*, a mother whose son was killed during the Cultural Revolution asks, "Why? Why? Can anyone tell me why?" Liu Binyan wrote

Chinese Communist leader Deng Xiaoping
(1904–1997).
[Getty Images Inc.—Hulton Archive Photos]

of a corrupt officialdom that had "degenerated into parasitical insects that fed off the people's productivity and the socialist system." But criticism of the government was not allowed. Writers were regularly enjoined to be "led by the Communist Party and guided by Marx-Leninism." When a writer in 1983 overstepped the invisible line separating what was permissible from what was not, a short campaign was launched against "spiritual pollution." It was followed in 1985 and 1987 by other campaigns against "capitalist thinking" and "bourgeois democracy."

Universities returned to normal in 1977. Entrance examinations were reinstituted, purged teachers were allowed to return to their classrooms, and scientists and scholars were sent to study in Japan and the West. Students still spent one afternoon a week studying party directives or the *Selected Works of Deng Xiaoping*, but the new openness within China and growing contacts with the wider world proved far more influential. Students became aware for the first time of the prosperity achieved by Japan, Taiwan, and Hong Kong. They began to demand still greater freedoms and even political democracy for themselves. During the late 1980s, the ferment that marked eastern Europe and the Soviet Union under Gorbachev also appeared in China—almost as if a new virus had entered the Communist world.

Student demands came to a head in April and May of 1989, when hundreds of thousands of students, workers, and people from all walks of life demonstrated for democracy in Tiananmen Square in Beijing and in dozens of other cities. Hunger strikes were held. Students published prodemocracy newspapers. Banners proclaimed slogans, such as "Give us freedom or give us death." A twenty-seven-foot, polystyrene-and-plaster Goddess of Democracy and Freedom was erected in the Square. Initially, government leaders could not agree on a response, but the hard-line faction led by the eighty-five-year-old Deng won out and, in early June, sent in tanks and troops. Hundreds were killed, and student leaders who did not escape abroad were jailed.

The suppression of the democracy movement at Tiananmen defined the political balance in China for the era that followed: No challenge to Communist Party rule was tolerated, but considerable freedom was allowed in most areas of life, even intellectual life.

Since Mao's death in 1976, Chinese policies have been fairly consistent. Deng established the baselines. Deng stepped down in 1992 (five years before he died) and was followed by Jiang Zemin, who had been born a generation later in 1926. Jiang propounded the "Three Representations": the Communist Party, he argued, must represent "the most advanced economic forces in society, the most advanced elements of culture, and the interests of the people." One newspaper focused on the first representation and announced, not wholly inaccurately, "China's Communists Recruit Capitalists." A Communist Party chief in Guangzhou declared publicly that the new policy would have been inconceivable in times past and had "a profound historical significance."

In 2002, after ten years in office, Jiang retired and Hu Jintao, born in 1944, became president of China. The transition was peaceful and according to law. Though

President Obama meets with President Hu Jintao during the G20 summit in Pittsburgh on September 25, 2009.
[Jim Watson/AFP/Getty Images]

of a new generation, to date, Hu's policies differ only slightly from those of Deng and Jiang. He carefully controls the media. But he has also invited leading economists and other scholars to discuss China's problems with government leaders, and the results of the meetings have been made public. Such openness conceivably may lead to greater transparency in policy formation—as long as no threats emerge to challenge the Communist Party's monopoly of power.

Economic Growth

Deng, on taking power in 1978, repudiated the Maoist command economy that had kept China poor. "To be rich is glorious," he said in a speech (or is said to have said), and he acknowledged that, "some must get rich first." The Chinese economy did not suddenly become a market economy. Five-year plans continued. The role of the state continued to be larger than in Japan, South Korea, and Taiwan—nations in which the state role was greater than in most Western countries. Still, in the years after 1978, the results of Deng's policies demonstrated the superiority of market incentives to central planning. Other leaders flocked to his banner. In 1985, Hu Yaobang, the General Secretary of the CCP, stated that China "had wasted twenty years" on "radical leftist nonsense."

THE CHINESE ECONOMY IN TRANSITION

In this document, Executive Vice-Premier for the Economy Zhu Rongji discusses key issues facing the Chinese economy at the end of 1995.

What does Mr. Zhu mean by "a socialist market economy"?

Pace of Reform

"At the 14th national congress of the Chinese communist party [October 1992], we decided to establish a socialist market economy. The pace of progress has generally been the same as we envisaged. Originally, we had anticipated more risk—but, as it turned out, we have seen less risk and more success."

State Enterprise Reform

"In 1994 we carried out extensive reform measures in accordance with the market economic principles. So far, all these are concentrated in macro economic areas, meaning reforms in fiscal, banking, taxation, foreign trade, foreign exchange and investment sectors. We have not had time to focus on the micro aspects of the economy, and one of the key issues of the micro reforms is the state enterprises. Next year, we will spend more time and energy on the reform of the state enterprises."

Regional Disparities

"The regional economic gap has always been a matter of concern to us, but this problem is caused by history. I am afraid in the short term the gap will not be narrowed—on the contrary, the gap might widen. At present, the focus in our work is to bring about rapid development in China's mid-west. However, we should not seek this objective at the expense of growth in the coastal areas."

Tariff Reduction

"The current tariff level of China is very high. . . . The average tariff level for developing countries is about 15 per cent, but now for China the level is 35 per cent. To be consistent with international practice, we will have to reduce tariffs to at least the average level of developing countries, 15 per cent, that is a must."

Reprinted by permission from the *Financial Times' Survey of China,* 20 November 1995. The Financial Times Ltd., London.

The next three decades saw amazing growth. Consider China's gross domestic product (GDP) as presented in the two columns below.

1980	$301 BILLION	$455 BILLION
1990	388	1,583
2000	1,081	5,019
2009 (est.)	3,200	12,000

The left column, which is based on the actual cost of goods and services at the current exchange rate, tells us that the Chinese economy was more than ten times larger in 2009 than it was in 1980. The right column, which corrects for lower prices in China and an undervalued *yuan,* suggests that it was actually twenty-six times larger. Both columns agree that China has grown faster than any other nation during these decades. By most measurements, in 2010, China's economy will be the second largest in the world.

Incomes also shot up rapidly from a very low base. In 2010, the estimated per capita income as measured by current exchange rates was about $3,400, or $6,400 as measured by purchasing power. This puts China ahead of India, Indonesia, and Vietnam, but still behind Malaysia and Thailand. In Japan, South Korea, and Taiwan, double-digit growth continued until the average income reached about $14,000. If their experience applies to China, rapid growth may continue for another decade.

China's trade, an engine of growth, also soared. In 2010, China is expected to pass Germany and become the number one exporter in the world.

1988	$100 BILLION
1994	200
2001	500
2004	1,000
2008	2,400

Deng abolished collectives in China's villages and made the farm family the basic unit of production. A local leader commented, "When people work for themselves, they work better." Standards of living went up. Grain production rose from 300 million tons in the early 1980s to more than 550 million in 1997, an increase of about 80 percent. After that, it declined slightly as farmers living near cities found it more profitable to grow fruits, vegetables, as well as feed grains for China's rising consumption of meat. To counter rising imports of grain from abroad, the Chinese government began a program of agricultural subsidies to encourage home production. But as local industries were established and village incomes rose, imports of grain and other foodstuffs rose further. They will likely become a permanent feature of the Chinese economy.

State-operated enterprises had been the showpieces of the old centrally planned economy. As late as 1982, their output was 74 percent of Chinese industrial production and included defense industries, mining, steel, petrochemicals, and shipbuilding. These industries, however, employed twice the labor needed to run them efficiently, and more than half ran at a loss. They drained the resources of the state-owned banks and became, in effect, welfare establishments in which workers were paid little and had little incentive to work hard since they enjoyed the security of the so-called "iron rice bowl."

Serious reforms began in 1997, by which time the state industries' share of industrial production had already declined. The government announced that the "state ownership" required by the constitution would give way to "public ownership." Some industries were sold to private entrepreneurs; others sold shares to the public. Defense industries and others the government deemed strategic remained in the hands of the state; but their managers were given the power to fire excess workers and make whatever changes were necessary for profitability.

The driving force in China's economy was the "free market" sector. The term is slightly misleading in that the sector includes not only businesses run by private entrepreneurs but also those managed by villages, municipalities, the military services, and other public bodies. During the 1990s, as investments poured in from Taiwan, Japan, South Korea, and the United States, joint ventures with foreign firms also became increasingly prominent. All of these businesses, whatever the ownership, produced for national and international markets and depended on profits for growth and for their continued existence.

The surge in new enterprises began in "special economic zones" along the border with Hong Kong and up the coast. But growth soon spread outside these zones. Shanghai, with a population of more than twenty million (2010), became a city of skyscrapers and industrialists and the site of China's first stock exchange. Shandong and Manchuria in the northeast attracted huge investments from abroad and achieved stunning growth. Growth gradually moved inland. Wuhan, a large city on the Yangzi that manufactured automobiles, averaged growth of 17 percent during the 1990s. (In 2010, China became the largest automobile manufacturer in the world.) In the hinterlands, large regions lagged behind and clamored for government assistance but to no avail: to achieve growth the government was willing to tolerate personal and regional inequities.

China since 1949

1949	Communist victory; People's Republic of China established
1950	Sino-Soviet alliance; China invades Tibet
1953	First five-year plan
1958	Great Leap Forward
1960	Sino-Soviet split
1966–1976	Cultural Revolution
1972	Nixon visits Beijing
1976	Mao Zedong dies
1978–1992	Deng Xiaoping in power
1979	United States recognizes China
1989	Tiananmen Square incident
1992–present	Rapid growth continues
2008	Beijing Olympics

The factors propelling China's growth are clear: the entrepreneurial talents of the people; a huge surplus of good-quality, cheap labor; rising education; a high savings rate; open world markets; a government that demands results; the infusion of capital from abroad; the stipulation that investments from abroad be accompanied by a transfer of technology. Under these conditions, China shielded its own markets with high tariffs and cheap currency while flooding foreign markets with its goods. The result was a steep rise in Chinese foreign currency reserves, to $2.4 trillion early in 2009, the highest in the world. These reserves are increasingly used to buy up natural resources abroad. Since joining the World Trade Organization in 2001, China has shifted away from overt tariff protectionism but continues to undervalue its currency.

Social Change

During the Mao years, farmers were locked into the collective or village production unit. Cities were closed to those without residence permits. City dwellers, whether they worked in factories, hospitals, schools, newspapers, or government offices, were

Cheap Labor. Wages at this Beijing shirt factory are low by Western standards but high by Chinese standards. This is not a sweatshop but a modern factory. Should Western nations leave the production of textiles to low-wage nations? What of steel or micro electronics?
[A. Raney/Photo Edit]

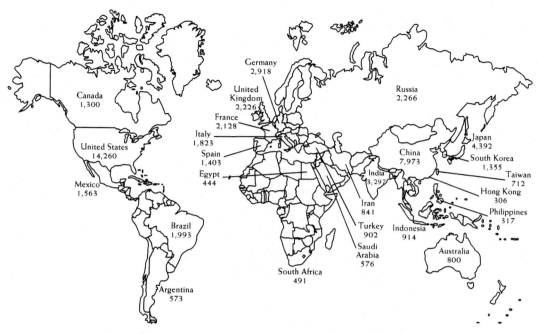

Map 6–2   "How big is China's economy?"   According to the GDP figures on this map, China was the world's second largest economy in 2008. The Chinese people are justly proud of their progress. (The figure given on the map corrects for the cheap yuan and for low prices in China's domestic markets. If the figure were based on the yuan–dollar exchange rate—another legitimate calculation—the GDP would be half as much and China would be third, after the United States and Japan.)

members of units. The English word "unit" is a colorless term, but in China, the *danwei* was the primary focus of life. Whether a factory, government office, or university, the unit provided its members with jobs, housing, food, child care, vacations, medical services, and pensions; it was like the company in a "company town." Party cadres controlled the units and, through them, every aspect of their members' lives. Block organizations exercised surveillance over the inhabitants and reported any infractions of "socialist morality" to the authorities. Even when "campaigns," such as those of the Cultural Revolution, were not under way, the social pressures brought to bear on the individual were intense.

Controls relaxed under Deng. The police became less active—except against political dissidents—censorship was reduced, and ties with the outside world were allowed to develop. The "unit" and the total social coercion it exerted diminished in importance as food became widely available in free markets and apartments were sold to their inhabitants on easy terms. Private housing brought with it the freedom to change jobs. Those with the means began to purchase medical care and other services. Workers with higher salaries began to provide for their own needs, and life became freer and more enjoyable. The replacement of the "unit" by the market opened the way for individual decisions and initiatives.

Prosperity and changes in the life pattern became increasingly visible. The blue Mao uniforms of the 1960s and early 1970s were followed by suits, however ill fitting, and later, for the young, by blue jeans, sneakers, and colorful jackets. From the 1990s, innovative Chinese designers held fashion shows in Shanghai and Beijing. Artists experimented with new forms. Young people associated more freely; in urban areas, the taboo against public displays of affection slowly relaxed. The "household treasures" of the 1960s, radios and bicycles, gave way to stoves and refrigerators in the 1970s, and in the next decade, to washing machines and color televisions. In the early 1980s, crowds gathered in department stores to admire displays of shiny, new motorbikes. By the early 1990s, motorbikes and increasing numbers of privately owned cars competed in crowded streets with the ceaseless flow of bicycles. After the turn of the century, bicycles in large cities were relegated to bike lanes, and the term "household treasures" had become obsolete. Private restaurants increased in number, and travel for pleasure became commonplace. In 1988, most passengers on airline flights within China were foreign; ten years later, flights had multiplied and passengers were mostly Chinese, and this trend continues.

Not all is rosy, however. Rivers are polluted by sewage and runoff. The water table in north China is sinking. Most electrical power in China is still produced by soft coal, and smog floats over the countryside near power plants. To counter pollution and to meet the demand for electrical power, China constructs nuclear power plants and solar power facilities at a more rapid pace than any other nation. But the soaring demand requires new coal-fired facilities as well. In cities, automobiles now cause 70 or 80 percent of the air pollution; in Beijing, winter dust and smog obscure buildings only blocks away. Pollution and traffic jams led the Shanghai government to levy a registration fee of $4,600 on each new vehicle. Despite the fee and an expanding network of elevated highways, the city's more than two million cars produce a regular 6:00 P.M. gridlock. Smog from China's northeast occasionally reaches the American west coast.

China's legal system has improved but slowly. Under Mao, the state had established "labor-education camps" to which criminals and drug offenders were sent without trial. The prison camps were also used for political prisoners and, from the 1990s, for members of the Falun Gong religious sect, who, like criminals, were viewed as a threat to the social order. Since Deng, new courts have opened, more judges and lawyers have been trained, and greater attention has been paid to proper legal procedures. But the ideal of an independent judiciary competes only feebly with the actual power of the state.

Education has made enormous strides since 1978. More than 90 percent of the population is literate. In 2008, the average Chinese had ten years of schooling; 2,000 colleges and universities had six million students, and various technical institutes had even more. Each year, the numbers increase. Students are admitted not to a university but to a university faculty: The best usually study the sciences, engineering, and medicine, and the very best are admitted to departments of business and economics. The numbers of students studying abroad increase geometrically. In 2000, a manual on how-to-train your child to gain entrance to a foreign university, titled *Harvard Girl*, was published. (The girl in question actually studied applied mathematics and economics at Harvard.) The book became wildly popular, selling 1.76 million copies, and was followed by a sequel, *Harvard Boy*, and others of the same genre. Chinese educational standards are rising faster than in other nations with comparable standards of living, but are still considerably lower than those of Europe, Japan, and the United States.

During the era of Mao, poverty in China was equitably distributed—except for the rulers, their helpers, and the upper levels of the military. In the years since Mao, the much higher incomes were unevenly distributed. Successful entrepreneurs buy luxury apartments, foreign cars, and computers. They travel abroad and sent their children to private schools. They are China's new upper class. Below them is a new middle class of managers, mid-level bureaucrats, scientists, and, perhaps, academics. They own apartments, cars, computers, and cell phones. They expect a steadily rising income, and this expectation conditions their support of a less than democratic government. Other city dwellers have also benefited from the new prosperity, but many, and particularly the floating population of immigrants from rural areas, barely scrape by. The pace of change is slower still for the majority who live in the countryside, where income levels are a third of those in cities. Villages near cities are prosperous with large brick houses and tractors, but an older lifestyle and lower standard of living persists in more remote regions.

Population remains critical. The story of population during the years after 1949 might begin with the four Ma's: Malthus, Marx, Ma Yinchu, and Mao Zedong. Malthus claimed that population would expand geometrically, whereas food would increase only arithmetically. Marx rejected the Malthusian hypothesis, along with classical economics, as myths of the capitalist stage of history. Professor Ma Yinchu (1882–1982), the chancellor of Beijing University, in 1957 published *New Principles on Chinese Population*, in which he argued that unchecked population growth would impede capital accumulation and depress living standards. Mao Zedong, faithfully following the teachings of Marx, purged Professor Ma and closed down population institutes at Chinese universities. There followed a population increase from 550 million in 1949 to nearly a billion in 1981.

The extra mouths ate up most of the economic growth that occurred during the 1960s and 1970s. Consequently, Deng in 1981 adopted a national policy of one child per family. Without such a policy, he argued, China's future would be bleak. Thereafter, the increase slowed, though by 2009, the population reached 1.34 billion. Over one hundred cities in China have populations of more than a million. Demographers predict the population will peak in 2030 at about a billion and a half. In recent decades, Chinese parents, not unnaturally, often spoil their single child; Chinese sociologists speak of a new generation of "little emperors."

THE CONDITION OF WOMEN: A POSITIVE APPRAISAL

Chinese women have made huge gains during the Republican era, the Communist revolution, and the decades that followed the years of Mao. In the passage that follows, Wang Anyi, an often translated, contemporary novelist writes of her own life experiences.

Does city life in Shanghai insulate Wang from the lives of the majority of her countrywomen? Will the freedom she has enjoyed become the norm in an increasingly urbanized China?

I consider myself fortunate. From the time I was born, equality between the sexes was always regarded as normal and desirable, even something protected by law. My grandmothers sit stiffly and solemnly in their photographs, their misshapen feet so remote from me they seem unreal: I can hardly believe we belong to the same century. . . .

I lived in this society of gender equality in innocence, and even ignorance. In the classroom we drew "38th Parallels" on our desks to mark a clear boundary with the boys who shared them with us.

That was how the buds of adolescence swelled. At work, women performed the same tasks and received the same wages as men; they were proud they were not judged inferior. In the family, because they were economically independent, they were on an equal footing with men. Where I live, in Shanghai, husbands are affectionately regarded as henpecked. . . .

With the eighties came an ideological emancipation that brought various philosophical trends to us, bearing the fruits of centuries of thought. . . . Thinking was restored to health. That was a more dynamic period, the vigour of which resonated with my desire for freedom and growth. For a woman writer, it was especially favourable. I was not only able to observe the world as any man might; I had a further perspective on it, as a woman, from an angle that made it clear men and women were not yet truly equal. To some measure, women were still dissociated from the centre of society, wandering in its margins.

A. Wang, "Tales of Gender," in C. H. Wang *One China, Many Paths* (New York, Verso, 2003), pp. 250–251.

THE CONDITION OF WOMEN: A NEGATIVE APPRAISAL

In China, parents traditionally relied on sons for support in old age. Daughters married out and became members of other families. This pattern still prevails in rural China. But today, because of the one-child-per-family rule, a couple whose firstborn is a girl cannot try again. The following responses by rural women who gave birth to girls are in answer to queries by Chinese sociologists.

What institutional changes will be required to change this pattern? What cultural changes?

"I was sterilized after the birth of two girls. My mother-in-law condemned me by saying: 'I have only one son who married a bitch like you. You have extinguished our family. Get out of here and get yourself killed; otherwise we will never turn around.' My husband abused me,

beat me, and threatened to divorce me every day. He angrily reproached me: 'If I can get rid of you, you ugly woman, I'll get another woman who can bear me a son. I'll kill you if you do not clear out.'"

"When I was pregnant, both my husband and my mother-in-law took good care of me. When they saw I gave birth to a girl, they were all disheartened. I also felt guilty toward my husband and my parents-in-law and was ashamed of myself. When I saw other people explode firecrackers and make feasts to celebrate the birth of a son, I felt even more sad. I want to give birth to another child, hopefully a boy and not a girl. People will look down upon you if you give birth to a girl. What a difficult lot we women have!"

P. Ebrey, ed. *Chinese Civilization, A Sourcebook* (New York, Free Press, 1993) pp. 481, 482–483.

If population peaks in 2030, for several decades, there will be too few workers to support the many who have retired. Japan and Germany will face a similar problem sooner. (One constructive solution might be a later retirement.) The second demographic problem is "missing girls." Pregnant wives are often tested and female fetuses sometimes aborted. Nationwide, 114 boys are born for each 100 girls; in one area of Fujian province, the ratio is 134 to 100. As one resident put it, "A son is the equivalent of a pension." The government has prohibited sexual selection by abortion but the law is difficult to enforce.

China and the World

China's international relations reflect its political economy. During the age of Mao, China was isolated. The Cold War defined its relations with Japan, South Korea, Taiwan, and the United States. As a Communist state, it was close initially to the Soviet Union, North Korea, and North Vietnam; it borrowed Soviet institutions and engineers; it sent Chinese troops to rescue North Korea during the Korean War. But in 1960 it broke with the Soviet Union, its most powerful ally, and went its own way. It gave material aid to North Vietnam during the Vietnam War (1959–1975), but when Vietnamese anti-Chinese sentiment resurfaced after the war, in 1979, China briefly invaded Vietnam's northern provinces. Deng Xiaoping's comment was "Vietnam is a hooligan. We must teach it a lesson." China also gave support to the anti-Vietnamese Khmer Rouge in Cambodia. It will not exaggerate to say that during these years China's internal political radicalism poisoned its relations with other nations.

The second phase of international relations, China as an emerging nation, began soon after the advent of Deng Xiaoping. New economic policies required an opening to the world, an opening that became wider as the Cold War drew to an end after 1989. China began trade with the United States, Japan, South Korea, and even with Taiwan. It established ties with the European Union and with oil-producers in the Middle East. Relations with Russia became amicable, if not close: border disputes were settled and trade grew. Trade ties and participation in international organizations led China to adopt an increasingly moderate stance.

The third phase of international relations was China's emergence as a power to be reckoned with in the world. This phase began soon after the turn of the century, though it is difficult to say precisely when. Was it when China's per capita income reached a certain level, or was it when the GDP became greater than that of leading European states? Was it sometime during the first decade of the new century when China began buying up natural resource companies in Africa, Australia, and elsewhere? Should it be defined by China's purchase of submarines from Russia and the continued drive to modernize its military and nuclear weapons? Was it inaugurated by the 2008 Beijing Olympics, which were more extravagant than any Ringling Brothers circus? Was it in 2009 when foreign currency reserves passed the $2 trillion mark and

China produced more automobiles than any other country? Taken together, these mark an impressive advance in China's stature.

The United States, which extended diplomatic recognition to China in 1979, soon became China's most important export market. In 1985, China's exports to the United States, about $4 billion, just about matched its imports from that country. Trade was just beginning. Twenty-three years later, in 2008, China's exports to the United States were 338 billion, but its imports from the United States were only 70 billion. The $268 billion deficit was of course a consequence of the U.S. appetite for cheap, good-quality, Chinese products. But the products were cheap partly because the Chinese government held down the value of its currency. The United States was unhappy at this imbalance and at the blatant Chinese piracy of computer software, movies, and CDs. It was also critical of Chinese human rights abuses, nuclear testing, and arms sales to Iran and Pakistan. For its part, China was critical of U.S. military alliances with Japan and South Korea, and the support of Taiwan and the non-Communist nations of Southeast Asia; these relationships were the main countervailing force to Chinese hegemony in a region that China felt—in Middle Kingdom fashion—was its proper sphere of influence. Chinese and American presidents regularly exchanged visits. Little by little, in the WTO, the UN, and elsewhere, China began to adapt to the standards of the larger international community.

Japan was China's second largest export market. Because China remembered Japanese aggression in World War II and found it politically expedient to keep these memories alive, relations with Japan were not easy. The villains in historical dramas on Chinese television are often Japanese soldiers. Chinese newspapers attack Japanese prime ministers who honor their war dead at Yasukuni Shrine, where sixteen war leaders are also enshrined. They criticize Japanese textbooks for their treatment of the war, and demand from them a standard of objectivity not approached in their own. China condemns any strengthening of the Japanese non-nuclear Self Defense Forces, even while rapidly modernizing its own military and nuclear weaponry. In 1995, China exercised its Security Council veto to block Japanese entry to that body. None of this, however, is permitted to interfere with Japanese imports of Chinese goods or Chinese imports of Japanese technology.

China's relation to the two Koreas has changed. During the era of Mao, China was allied with Communist North Korea—which would not exist had China not come to its aid during the Korean War. But from the 1980s, trade with South Korea grew, until in 2010, South Korea was China's third largest export market. The government of North Korea, in the meantime, continued its cult of personality, and policies that were harsh, ideological, and eccentric. China liked the idea of North Korea as a buffer state, and worried that its collapse might flood Manchuria with North Korean refugees. But it did not like having a poor and unpredictable nuclear power at its doorstep. This led it from 2003 to cooperate, somewhat reluctantly, with the other four concerned powers (South Korea, Japan, Russia, and the United States) to negotiate an end to the North Korean nuclear arms program.

TAIWAN

Nowhere is the strange chemistry of international relations more apparent that in China's changing relation to Taiwan. A mountainous island less than a hundred miles off the coast of central China, Taiwan is little larger than Belgium or Massachusetts, with a population of 23 million. It became a part of China in 1683, and then a Japanese colony in 1895 as a spoil of the Sino-Japanese War. The Japanese found it relatively easy to rule since the Taiwanese lacked a modern sense of national identity and were accustomed to rule by officials who came from across the sea and spoke a language they could not understand. (Standard Chinese and the Fujian dialect spoken on Taiwan are mutually unintelligible.) The Japanese colonial government quickly suppressed opium and bandits and eradicated epidemic diseases. It built roads and railroads, reformed the land system, and introduced improvements in agriculture. By the early 1930s, little Taiwan had 2,857 miles of railroads compared with China's 9,400. Before becoming a colony, education in Taiwan had been the privilege of a tiny elite; by World War II, 71 percent of school-age children attended the "common schools." (In the Dutch East Indies and French Indochina, the figure was about 10 or 15 percent.) The Japanese introduced light industries, built power plants, and, during the 1930s, developed textiles, chemicals, ceramics, and machine tools. Though owned by Japanese and run in their interest, more benefits accrued to the local population than in Japan's other colony of Korea, and the standard of living was several times higher than that of China proper.

Anticolonial feelings rose slowly. During the 1920s, Taiwanese petitioned for political reform and greater personal freedom. The Japanese made a few concessions, but after the China War began in 1937, they reverted to strict controls and policies of assimilation. Taiwanese were conscripted into the Japanese army. By the end of the war, Taiwanese were happy to see the Japanese leave and welcomed mainland Guomindang (GMD) officials as liberators.

The GMD officials, however, viewing the Taiwanese as Japanese collaborators, looted the economy and ruled harshly. When Taiwanese protested in February 1947, the new government put down the demonstrators and over several months killed almost 10,000 Taiwanese, many of whom were community leaders. By the time Jiang Jieshi (Chiang Kai-shek) and two million more military and civilian mainlanders fled to the island in 1949, Taiwan's economy and society were in disarray. The newly arrived Chinese looked down on the Taiwanese, who, in turn, hated their new rulers, and, in private, often compared them unfavorably to the Japanese. Positions formerly held by Japanese were taken over almost entirely by mainlanders.

In the mid-1950s, order was restored, and rapid economic growth began. Heavy industries were put under state control, others sold to private parties. With the outbreak of the Korean War in 1950, U.S. aid became substantial. Foreign investment was welcomed. Light industries were followed by consumer electronics, steel, and petrochemicals, and then by computers and semiconductors. From the late 1980s, trade and investments in China began. By the late 1990s, Taiwan was the world's largest producer of monitors, keyboards, motherboards, and computer mice; the second in notebook PCs; and the fourth in integrated circuits. Some of these products were actually manufactured in Taiwanese-owned plants in China. Taiwan invested hundreds of billions of dollars in China, and by 2005, a million Taiwanese lived and worked in China. Per capita product in Taiwan rose from $200 in the early 1950s to $1,800 in 1982, to $5,000 in 1987, and to $17,000 (or $31,000 in purchasing power) in 2009. That this was five times higher than China's was not lost on the Taiwanese.

Social changes began early. Land reform in 1949 led to a steady growth in agricultural production, benefiting Taiwanese who owned land. Entrance examinations to universities were equitable; rising numbers of both Taiwanese and mainlanders obtained a higher education; the percentage of female students rose from 11 percent in 1950 to 36 percent in 1970, and higher thereafter. Taiwanese and mainlanders began to intermarry, further breaking down the distinction between them. As a new, educated middle class emerged, Taiwanese began to enter the GMD and attain political office.

Initially, GMD rule in Taiwan was authoritarian. The GMD maintained that its government, which it called the Republic of China, was the legitimate government of all of China. Posters on Taipei billboards proclaimed the official goal of retaking the mainland. As the self-proclaimed government of all of China, the GMD mainlanders who had fled China controlled the military and dominated the native Taiwanese. Jiang Jieshi died in 1975, a year before Mao. Under his son, Jiang Jingguo, who became president in 1978, Taiwan inched toward representative government. Jingguo began as a figure of repression but ended as a populist, touring the countryside and appointing native Taiwanese to important posts. In 1987, a year before his death, he ended martial law and permitted the formation of opposition parties.

Thirty-nine years of rule by mainlanders ended in 1988 with the selection of Li Denghui as president. Though a member of the GMD, Li was a native Taiwanese, who had graduated from a Taiwanese high school, attended Kyoto Imperial University, Taiwan National University, Iowa State University, and Cornell University. His presidency marked a shift in political power to the majority population of Taiwan. Li described the March 1996 election, in which he once again became president, as "the first free election in 5,000 years of Chinese history." During the election, China tried to intimidate the voters by firing missiles into the waters off Taiwan. The voters reacted by giving Li a substantial majority of votes. Four years later, in 2000, fifty-one years of GMD rule ended when Chen Shuibian was elected president. Chen was both a Taiwanese and the leader of an opposition party. His election marked the arrival of full democracy in Taiwan. Chen, who had been born in poverty, became a corporate lawyer and, in 1994, was elected mayor of Taipei. His election was hailed by one scholar as "the first peaceful transition of power from one political party to another in Taiwanese history, and probably in all Chinese history." In 2008, Ma Jingjiu was elected president of Taiwan. Born in Hong Kong in 1950, he was a graduate of Taiwan National University and Harvard Law School, and had served earlier as justice minister, mayor of Taibei, and chairman of the GMD. When he ran for president, his platform stressed economic growth and better relations with China. He opposed Taiwanese independence, but also opposed reunification with mainland China.

Since 1949, China has never wavered in its claim that Taiwan is a province of China, unlawfully controlled by a "bandit" government. Insisting that its relation with the island was an internal Chinese matter, it refused diplomatic ties with any nation maintaining such ties with Taiwan. With the outbreak of the Korean War in 1950, the United States recognized Taiwan as the Republic of China, the legitimate government of all China, and gave it military aid. But in December 1978, the status of the island changed abruptly when President Carter recognized Beijing as the legitimate government of a China that included Taiwan. But U.S. policy had not changed completely. It ruled out reunification by force and passed the Taiwan Relations Act, which provided for continued arms sales to Taiwan and for continued "non-diplomatic" relations with Taiwan—to be handled by U.S. diplomats on leave from the State Department. It was during the years of diplomatic limbo after 1978 that Taiwan's economy grew and its society became democratic.

As the new century dawned, conflicting trends were apparent. China was concerned that a freely elected representative government would give Taiwan a claim to legitimacy in the eyes of the world. It worried that Taiwan's prosperity would make its people less willing to rejoin the mainland, a view lent credence by public opinion polls in Taiwan. China stated that should President Chen declare independence, China would take the island by force. The United States, hoping to play down the conflict, counseled Taiwan not to speak of independence. President Chen replied that a declaration of independence was unnecessary since Taiwan was already an independent state. The danger of war was not immediate, for China lacked the military power to take the island. But in a decade or so, it will be able to project its power across the Taiwan Straits. In July 2005, a hawkish Chinese general publicly opined that in case of a war over Taiwan, the United States "should worry more about Los Angeles than about Taipei." Since China possesses nuclear-tipped missile submarines, his view cannot be totally dismissed. The general's views were of course not those of the Chinese government. But even the government labeled a Pentagon report on the rising Chinese military strength as "crude meddling in China's internal affairs."

By 2010, however, the likelihood of conflict had diminished. Any Chinese attempt to conquer Taiwan, even without an American intervention, would invite sanctions that would halt China's economic growth. China has everything to gain by waiting. In the meantime, Taiwan's economic involvement in China grows deeper by the year. President Ma was elected in 2008 on a platform of "no independence, no use of force, and no unification." But he also argued for a common market with China and established direct air links with Chinese cities. If the Chinese standard of living continues to rise and if China moves toward greater political freedoms, a political solution to the problem of Taiwan may be possible.

MODERN CHINA IN HISTORICAL PERSPECTIVE

What China does affects other nations. Consider population. Our usual models are western Europe and Japan, where population quadrupled in the process of industrialization and then, almost as a natural process, began to level off. China was different: With a huge population to begin with, it could not afford a further quadrupling. Consequently, late in the day, it adopted tough policies to limit births. Many nations, overpopulated and poor, resemble China, and as they experience the negative consequences of soaring populations, they may look to the Chinese model.

China's influence on world trade grows. Prior to World War II, the advanced nations of the West sold manufactures to the world in exchange for raw materials and labor-intensive goods. They had no expectation that this pattern would ever change. After the war, however, Japan advanced swiftly to high technology, followed in rapid succession by Taiwan, South Korea, Hong Kong, and Singapore. Their combination of efficient production and cheap labor put great pressure on the United States and Europe, causing trade deficits, corporate restructuring, the relocation of jobs abroad, and a downward pressure on wages. The pressures lessened, however, as East Asian wages rose. Then, from the mid-1980s, China, with its enormous population and extraordinarily cheap labor, emerged as an efficient producer. First came labor-intensive products, such as toys and bicycles, but Chinese technology and engineering steadily advanced. By the turn of the century, four out of five mice for Apple Computer were made by a Taiwan subsidiary in Suzhou by women paid far less than wages in Taiwan. An experienced Chinese automobile worker earned less in a year than a new hire in Detroit earned in a month. If free trade remains in force, the impact of China on manufacturing and wages in industrialized nations will continue to be enormous.

China affects the world supply of natural resources. Consider oil. In 1973–1974, the first oil crisis occurred—a combination of politics and insufficient supply. Shortages occurred at the pump, the price soared, and wealth was transferred from industrial to oil-rich nations. Though the crisis subsequently disappeared, reserves continued to dwindle. The second crisis occurred in 2005–2008, as demand again outstripped supply and the price again soared. If blame is to be apportioned, the industrialized West, and particularly the United States, must bear their full share. Yet at the margin, it was the Chinese demand (India and Brazil also contributed), increasing at four times the rate of other users, which triggered the crisis. World demand continues to rise, while reserves decline.

What are the political consequences of economic growth? Will modernity inevitably lead to democracy, or is this mere wishful thinking? At present, the Chinese Communist Party justifies its dictatorial rule by arguing that party leaders and party technocrats can better manage economic growth and that the disorder attendant on democracy might interfere with it. Chinese leaders do not attack democracy as an ideal, but say that China is not yet ready. Since China's leaders jail their critics, control the media, and treat the army well, sudden change seems unlikely. But what of the longer term? Traditional East Asian culture, if it may be spoken of in the singular, is no bar to democracy. The advance toward representative government in Japan, Taiwan, and South Korea rested on higher standards of living, large and highly educated urban middle classes, the assimilation of key Western concepts, and considerable U.S. influence. Some of these conditions are appearing in China. The assimilation of Western ideas has gone on for over a century, and many educated Chinese desire democracy and greater freedoms. The standard of living and the educational level are rising rapidly, though they are still substantially below that of the Asian rim nations. And while the single influence of the United States is weaker, China is increasingly engaged with the international community, whose most influential members have representative governments. There are grounds for optimism, but even the most sanguine see Chinese democracy as decades in the future.

Lastly, there is the question of Chinese culture. To the extent that culture is organic, China, from the May Fourth Movement through the Cultural Revolution, cut its links to the past more drastically than any other nation. Present-day Chinese often seem adrift, influenced principally by a rampant consumerism and a potent nationalism. But to the extent that culture is information, it is a database that can be accessed at will. Schools of art already teach traditional methods and combine them with Western genres. A concern with Chinese history and parts of the cultural tradition is already evident. The *Analects* of Confucius or a poem by Du Fu will not have the same meaning to a factory manager living in a high-rise, two-room apartment as they did to a Ming scholar, but their humanism and aesthetic values may be reappropriated and reanimated in new forms. It is not inconceivable, for example, that the concern of Mencius for popular welfare will be joined to social democratic ideas in some future Chinese democracy. At present, however, there are so many crosscurrents that the future remains opaque.

REVIEW QUESTIONS

1. Was the Cultural Revolution the logical conclusion to earlier policies or was it an aberration?
2. What economic policies did Deng Xiaoping put in place?
3. Contrast Chinese society before and after 1976. Be concrete.
4. Where on the continuum between the most totalitarian society and the most democratic society would you place contemporary China? Discuss the factors involved in your choice.

SUGGESTED READINGS

BAUM, R. *Burying Mao: Chinese Politics in the Age of Deng Xiaoping* (1996).

CHAN, A., MADSEN, R., AND UNGER, J. *Chen Village: A Recent History of a Peasant Community in Mao's China* (1984). The postwar history of a Chinese village.

CHANG, J. *Wild Swans: Three Daughters of China* (1992). A superbly readable novel of three generations in a Chinese family.

CHENG, J. Y. S. *China in the Post-Deng Era* (1998). A multiple author view of the immediate future based on study of the recent past.

FAIRBANK, J. K. AND TWITCHETT, D., EDS. *Cambridge History of China*. Volumes 14 and 15 (1987, 1991) treat the People's Republic since 1949.

FEWSMITH, J. *China Since Tiananmen: The Politics of Transition* (2001). The 1990s.

FROLIC, B. M. *Mao's People: Sixteen Portraits of Life in Revolutionary China* (1987).

GOLD, T. *State and Society in the Taiwan Miracle* (1986). The story of economic growth in postwar Taiwan.

GOLDMAN, M. *Sowing the Seeds of Democracy in China* (1994).

GOLDMAN, M. AND MACFARQUHAR, R., EDS. *The Paradox of China's Post-Mao Reforms* (1999).

LIANG, H. *Son of the Revolution* (1983). An autobiographical account of a young man growing up in Mao's China.

LIEBERTHAL, K. *Governing China, from Revolution through Reform* (1995).

LIU, B. *People or Monsters? And Other Stories and Reportage from China After Mao* (1983). Literary reflections on China.

MACFARQUHAR, R. *Politics of China: The Eras of Mao and Deng* (1997). A summary of some of the best research.

PAN, I., *Sons of the Yellow Emperor: A History of the Chinese Diaspora* (1990). On Chinese in Southeast Asia and the rest of the world.

RISTAINO, M. R. *Port of Last Resort: The Diaspora Communities of Shanghai* (2001).

SAITH, T. *Governance and Politics of China* (2004).

WANG, H. *China's New Order* (2003). Translation of work by a Qinghua professor, a liberal within the strict boundaries of what is permitted in China.

WHITE, G., ED. *In Search of Civil Society: Market Reform and Social Change in Contemporary China* (1996). An insightful look at the society.

WOLF, M. *Revolution Postponed: Women in Contemporary China* (1985).

ZHANG, X. AND SANG Y. *Chinese Lives: An Oral History of Contemporary China* (1987).